With an Eye
on the Future

With an Eye on the Future

Development and Mission in the 21st Century

Essays in honor of Ted W. Ward

General Editors
Duane H. Elmer
Lois McKinney

Sectional Editors
Muriel I. Elmer
Robert W. Ferris
Stephen T. Hoke
Mark E. Simpson
Catherine Stonehouse

800 West Chestnut Avenue, Monrovia, California 91016-3198 USA

For their special contribution to making this book possible, the editors wish to acknowledge

E. Joe Gilliam
Dr. E. Stanley Kardatzke
Louise and James B. Castles
Board of NAPCE

With an Eye on the Future
Development and Mission in the 21st Century
Duane H. Elmer and Lois McKinney
ISBN 0-912552-99-9

Published by MARC, a division of World Vision International, 800 West Chestnut Avenue, Monrovia, California 91016-3198, U.S.A.

Manuscript editing and typesetting by Joan Laflamme.

Dedicated to

TED W. WARD
Visionary
Pioneer
Mentor
Colleague
Friend

with fondness
from your students
the beneficiaries of your life and teaching

Contents

SECTION III
GLOBAL MISSION IN CHANGING TIMES
STEPHEN T. HOKE, ED.

SECTION IV
CHRISTIANS IN INTERNATIONAL DEVELOPMENT
Muriel I. Elmer, Ed.

SECTION V
CHURCH LEADERSHIP AND RENEWAL
Catherine Stonehouse, Ed.

SECTION VI
TRIBUTES TO TED W. WARD

Beyond the Traditional and Familiar

A Glimpse of Ted Ward's Life and Work

MARGARET WARD

_____

From his growing up days in pioneering Central Florida of the 1930s until his retirement from Trinity Evangelical Divinity School in 1994, Ted Ward's life and career have been characterized by ideas beyond the traditional and love for people beyond the familiar.

Born in a small town in western Pennsylvania, he moved with his parents and younger brother to another small town in central Florida about the time he was starting elementary school. During those early school years, his parents became acquainted with a retired China missionary, Mabel Lee, who was an important influence in the lives of all the Wards. Through "Aunt Mabel's" teaching, Ted's parents became committed Christians with a vision for those beyond their little town. Aunt Mabel's stories of her lifetime of work in early twentieth-century China gave Ted an awareness and concern for people of very different cultures. After Mabel Lee's death, the Ward family purchased her home, and Ted completed his growing up years in that house.

Music became Ted's greatest love during his school days. As a teenager, he directed a young people's choir in a local church and

_____

Margaret Ward holds the master's degree in child development and educational psychology from Michigan State University. She has had extensive experience in Christian ministries to children. Margaret and Ted have been married for forty-five years. They have five married children and fourteen grandchildren.

was involved in all the instrumental music activities his school system offered. After high school graduation and a summer at Interlochen National Music Camp, he enrolled at the Wheaton College Conservatory of Music to pursue a degree in music education. As a student, he participated in chapel choir, concert band, marching band, and symphony orchestra. In the flute section of the band and orchestra, he sat next to his future wife, Margaret, and they were married the day after his graduation.

Even before graduation, Ted was putting into practice his music education ideas. As a college student, he organized the first concert band and taught instrumental music at a nearby Christian high school, where he continued to teach after his graduation while Margaret finished her degree.

The following year they moved to Gainesville where Ted began his graduate studies at the University of Florida. At first, he concentrated on music education, but he soon gained a vision of the broader field of education for teachers of all subjects. The University of Florida at that time was pioneering an internship program for teacher training, and Ted became a supervisor in that program while completing his master's degree and his doctorate in education. During these years, they worked in a little mission church as choir director and in various teaching roles.

During these first years after the end of World War II, colleges and universities all over the country were expanding to take in the returning service men under the GI Bill and offering new programs to meet the expectations of a society entering the longed-for time of peaceful growth and prosperity. Michigan State University, in that era, was training more new teachers for American schools than any other institution in the country. It, too, was using internship programs in numerous cities around the state. For his first five years at MSU, Ted lived and worked in the Pontiac center and also directed a church choir in Detroit.

In 1961, Ted moved to the main campus in East Lansing as assistant to the curriculum director for the College of Education. Just after the war, Michigan State had moved from a college to university structure. Now the College of Education was preparing to add a doctorate, and Ted was involved in the planning of that curriculum. Other administrative roles in those years were in the Learning Systems Institute and the Human Learning Institute.

As colonial powers granted freedom to their former colonies around the world, these developing nations experienced a severe lack of capable leadership. Because it is a land-grant university motivated by service, MSU began working in leadership-development projects all around the world. Over the next several decades, Ted found himself working for various government agencies with people in over sixty countries in the development of human resources. As he did his official job in those countries, he was often able to use his evenings and weekends in consulting roles for mission organizations and institutions.

During his first five years at MSU, Ted worked with undergraduate future teachers, but during the latter twenty-five years, he worked almost exclusively with doctoral students. The great majority of those students whose doctorates he directed were committed Christians who today are serving in leadership positions worldwide. Although several of his MSU faculty colleagues were evangelical Christians, most were not. The openness of the university setting and the willingness of that community to wrestle with ideas made it possible for students to develop their own Christian world view and to bring their Christian perspectives to bear both in and out of the classroom. The university dean of international studies, recognizing the contributions made by the church to international development, asked Ted to be a liaison between the Christian community overseas and the research projects conducted by the university faculty. During much of this time he also continued directing church choirs and teaching Bible classes in a local church.

After thirty years at MSU, with his five children grown and establishing their own homes and careers, Ted took early retirement and became professor emeritus. He then moved to Deerfield, Illinois, to Trinity Evangelical Divinity School, where he became director of the academic doctorate in education and intercultural studies and held the G. W. Aldeen Chair of International Studies and Mission.

As one of the designers of the doctoral programs, he once again had the opportunity to put into practice his innovative ideas to build a learning community.

Now that he has retired a second time, Ted continues to teach occasional courses at Trinity and to do seminars and consulting both at home and abroad. He is experiencing the joy of seeing many of his former students continuing in cooperative learning and doing the work of the kingdom around the world.

SECTION I

A VISION FOR THE TWENTY-FIRST CENTURY

Chapter One

With an Eye on the Future

TED W. WARD

G. W. Aldeen Professor of International Studies and Mission
Trinity Evangelical Divinity School
—and—
Professor Emeritus of Curriculum Research and Educational Administration
College of Education, Michigan State University

The honor of being recognized by one's professional colleagues through their labors of love and ministry in this book is gratefully acknowledged. When word of the tribute came to me, it was accompanied by an outline indicating that several pieces of writing sampled from across the forty-six years of my career were to be included. Although generous, this stirring up of old controversies was unsettling. Most of my writing has been focused on contemporary issues, and those issues change. They change in part because concerned people bring attention to them in a timely manner. Such is the responsibility of the educator.

I was asked to write a new piece that might help my other articles "make sense." Perhaps the invitation was intended to add a humorous touch, but I have taken it seriously. Always ready to take up a new challenge, I have indulged here in an autobiographical style, a form that I have rarely used and which my students know I generally disdain in serious professional literature. But this time it seems appropriate to write in a "warmer" first-person voice. Because most of the people represented by the new writings in this volume were closest to me during their doctoral studies, I have decided to pull back the curtains a bit and pass the tribute to several of my mentors whose influences, in turn, have come through to my students and to their students.

For many people *teaching* is defined in terms of content. What the learner needs to know—or know how to do—is at the core of the definitions of teaching, learning, curriculum, schooling, and ultimately of human competency itself. What do you teach? *History*. How nice! *And what do you teach?* French. *How nice.* Now and then a smug temptation drives the conversation to a deeper level: What do I teach? *People! That's what I teach!* The questioner usually has in mind the content field or the subject that is being taught. Fair enough. But as Ivan Illich and many others similarly concerned about depersonalization of modern education are quick to point out, the human task of teaching and learning focuses first and foremost on the learner. Content is but the instrumentation or the tools toward human fulfillment.

FINDING IDEAS TO SHAPE A CAREER

Early in the second half of this century, the Association for Supervision and Curriculum Development, a research and professional development division of the National Education Association, took as its motto, "The curriculum is people." The worthy intention was to stimulate and encourage redefinition of curriculum away from its preoccupation with *things* and toward a recentering of the importance of the human aspects of the teaching-learning environment. The simplicity of the motto provided something more important than an academic redefinition of the term *curriculum* could ever provide. Its appeal was to the heart more than to the head. For the Christian, it struck a valid chord: People are the creatures of greatest importance to God. As we treat creation with responsible embrace we honor God. Whatever we do in the cause of education must be done with respect and honor. We cannot violate people through coercion or manipulation. Human dignity, not intellectual content, is the highest value of education. As God is above those things he has created, people are above those things they have created.

In the midst of the resultant debates and ideological transformations, doctoral studies in the Department of Curriculum and Instruction in the College of Education at the University of Florida provided the conceptual framework for my career as an educator of educators. Heretofore, my early motives as a teacher were focused on knowledge and skills that I believed to be necessary and valid. Since I had enjoyed the worthy content that I was teaching, others should surely also find that enjoyment and worth. Especially for a music teacher, these matters of enjoyment and worth were matters of deep conviction. They provided a thoroughly ethnocentric and even egocentric frame of reference in which success and failure were defined in terms of the shortcomings of the students: lack of talent, immaturity, misguided taste, and lazy unwillingness to pay the stiff price for competency. Three mentors at the university were especially significant in the development of my conceptual framework.

Discovering Social Science

Kimball Wiles, the chairman of our department and subsequently dean of the college, through his seminars and his transformational book *Teaching for Better Schools* (1952), demonstrated the potential humanness of educational procedures through models that drew their foundations from social science. Until Kim and others of his associates in the "group dynamics research" movement came along, education was largely in the hands of the philosophers and historians, on the one hand, and tacticians of instructional delivery, on the other. The first took their foundations from the lore of human history; the second put little stock in foundations of any sort, choosing instead to focus on the simple pragmatics of "getting people to learn things." Kim Wiles showed a promising bridge between these two crude domains: the responsible study of human society. Following the pioneering work of Robert Havighurst and B. O. Smith (another University of Florida loyalist), and deeply drenching his new scholarship in the emerging social sciences (social psychology, sociology, and embryonic educational anthropology), which were augmenting the now-dated maxims from psychology, Wiles provided some of the strongest arguments for grounding educational theory in research of the human context. The impact of Christian values and teachings was there to see, if one took the trouble to probe and appreciate it.

Discovering the Ears of Teaching

Clara Olson was the chairman of my doctoral dissertation committee. (In those days one did not have a chairperson. Clara said that she was as good a chairman as anyone and saw no reason for a title different from the rest.) She was only a few years from retirement, and she poured into those of us closest to her in that period her newfound passion for the anthropology of education. She was instrumental in opening my eyes to the value of learning about human processes in education from intercultural experience. As I finished, she left (at age 70) for her first Asian assignment, a year with the Ministry of Education in Thailand. Clara Olson showed us that the only alternative to being trapped in one's own narrow perspectives and perceptions is deliberately to seek experience in other cultural contexts. She had grown up with the post-slavery biases of the very racist and segregated north-Florida society. Through her eyes we learned to see and to abhor the social violence, injustice, and inhumanity, which were all around us even at mid-century. She taught us how to work for change; we learned the importance of starting with the aspirations of those who were hurt by injustice. She taught us the futility of activism that started from our own views of the problems and their resolutions. In short, she taught us that educators who undertake basic problems in society need first of all to learn to listen.

What a delight it has been to see these values mature into the operational style and methods of several of the Christian mission and ministry enterprises we have helped to build, and now to discover the sharing of these insights in a new form of professional literature following from the work of Paulo Freire and others who have caught this message of truth. (See Jane Vella's *Learning to Listen, Learning to Teach—The Power of Dialogue in Educating Adults* [1994].)

Discovering Social Learning

Louise Hock was closer to my own age. After several years as a teacher in an outstanding laboratory school she joined the faculty in our department. Because her classroom experiences as a secondary school teacher overlapped with my early teaching experience, I was especially willing to listen to her. She was a nontraditionalist in her educational style but was ever so gentle and humane. Her profound thoughtfulness was a model worth emulating. Louise is one of the few people I ever really tried to copy. Most of my attempts were faulty, but I finally saw to the very heart of what her style represented: she actively believed that learning is a social process. She put into practice her conviction that people learn more effectively *and* more efficiently when they work and learn together through social interactions, joint projects, and discussions wherein helping one another is valued above surpassing one another. After one memorable experience in which Louise and I had been team-teaching a masters-level seminar, it flashed before me: God's evaluative judgment in Genesis 2:18 also relates to *teaching*: "It is not good for the man to be alone." This was the biggest "Aha!" of my years with Louise. What a teacher-learner!

Putting It Together

These three mentors encouraged the conceptual foundations that give structure to this Christian's lifelong spiritual quest as an educator. In brief, the principles formed through experiences with Kim, Clara, and Louise have provided a functional context for the doing of education as a Christian:

1. Motivation to learn comes from inside. The teacher cannot give it to the student. Whatever the reason or combination of reasons for wanting to learn, they do not come from the teacher. Nonetheless, the teacher has a transcendent responsibility for helping the learner discover and identify from within those interests, needs, and concerns that may be constructively related to the learning experience.

2. All substantial learning comes about as the experiences of one's past and the perceptions they have created come into interaction with new experiences in such ways as to encourage evaluation leading to the realigning or maturing of one's understanding.

3. Teaching and learning are most effectively experienced when the two are intertwined. A teacher should always be a learner; the learning process is enhanced by teaching. These two are most symbiotic when in a continuously rolling interaction rather than being sequential.

4. Learning to know oneself and learning about one's learners and their social contexts are never-ending tasks for the responsible educator.

5. Intercultural work experience is a major source of deliverance from narrowness and bias in the understanding of oneself, others, and the diverse meanings of human behavior.

HONORING CHRIST BY EMPOWERING OTHERS: CAN YOU RUN IN THE RAIN?

References to valuable friendships and professional mentoring at the university could continue for many pages, but there is space here for only one more, Charles Durrance. If it were not for the beyond-the-call-of-duty initiatives of this dear Presbyterian elder, our discouragement after departure from a seriously flawed experience in Christian education could have continued into deeper frustration. But no. In the providence of God the first encounter with the admissions process at the University of Florida was rescued by Charlie Durrance. We had arrived in a campus parking lot in mid-afternoon with a three-month-old baby, after having dragged a semi-functional trailer with all our earthly goods from Illinois through three days of nonstop rain. The decision to go to graduate school was one of very few options that had seemed feasible, once the school in which we had been planning to continue as faculty and staff seemed destined for self-destruction.

In those days not long after World War II, one's home-state universities provided almost tuition-free education. So we scurried to Gainesville—back to "gator land"—wet, exhausted, and emotionally drained. The first discovery at Gainesville was that we were stuck again. The close of registration was only two hours away, and since we had filed no preregistration documents—the decision to leave Illinois was made only a week earlier—the polite but firm assistant at the counter said, "Perhaps you could set things up now for next semester."

Margaret and little David were huddled in the steaming car, enduring the driving rain, and here I was, feeling very much alone. A door at the side of the counter suddenly swung open and out popped a man who turned out to be the graduate admissions director for the College of Education. He took one look at the pathetic sight at the counter and swung into action. "What seems to be the problem?" he asked with a gently reassuring smile. I told my story once again, assuming that smiles notwithstanding, the logistics of my registration as a graduate student were insurmountable at this time.

His next question provided a flicker of hope: "Do you happen to have your Wheaton College transcript?" Knowing full well that you can't be admitted on the basis of an "unofficial copy," I felt almost foolish pulling a rather wet and sweaty copy out of my shirt pocket. He scanned it for all of ten seconds then quickly scrawled across it: "Approved as official. Charles L. Durrance." He handed it back swiftly, glanced at the clock, and asked: "Isn't Gil Dodds the track coach at Wheaton?" Whatever that had to do with anything wasn't quite clear, but I affirmed his recollection. "Did you run for Gil?" "Yes, but not well enough to make the team." "Feel like running in the rain?" "Sure, whatever you suggest." I would have run to the moon and back for this man, so instantly did his "can do" spirit fill me with hope.

With about fifteen minutes to spare, I was back in front of that same counter. Charlie's smile had turned into a huge grin: "You made it! You're in." I had run well, following the route that Dr. Durrance had hastily sketched over a campus map torn from a university catalog. At each planned stop he had put the name of a person I was to see. "Trust me," he had said, "each of these people will have heard from me, and I will tell them your story. They may not ask you much. Each will have a signature ready or will put it on one of the papers you will be carrying by then. And here's my rain bag; carry the stuff in there to keep it dry." I could hardly believe that a stranger could take such an interest in *anyone*. I ran from one unfamiliar building to another, paying extraordinary attention to the map my newfound brother had drawn.

For years I had been steeped in the propaganda that is passed around so convincingly in small colleges and among conservative Christians that you must fear and, if possible, avoid large universities. And here, in my first hour inside a big state university, I had discovered an important truth: God has his faithful followers planted all over the place, even where you are least likely to hope. On this first day I began to learn something else: God builds the bridges. It isn't that we are so clever or so lucky as to be able to cash in from time to time on some holy lottery; the truth is that God prepares the way and builds the bridges. Our task is to seek them out as we walk—and occasionally *run*—day by day, allowing God's guidance into our lives.

Every lesson we learn in life has implications for our future. My professional commitment to being a "can do" educator began that day. Even during my most bureaucratic institutional assignments I have tried to pass along to others the model of Christian values and behaviors that I saw in Charles Durrance. Here was a respected Christian layman fulfilling a series of responsible positions within the university, and quite well liked by everyone. He placed people above bureaucracy, human needs above institutional regulations, and he always started with the challenge, "Let's try!" It wasn't that he did things *for* you; Charlie did things *with* you—always helping you identify your part in the effort, always tuned to what you could do rather than to where you failed or what you could not do. "Let's try!"

Teaching Touches the Future

The teacher's task is inherently future oriented. Only an overwhelmed or pedestrian educator could be so concerned with maintenance and survival as to block out the insistent preoccupations with things to come. It is in the "something evermore about to be" of which Ellen Glasgow wrote in her marvelous Christian novel *Vein of Iron* (1935) that the true educator finds inspiration and purpose. Without a future-directed orientation everything becomes hum-drum repetition. Early on, I learned the importance of *hope*. So much of life carries disappointments and jolts. If one loses the perspective that comes from awareness of God's control of the future, there isn't much to hold at the end of the day.

Two propositions about curriculum have guided my professional development since early in my career. To the informed educator, curriculum is the meeting point between purpose and content. Purpose must always have priority. The quality, relevance, and contextual worth of purpose is the key to good educational planning. As Peter

Drucker says, *efficiency* is concerned about doing things right, whereas *effectiveness* is concerned with doing the right things.

Proposition One

Every curriculum reflects an image of the future. More precisely, in every educational plan there is some sort of assumption about the *value* of the learning experience. This notion of value has its roots in the future of the learner or the context in which the learning will be of use and will make a positive difference. The guiding imagery of the intended outcomes is often left in a vague and amorphous state; many teachers do their teaching from habit or as a mere fulfillment of formal customs. Many times students wonder, Is there really any intention or purpose at all? Even then, a view of the future, whether wise or foolish, lies implicit, deeply embedded in the process and its activities, having its effects on the learner for better or worse. The responsible educator learns to live with these images of the future, weighing them against evidence and trends, sharpening and clarifying. Is it any wonder that educators are second only to economists in the extent of time and effort given to the emerging derivative science of futurism? Christians in education have an even more profound reason for stretching their perceptions into the future tense: biblical Christianity provides insights into God's intentions and God's plans for bringing this creation into an ultimate judgment and newness. How we teach reflects a concern for partnership with God in the matters of fulfilling God's plans, surely not taking them into our own hands, but becoming ever more conscious of God's transcendence in the maturing of all things.

Proposition Two

The planning of curriculum is a concern for the decisions about what should be taught why, to whom, and under what conditions. I will admit authorship of this action-definition of curriculum. It has found its way into the literature, usually identified only as being from an anonymous source or simply common lore. This lack of attribution is no more worrisome than other uses of material from my seminars, lectures, and sermons, which appear as if by magic in the writings and speaking of many of my most loyal students. (Perhaps we could all be happier if we accepted a Muslim view of plagiarism: to quote from another is to give honor to Allah's communicator. Whether or not that person is named, Allah is the source of truth. Allah knows the communicator. It is enough that Allah knows.)

This proposition has its roots in the pioneering work of Florence Stratemeyer, Bunnie Smith (B. Othanel Smith), and Robert Havighurst, people with whom I was a very junior partner but was always accepted as having worth in my person and my ideas. The first component of the action-definition is *concern for decisions*. It raises to a high level of consciousness that someone must take responsibility and must decide how best to share that responsibility of deciding. Jane Vella uses the abbreviation *WWW* to focus the three key questions into one: *Who needs What according to Whom?*

The second element of the action-definition is the *What-Why connection*. A responsible educator cannot decide *what* should be taught apart from the issue of *why* it should be taught. Thus I deliberately leave out the comma to make one question, *What should be taught why?* One cannot responsibly determine the content or specify the objectives without accountability for the issues of worth, need, and appropriateness.

The third element pushes the issues of appropriateness forward by linking the *what-why* with the *to whom*? The responsible educator always seeks to determine the appropriateness of a learning experience to the developmental capability and the social maturation of the learner. Not everyone can learn everything. The elegance of a curriculum depends extensively on the fit between the intended outcomes and the planned learning experiences, on the one hand, and the readiness, fitness and awareness of need in the learners, on the other hand.

The fourth element is the connection of all of these careful decisions to the question, *under what conditions*? Here the focus is on the learning situation itself. What amount of time? What sort of social relationships while learning? What physical situation? What resource materials? What learning exercises? And perhaps most important, exactly *where*? It is in the careful study of nonformal education that this set of issues becomes most clear. Typically, the presuppositions about place, space, time, and task that discourage imaginative curriculum planning are a direct outcome of narrow thinking conditioned by extensive experiences within formal education. It grieves me to discover over and over again that for many who engage in educational leadership, imagination about learning contexts is limited to classrooms, clocks, hierarchical formal relationships between teacher and learner, and physical space in which the knowing person looks in one direction and the ignorant look in the opposite direction.

How sad to see people limit Christian education to situations that emulate schools. Even the most powerful context of the church's nonformal education options, church camping, often ends up looking like a series of school classes punctuated by swimming, eating, bed-making, and more eating. Camping is a great learning environment precisely because it is a whole context in which learning can be talked and walked at the same time.

INTO A NEW ARENA FOR LEARNING

When I took early retirement from Michigan State University in order to move to Trinity Evangelical Divinity School, most of my closest associates were startled. Even some of my closest partners in ministry were alarmed, fearing that I was accepting the invitation without adequately considering the consequences. Surely it was a matter of great curiosity at both schools. What was the "fit?" Was the Divinity School ready for what it was likely to discover? Was I knowledgeable about what I would face?

Having consulted extensively in theological education institutions for about fifteen years, and having taught myself many of the content fields expected in a theological faculty member, I felt that both the senior administrators at Trinity and I were reasonably well-suited to each other. The tasks that they had laid out for me in the development of their doctoral programs and the institution's development of international relationships among similar theological graduate schools were matters that I could be expected to handle with fair competency. So Margaret and I followed God's hand with no fundamental reservations. We have been confirmed and reconfirmed; it has made sense to us. I can recall no conversations in which either of us has said, "Maybe we shouldn't have done it." But for many of my colleagues in the Divinity School it has not been so easy. Clearly, for some, I am still a misfit. Nevertheless, Christian grace and a sense of family have been transcendent. Trinity is a great educational institution.

In the earlier years the misgivings of some of my faculty colleagues were revealed mostly as curiosity. Far too often I was asked to tell about the differences between teaching in a large public university and at a much smaller church-affiliated theological school. I could occasionally detect what people wanted to hear: that it was indeed a blessing now to be among the safe and sanctified halls of ecclesiological ivy; that it was an emotional relief; that students at the seminary are much more purposeful and better scholars; and that it was more gratifying to be doing work for the kingdom of Christ. But I rarely took the questions seriously enough to respond other than in trite ways: "Don't worry about me. I can make it."

Only once did I let it fly. One of my closest faculty friends baited me with the question. He knew how I despised the question and the temptation to make invidious comparisons between the university and the theological school. We were sitting in his office musing about a currently disturbing political issue and being very unguarded in our conversation. With a chuckle, he asked, "Tell me just once more, what makes this place different from the university?" I sat quietly and gave the question some of the most careful reflection I had allowed myself. This friend deserved to hear from my heart. Then it popped out. Without even refining the words to express my thoughts, I blurted, "It is so hard to work day after day among people who are so _____ right all the time!" (The deleted expletive is a word often heard as theology professors lecture on the status of the nonbeliever.)

After a shocked moment of surprise that I had uttered such a foul judgment, I noticed that my friend had doubled over in gales of laughter and was struggling to stay on his swivel chair, which seemed itself also to be out of control for the moment. My next words were not really repentant but instead reflected on the insight of the "Aha!" moment: "Sorry, it just came out. But maybe that's the deeper truth of all this." I had never reflected cogently on this possibility before. But I surely have done so since.

Perhaps there lurks a sort of "Inquisition anxiety" among theology professors: They once burned people for religious error; maybe they still do. Better not say it wrong—they might burn me. Better not utter anything I'm not ready to defend—they might burn me. Better not admit that I'm wondering about the accepted way to look at this issue—they might burn me. Better not spend too much time in unsafe conversation (stick with the Bears and the Cubs)—they might burn me.

The resultant forms of dialogue and verbal interaction thus sound more structured than spontaneous, more contrived than natural, and more defensive than expansive. Of course, theology is not the only discipline where the truth is revered, but especially in conservative Christianity and in orthodox Judaism, the Word is Truth. And indeed, I have no quarrel with this maxim. But in the handling of the Word of God, as in the handling of empirical information from other facets of God's revelation, there simply must be scholarly dialogue and sober reflection on the ways that our perceptions and previous presuppositions color and even blind us to new or deeper truth.

While at Michigan State University, and before that the University of Florida, I had inadequately valued the importance of the open dialogues we had about ideas. Only after I came into the divinity-school situation, where such dialogues rarely allow for free association and seem to discourage the teasing out of a new hypothesis, did I realize how much I missed this freedom to talk and think at the same time. For a person committed to the values of social learning, this is indeed a handicap.

On the other hand, it is so exciting to share a common ground of "bottom line" convictions with one's colleagues. Even when debate and discussion seem most fruitless, we come to resolutions with a sense of deep confidence when we seek wisdom and common ground in the truth revealed in Scripture. We come to rest there as a family. In today's confused world, where hardly any common agreement on any moral issue seems feasible, being *the people of the Book* is very much a source of real peace and hope.

The Realization of a Deliberate Learning Community

The most significant discovery since moving into the development of doctoral study programs at Trinity is perhaps the capstone of my professional career. Much to my delight, joy, and intellectual satisfaction, I have found here the reality of a true learning community. We came close from time to time at Michigan State, close enough that I knew it could happen. Thus, in making the move to Trinity, one of my greatest hopes, one for which I fervently prayed, was that we could find that crucial balance between trust and compulsion to wrestle with ideas, between concern for one another and respect for personal responsibility, between honest intellectual exercises and profound spiritual maturation, and between warmth of relationships and toughness of reasoning that would fulfill the highest images of graduate study and the highest images of social learning all at the same time.

It has happened, and beyond my hopeful imaginings. We have seen the goal of a learning community come to pass. Partly because of the widely shared common ground among faculty and students at Trinity, and partly because of the characteristics of the doctoral students who have joined us here, the dreams, hopes, visions, and motives of a lifetime quest for optimal learning environments have been overwhelmingly fulfilled here in the doctor of education and the Ph.D. in intercultural studies programs.

These programs, each in turn, surged forward so quickly that we were suddenly launched into the enviable position of needing to select candidates carefully. As we tell the students whom we do accept, less than 25 percent of applicants, "You are here because we want you. We will see you through to fulfillment of your intentions." Thus a covenant of mutual responsibility provides the basis for this community of learners. I believe that under such circumstances if we cannot select really superb doctoral students from this reservoir, we have only ourselves to blame. Then in true Harvard style, having selected the best, we try hard not to hurt them much, and thus ultimately we can take institutional credit for anything good they may ever do. (Get thee behind us, Satan.)

More to the point, an ethos emerged smoothly in which the students recognized quickly that they were free to put aside the competitiveness and self-serving that are commonly part of the learned habits of the formally educated. With this inhibition to effective learning laid aside, a supportive relationship of peers developed among faculty and students in which the valuing of learning together is shared and appreciated. It really works. Recently this characteristic of our work together as faculty and students has been documented in a highly scholarly and elegantly researched ethnographic study by Laurie Bailey (1996).

A BRIEF AGENDA FOR CHRISTIANS IN THE TWENTY-FIRST CENTURY

Humankind is leaving the twentieth century painfully unprepared for the twenty-first. The quagmire of hopelessness, lawlessness, immorality, anger, frustration, and inter-ethnic hostility is indeed frightening to any honest assessor. The public arena suffers from loss of confidence and respect for institutions. The private sector suffers from rampant autonomy and self-seeking in which personal values are largely floating on pragmatic foam thrown about in the turbulence of parental and community ineffectiveness and guilt, expressed at every turn as denials of social accountability and insistence on liberty without reciprocal responsibility. Has there ever been a time when responsible public education and effective religious education for people of all ages have been more needed?

Ethnic Strife: Unprepared for the Rising Water Table

Undoubtedly, it is more *natural* for human beings to prefer to be grouped with people who are as much like themselves as possible. Tragically, the people of the church of Jesus Christ have more often preferred to live *naturally* than to accept the transcendence across racial, gender, and status lines that is held up in Scripture as the model for the church (Gal. 3:26-28). Thus today's Christians are very little more prepared than the general society to deal positively with the racial and intercultural tensions of our time. It is not enough to shrug, "This problem has always been with us." Of course it has. And it always will be until Christians show the way through it.

   What makes our period in history different is the acuteness and persistence of inescapable problems created by racial and social divisiveness. In centuries past, people-clusters—*natural* and rather exclusive units within communities and neighborhoods, across towns, cities, and nations—could find ways to distance themselves from those they disdained. The world was like a great plateau pockmarked by ponds—little ponds, big ponds, everywhere ponds and puddles. But with massive increases in population and the creation of helter-skelter interconnections through the technologies of travel and communication, the water table is rising and the puddles and ponds are all flowing together. This confluence produces turbulence more than homogenization, swirls more than smooth mixtures. Few today can pull apart and escape. Fewer yet have the will and the skills to cope effectively. So chaos reigns.

Agents of Reconciliation

If the fragmented and destructive environment of the former Yugoslavia is ever restored to peaceful productivity, the historians will surely note respectfully the effectiveness of a genuine peacemaker, Richard Holbrook. This competent negotiator and arbitrator, with skills honed through appropriate education and the experiences of his early career and his service as the U. S. Ambassador to Germany, has demonstrated an ideal of service that should be recognized and valued by every Christian. Like the Apostle Paul, Christians should see themselves as the ambassadors of Christ, working skillfully as agents of reconciliation, reconciling human beings to God through the finished work of Jesus Christ and reconciling human beings with one another in the name and service of the Prince of Peace.

If only Christian higher education could grasp this vision. What need there is! What a task could be undertaken by the Christian community's educational institutions! Why not become the source of well-prepared negotiators and peacemakers? As we endure the sounds of this roaring overture to the new century, humanity is splitting and crunching along this fault line and that. The world is crying out for help and healing, but competent, trained, experienced, and motivated peacemakers are in very short supply. And grief upon grief, some Christians, in their preoccupation for self-preservation and craven desire for separateness from the dirty tasks of this world, sometimes even disdain those Christians who do dedicate themselves to the ministries of relief, development, reconciliation, and public service. The name Jimmy Carter comes to mind. I make no secret of my admiration and respect for this man of God.

Putting Christian Education Together

Christian education, at all levels and for all purposes, is beginning to emerge from its bondage to traditionalism. Undertaking reform, restoration, remediation, and rejuvenation is the necessary task of educators who participate in God's continuing redemptive involvement with human society. Helping to interpret new visions and to carve

out new models are exhilarating prospects for the twenty-first century Christian educator. This prospect calls for readiness. One important starting point is to come to a clearer understanding of how
the church came to embrace such dysfunctional educational motives
and forms.

Teaching for Foundation-Building

Seeing learning as an end in itself is a common problem within formal education. Two contrasting positions are commonly taken by
teachers: some assume that anything that the person will ever need
to know should be at least represented and given attention in the
formal curriculum; others assume that trying to anticipate and deal
with every learning and information need within the scope of even
three or four years of formal education is futile. Teachers holding the
second position are more inclined to find ways to introduce channels
of inquiry and to teach the means and procedures by which the student can begin a process of lifelong learning. By contrast, those holding the first position tend to organize and deliver great quantities of
information, often overwhelming the students and leading them toward frustration and resentment.

Within much of higher education it is not unusual for faculty members to keep themselves so thoroughly informed in matters of the
content of their specialties that they have little mental energy or professional time left to come to any sort of professional understanding
of the learning processes and the art and science of teaching. These
are the professors who try to cover everything they think a student
will ever need to know. When such professors are in the majority
within a department, they usually control the departmental examining process. Their examinations often sound like the script for a
"trivia" game. Students in their sections will likely perform better on
the examinations than the students of the second type of professor.
But students who are more likely to continue their learning from the
foundation provided in their earlier learnings are not always hold-
ers of the best grade records.

Follow-up studies of graduates show that those who continue to
learn—in contrast with those who go stagnant after completing a
degree—have acquired an integrative style of learning. For these
learners it is more important to *think* than to *recall*. At some point
they began to resist the cognitive overload by spending more time
with the underlying questions: *So what? What difference would it make
if? How does this relate to that?* If this is so, then what happens to the
other? Intellectual exercises of this sort may jeopardize the getting of
higher grades, but such a student later rises up to applaud the pro-

fessor who encouraged this sort of mental process. The bottom line is that professors who give more attention to laying a sound foundation of learning skills and put substantial trust in the students' prospects for continuing education are more often the ones whose students later attest to continuing to learn.

Sustainable Habits

Academic jumping of hoops is futile. If learners strain and stretch in unnatural ways, they may achieve good grades, but they often end such an experience with a sigh of relief and a murmur of "never again." Graduate education in any applied discipline such as theology or education is a professional development experience; thus it must meet the tests of applicability and functionality. For the leader in the community of faith nothing is more practical than the skill and habit of reasoning theologically. People who cannot or will not think in God-centered abstractions and theoretical constructs are seriously undereducated. Tragically, it is possible to hold even a four-year graduate theology degree without having built the habits of thinking theologically. Academic theology, or academic education for that matter, should be held accountable for helping to develop in its students the sustainable habits of reasoning and thought. This outcome is far more important than merely causing students to demonstrate on some Olympian field of memory and verbiage that they have all the right answers to a set of rather predictable questions.

The False Dichotomy Between Word and Deed

Since childhood in a Christian home with concerned parents, I have been struggling with a stubborn question. Even after discovering the Epistle of James and relishing its blunt condemnation of fruitless belief, the struggle has continued. *Why is it so easy to be a Christian? More to the point, why do so many Christians let their kinship with Christ count for so little in their lives?*

The looseness of the uses of the word Christian is appalling. This is not to argue for some absolute litmus test of behavior beyond the tests provided in Scripture, but rather to assert that if evangelical Christianity is to make its appropriate contribution, we must take far more seriously the contributions we make toward godliness in human society. Some seem satisfied to take stands against things they judge to be evil; I appeal for taking stands with equal fervor *for* things that God advocates. The issue that differentiates among species of Christian lifestyle is whether it is more important to stay away from things or to become involved. *Social action* is a term that still divides the house. Pity. Pity.

The days ahead will severely test the adequacy of one's Christian roots. If the roots are shallow, based in cognitive information about what the Bible says, falling away will most likely be the consequence. If the roots are deep, nourished by *doing* the things of faith, the prospects for making a worthy contribution to society and thus deserving a hearing for one's faith-claims will surely be greater. The way we look at education will have much to do, therefore, with the quality of our Christian maturity.

> He has showed you, O man, what is good.
> And what does the LORD require of you?
> To act justly and to love mercy and to walk humbly
>   with your God.
>
> (Mic. 6:8)

A BASIS FOR DEALING WITH THE FUTURE

The Christian community has done as well as almost any of the other broad subdivisions of American society in the matter of lifelong learning. The Christian church has long embraced a lifelong encounter with exposition and application through regular exposure to sermons. Christians assume that there is always more to know. Quite recently there seems to be an increasing interest in learning things of God among those who are coming to recognize the dangers and turmoil in human societies that arise from denial of ultimate truth. The church, at home and abroad, faces a more comprehensive task in teaching and learning than ever before.

Learning Across a Lifetime

The concept of learning as a lifelong task is well supported in biblical teaching and in Christian theology. Lifelong development is given far more space in the Bible than is the somewhat more popular material on the conversion experience. The cultural contexts and mandates of both the Old Testament and New Testament assume that the progression toward wisdom is a function of maturing across life. Even our Lord's final instructions to his disciples brought up the issue of lifelong learning as a fundamental part of disciple-making: "Teaching them to obey [do] everything I have commanded you" (Matt. 28:20). How long does it take a person to learn, in the Hebraic sense of *doing* as the evidence of having learned, to do all things that our Lord has taught? It takes a lifetime, no less.

Unfinished Business: Dialogue

The agenda for Christian education in a more demanding future will surely carry some surprises beyond our power to predict. But, just as surely, today's unfinished business will find its way, perhaps with increased urgency, into the agenda for the new century. The word *dialogue* still frightens some Christians. It suggests an openness and willingness to get in touch with people who hold different views. And so it should. Among Christians, dialogue—processes of systematic and focused conversation and explication of mental paradigms—is an enriching and fulfilling part of the learning process. Through dialogue we not only hear other ways of expressing ideas and gain insights through others' perceptions, but we gain facility and confidence in the organizing and expressing of our own understandings. One of the best arguments that can be made in support of residential study is the deeper quality of dialogue that it can encourage—assuming that the academic environment is used for that purpose. Further, the Apostle Paul demonstrated in several situations that were new to him, in Athens for example, that dialogue concerning people's culture, religious presuppositions, and world view is a basic necessity for effective evangelization.

Unfinished Business: Culture Learning

The most pressing social need within every nation and across every international connection in this post-ideological world is for intercultural and especially inter-ethnic reconciliation. Leaders in the church face an increasing challenge to help the people of God learn within the church the rudiments of intercultural reconciliation. The example in Acts 6 when the church acknowledged its own internal bias and prejudice becomes more important with every passing year. Leaders must be good culture learners and effective teachers of culture learning.

The Crucial Rudiment: Lifelong Spiritual Development

Continuing education and lifelong learning are the ways and means by which a godly leader keeps sharp and fit. Spirituality is reflected in worship, a fountain of responsiveness to God's holiness. It is reflected in the humility of a Christlike walk of life, extending into the good works of life as evidence of faith (as emphasized in James). At the bottom line, such stewardship of life, its spirituality, mission and resources, is an appropriate response to the grace of God shown through the Lord Jesus Christ. Learning must first and foremost be concerned with the relationship of God's Word to life and experience. If the Word of God is to be of any significance in the maturing of faith, it will need to be put into action. The context of social life is where the best learning takes place. Donal Dorr, in *Spirituality and Justice* (1984), focuses on the place of godly work, surely the most controversial of the exercises of spiritual development. Dorr's effectiveness in connecting biblical materials to the ministries of Christian help and witness in an unjust world is outstanding. For many evangelicals the rediscovery of the Epistle of James has aroused social consciousness and has led to the recognition of the importance of applied ministry and the works of the gospel in the life of every maturing believer. To come into a fullness of relationship with the Lord Jesus Christ requires a commitment to lifelong spiritual development.

I HAVE NO DISCIPLES

I must hope that somewhere in God's grace there is a special forgiveness for pride in one's students. I thoroughly enjoy the warm and joyous thanksgiving that bubbles up from seeing one's children and one's students as especially worthy people. This pride is constrained by the recognition that I have not caused the success of another. I can take no credit for the gifts that God has given. I dare not see myself as more than God's instrument for a time and for a purpose. It is tempting to take credit for the meritorious accomplishments of others. Whatever God has allowed me to be and to do for another person is but one piece in the grand tapestry of God's providence in that person's life. I am but one parent to my sons and daughter. I am but one teacher for my students. Perhaps too often I speak of "my students" or "my former students" with that selfish and possessive word *my* revealing just how close to manipulative control I may wander. Am I eager to add to my stature through claims upon the excellence of someone else?

Do I see my students as being my disciples? Sometimes this word *disciple* is used very loosely. The teachings of Jesus revealed in the first twelve verses of Matthew 23 have become very important to me. I hear our Lord warning against loose use of titles and against relating to one another in any hierarchical manner that would obscure the basic truth that we are all brothers and sisters, under one Father and serving one Lord. We should understand discipleship in this manner: my students, Jane and John, are disciples of the Lord Jesus Christ; I too am a disciple of the Lord Jesus Christ. We share our discipleship. We stand side by side before our Lord. We help each other in our discipleship because we three are disciples of the same Lord. Thus, quite surely, I have no disciples.

Through the generous providence of God I have enjoyed the satisfactions, pleasures, and the disciplines of the teacher's calling. As a further grace, I have been given marvelous students—many, many of them with their own intensity of awareness of God's calling and the rich experiences of their walk of faith under the Lordship of Jesus Christ. For all of these things I would claim no recognition except for a small note of identification with another hero of my Christian faith—Johann Sebastian Bach—whose final wet ink on every completed work spoke of his true motivation: doing all for the glory of God.

Soli Deo Gloria.

Chapter Two _____

Servants, Leaders, and Tyrants

Ted W. Ward

_____

From the topic "Servants, Leaders and Tyrants," you might surmise that I intend to deal with either of two areas of concern, both of which happen to be very close to my professional role and to my consciousness as a Christian involved with the development of the church. The emphasis could be on leaders and tyrants in the sense of the politics of the state, or on the Third World, where one of the greatest problems is political tyranny. Or the emphasis could be on the task of American Christians in raising an ever more steady voice in matters of social justice. But no, it is not my intention to discuss leaders and tyrants in the sense of the politics of the state, but in reference to leadership in the church. Indeed, of the three words, servants, leaders and tyrants, the greatest concern is for the first two—servants and leaders—and through the servant-leader relationship, the avoidance of the third, tyranny.

The church is the institution through which God provides for the redemptive development of human beings—particularly of the ones who are called by His name and, through them, of all mankind. Therefore, we need constantly to ask questions about where we are in history and what is happening to the church in our time: what is its social context, within itself and within its larger human circum-

_____

stances? All of this can tell us something about leadership in and for the church, what it is and what it must confront.

PROBLEMS

Servanthood and leadership are basic concepts in biblical Christianity. How servanthood and leadership relate to each other is an especially important issue in the development of the church in our time. But discussion of servants and leaders sometimes leads to consideration of tyrants; indeed, tyranny within the church is one of the historical and contemporary problems of Christianity. Much that we assume and much that we tolerate (and sometimes embrace) within the church and especially within the educational functions of the church is tyrannical.

The criticism is that of a sympathetic "insider," and a member of the family; it is not intended as a diatribe to send you reeling in revulsion. I wish to share the concerns that are very deep, concerns that can be accepted in a spirit of community. There are many ways of viewing the particulars that are described following, and I do not claim to see the evidence in its most clear light. But if I am even partly right, in light of the Scriptures there are some things here about which Christians need to take action. These are matters of importance, with implications especially for Christian education for the near future, if the Lord should tarry and if the church should hold firm in this era.

Five problems are identified, each of the five related to leadership. What the problems may mean is suggested in the two propositions that follow.

Passivity

One of the characteristics of certain sectors of the church today, speaking primarily of symptoms in North American Christianity, is passivity of the laity. This issue is commonly discussed; it is generally accepted to be a problem. Why should it be that some Christians are so willing to delegate—to let others take care of responsibilities—while being so passive and apparently so disinterested in the things of God? We hear such criticisms as, "The people push responsibility onto their pastors" and, "They hire pastors in order to get certain jobs done that they themselves are not willing to carry out." This problem of passivity of the laity seems to be widely recognized by the clergy and is acknowledged by the laity.

Hierarchy

Much of the church today is essentially as hierarchical as any secular organization. Yes, the Protestants, evangelicals and even the Baptists (!) have accepted hierarchy as the keynote of organization. Some clergy are sensitive to this. Laymen are even more sensitive and concerned about it. There is a mounting criticism that the church, established as a community of God's children ("you are all brothers" Matthew 23:8) has *fallen* into hierarchical structures. Historically, we can be more accurate than that; we can observe that it hasn't fallen into it, at least certainly not in recent times. It just never reformed *out* of it. The hierarchical structure of the church was one of the earliest secular "innovations" within Christianity; at the time of the Reformation, it was not significantly altered. The Reformers brought over into Protestantism much of the hierarchical organization that was characteristic of the Roman Church up until that time. We still suffer today with the Chiefs-and-Indians syndrome. There are an awful lot of Indians and relatively few Chiefs; but the Chiefs make most of the decisions—directly or manipulatively. This complaint does not argue against the doctrines of offices in the church. Biblically, the offices are not hierarchical but are functional. They are described in terms of the needs of the particular church. The offices are intrinsically related to the gifts of the Holy Spirit to the church. And the gifts are broadly distributed among the people of God—not concentrated on a prestigious hierarchy.

This particular criticism is focused on the ranking systems that exist in the church. The assumed legitimacy of ranking itself, and the resulting notion that there are some people who are more important and other people who are less important, is debilitating, and undercuts the work of the Holy Spirit.

Intellectual Meritocracy

The third criticism is more widely heard among laymen than among the clergy: leadership education for the church is dominated by an intellectual meritocracy. In the church, status is earned by knowing; what is required for leadership is the possession of a magic bag of merits. These magic bags of merits are systematically dealt out only to relatively few players in the game. The dealers are the theological seminaries. Once a magic bag of merit is in one's possession, it can be traded for honor and prestige (plus a salary) at the friendly local church, and thus one maintains oneself—career and salary—more in terms of what one knows than what one *is*. The Bible suggests relatively *few* criteria for the elder or the pastor (or for the deacon) that relate to what one knows. Many *more* criteria relate to what a person is and how a person is functioning within the community of Christ. Yet Christians today seem reluctant to challenge the sort of ordination that is dictated by the educational establishment. Intellectual meritocracy is a kind of aristocracy; it should be challenged within the church because it falls short of the standards for community that are described biblically as the community of Christ.

Pride and Status

The fourth of the criticisms is also heard mostly among the laity: leadership in the church itself has become something of a proud self-serving status in which one takes pride in the leadership role and serves oneself through the various kinds of privileges and prerequisites of leadership. In other words, leadership has become something of an end in itself. Leadership is a cause for pride and self-service much more than a cause for service to the community. The teachings of Christ about servanthood are confused in some minds with the Horatio Alger Americanism: one begins low in order to become great. Servanthood becomes a temporary or transient period of initiation or demonstration of eligibility.

Manipulative Tactics

The fifth criticism is of the style of leadership—a style increasingly characterized by manipulative leadership tactics. It takes no diligent search to find the use of manipulative strategies and procedures on the part of leadership people, particularly the manipulation of guilt in order to get certain kinds of conformity: the use of fear; the playing upon "divisions" that occur within the household of faith; and the old-fashioned technique of manipulated gossip. These concerns are rarely voiced among the clergy, but they are discussed increasingly among laymen.

The new wave of "management skills" in church leadership may be partly responsible, since management technology takes as its basic value pragmatic goal-seeking. But there is an easier explanation: at least some of the problems of manipulative leadership can be traced to an impoverishment of leadership logic and leadership skills. Just as a person who swears a lot is probably a person with a very limited vocabulary, some leaders are manipulative because they have a limited "vocabulary" or understanding of leadership. They lack awareness of the possible range of approaches to people, and therefore, they resort to tactics that are impudent, and in the final analysis, childish. They resort more to manipulation than to true leadership.

WHY?

Consider these five problems again: 1) passivity of the laity; 2) hierarchical organization; 3) domination by intellectual meritocracy; 4) proud and self-serving valuing of leadership; and 5) manipulative leadership style. The problems all can be traced to the first: passivity of the laity. It is both cause and result. So long as any of the other four persist it will produce passivity; and so long as passivity persists, the others cannot be effectively solved.

How do the people of God get out of their lethargy and into action? There are two ways to view the problem: 1) there is something wrong with the people, or 2) there is something wrong with the leadership. We are much more likely to see the gifts of the Spirit develop in God's people if the latter view is taken. The question to be posed is, "What is wrong with leadership that results in passivity in the laity?"

Proposition One

The five problems are cyclical. In the sense that they each feed each other and the whole thing keeps coming back onto the first problem, it is a self-perpetuating cycle and extremely difficult to break into.

Proposition Two

The conditions in the church today are a reflection of conditions in the secular society. Many people in the church demonstrate the same needs felt by people in the secular society. In other words, these needs—to be dominated, to be manipulated, to be passive, to let somebody else do it, and to transfer obligation and responsibility—are very symptomatic of our secular society. Ours is a society of largely passive participation. Americans have an intense interest in sports, for example, but it is mostly at the observational level. From time to time there are upsurges of handball, racquet ball, tennis, golf and whatever, but the persistence of the beer can and the television tells us what the real interest in sports is; it is not athletics so much as it is observation. To be part of something by simply watching it is characteristic of our society.

Some of the needs to which the church is catering are basically non-Christian needs; when the church is catering (or pandering) to non-Christian needs, the church is on dangerous ground. For example, among the non-Christian and sick needs of fallen humankind are needs for status, needs for individualism and needs for being powerful or being dominated by power. The psychological condition of a person who has the need to be dominated is not really all that far from the person who has the need to dominate. These are sick needs; they are unredeemed needs. They are not characteristic of the people of God in any normative, biblical way. Instead, they are characteristic of the secular society, and yet the church has accepted them as normal.

Consider what the issue is and what the issue isn't. In reference to the biblical teachings on leadership, the issue is not whether or not there should be leadership. Indeed, the Scripture is very clear that there are leadership roles in which to serve and leadership tasks to be performed. The salutations in the New Testament indicate that at the time of the apostles there were leaders, and they were recognized as such. In Hebrews 13:24, for example, "Greet all your leaders and God's people." (The reader is anxious that already there was a distinction between leaders and saints!) The leadership persons were identified. Thus, the issue is not whether there should be leadership, but the issue is what kind of leadership. What *kind* of leadership furthers the cause of Christ, honors the cause of Christ, honors the name of Christ, furthers Christ's church?

Further, the issue is not that the seminaries are creating this problem, but whether or not the seminaries today can serve to relieve the problem. There is little to be gained by pinning the blame somewhere. Instead, we need to face up to the situation as we find it, and to ask what we can do, what the various institutions that serve the church can do, and particularly, what higher education and seminaries can do to relieve these problems. Christian higher education, in general, may indeed be culpable, but far more important is its potentiality for helping to get the church out of the current leadership crises.

Despite the positive orientation toward education and a preference for constructive propositions, one word of warning must be sounded at this point. We should not rely too much on formal education. (I am uneasy about Christian higher education in general, and the Christian liberal arts college in particular, but that is another story.) In this discussion it is enough to warn that since the time of Thomas Aquinas, Christianity has been holding hands with formal education largely oblivious of the dangers it poses especially in relation to the development of the church. The dangers are inherent. When you accept the schooling model, its assumptions about knowledge, learning and human relationships, you get some non-Christian values in the bargain. Much that is secular in the church can be traced to its drawing of crucial values from the academy of pre-Christian Greece.

The issue is not that the secular society induces the sort of leadership that we find in the church. Indeed it does, but that is not the issue. Instead, it is our productive task to seek ways that will help the church to withstand secular perversion and to be about its task of confronting culture. *Semper Reformanda.* Are we indeed about the business of reforming? If we are, the question of the secular perversions in the church must be raised. "Secular perversions" does not refer to going to the movies, not even to chopping wood on Sunday. Instead, it refers to those things that are organismic and more deeply functional in our institutional forms—violations of justice, truth, responsibility and unity. Whatever is secular in its origin and whatever is justified (rationalized) in secular terms must be disciplined in the light of the Word and the reforming work of God in the world. The complaint is not so much against the secular Society, but is in reference to ourselves, as those who stand against the worldly order to see that the work of Christ is carried out in the power of the Holy Spirit.

A NEW FRONTIER

The issue is not that the church is confronting some new problem, but that the church historically has never dealt adequately with an old problem: institutionalism, and especially formal education. Jesus' teaching on servanthood has rarely cut through institutionalism in historical Christianity. Take a look from the earliest times. The warnings of Matthew 23 were laid down in order that there could be some advice available at the very beginning of the church. Jesus said, in effect, "Beware of the dangers of institutionalism." And yet through the years of Christendom we have seen institutionalism dominating Christianity. In our time, the problem is becoming acute or at least more deeply felt. God may be sharpening the focus on leadership as servanthood.

Several factors underscore this possibility. First of all, pragmatism is replacing more principlized sorts of valuing in historical Christendom. The western cultural, moral and legal traditions since the time of Christ, have, on the whole, held to a kind of principled valuing. Thus even the secular society has reflected something of the teachings of the Scriptures in reference to morality. But today that has degenerated to the point where almost all valuing is pragmatic. Pragmatic valuing has crept into the church—creeping in somewhat as an elephant creeps. And the pragmatism in even such important elements and movements as evangelism, missions and "church growth" is often frightening. Concern over the issue of pragmatism is forcing the re-examination of the values underlying leadership. These are questions that the church historically has not had to focus quite that sharply. Other issues were bigger. In our time, the questions of what constitutes valid leadership in the church seems to be a transcendently important issue.

A second factor today is a widespread denial of God. Secular people no longer simply curse God; they deny God. God does not need to be cursed, because God is irrelevant. God is either not there or not at all in the process of thought. In such a state, even the church is left with a humanism that is becoming rapidly more absolute, a humanism that even lends itself to a congregational democracy which is more rational than spiritual. Authority is not thought to come from God. Thus leadership of the church is as relative as anything else. The denial of God may thus be raising the question of leadership to a higher level of importance among the various matters of concern to the church.

A third factor, confidence in institutions—in general, in western civilization—is waning rapidly. The various sorts of anarchy that have been sporadic and localized in the past are now becoming international and societal in the largest sense. Institutions have lost credibility. In the 1960s we saw it in our own nation: a tremendous loss of confidence in institutions. All sorts of institutions were affected: the military; government; educational institutions; the justice system; even our health institutions. Everything came to suspicion or disrepute. This rampant individualism, nurtured by the American psyche, is still advancing, replacing institutional trust with a kind of egocentric acquisitiveness. So you don't need to trust institutions nor to see them as having an important place; you just reach out for what's yours. Surely this is not socially cohesive; perhaps it is the threshold of widespread anarchy.

Leadership, in general, is in disrepute. Even among the people of God and within the community of Christ there is a challenging of leadership that promises to go far deeper than at any time previous. The question of what is proper leadership in the church, has probably never been a more dynamic question.

BIBLICAL LEADERSHIP

The Bible deals with leadership in a peculiar way. In the New Testament, the contrast with secular leadership is sharp. The Old Testament is not quite so precise, except for the inescapable God-presence shown through His selected leaders. Models of leadership can be drawn from Noah, Abraham, Joseph, Nehemiah, Moses and other illustrious characters of the Old Testament. These are pre-Christian, some are even pre-scriptural, and they can send us off on the wrong foot. It is alarming how many Christian education textbooks draw an out-of-context model of leadership from Moses. Until Sinai, Moses did not have the Word of God except in oral form. Moses is seen as leading through his adjudication. Of course! People came to Moses for adjudication because they lacked objective testimony. But is there need for Moses-style of leadership today?

In the New Testament leadership is less dramatic. It is seen as less concerned with the huge and momentous movements of history and more concerned with the step-by-step development of the people of God. What is most striking is the attunement between the leader and the community.

In Hebrews 13:7 for example, leadership is more than knowing and telling: "Remember your leaders, who spoke the word of God to you. Consider the outcome of their way of life and imitate their faith." Leadership is a behavior—a lifestyle—that is worthy of being inspected; it is even worthy of being emulated. Leadership is not just what a person knows, not just what a person says. Look again at Matthew 23. Note how contrasting is Jesus' criticism of the secular (Greek) model of leadership demonstrated by those who have seated themselves in the seat of Moses: "they talk a good line but they don't behave consistently, they are not worth modeling on" (Matthew 23:3). In Hebrews 13:17 we read: "Obey your leaders and submit to their authority. They keep watch over you as men who must give an account." Leadership in New Testament terms is reckoned in terms of accountability, not just in terms of authority. It gets its authority as it has accountability. Taken as a whole, biblical teaching on leadership deals more with criteria than with privilege; and beyond responsibility is accountability.

Leaders

Who are leaders? Who are tyrants? Who are servants? First of all, in reference to leaders of the church, the model of leadership must not be drawn from secular sources: it must be drawn from the Scripture and evaluated in terms of accountability to the Lordship of Christ.

Among the various pragmatic incursions into the planning of church development, church polity and Christian life in general, is the American Management Association—coming through like a rhinoceros on an escalator. The American Management Association tells us that leadership is "Getting work done through people." And there are plenty of people in almost all denominations today doing a slightly baptized version of pragmatic manipulation and calling it "Christian management." Selling at a fairly nice price, leadership seminars for the clergy are available at many local motels. These are dangerous when, in the cause of efficiency, answers to human development and human relationship questions are drawn from secular sources.

When leadership is disciplined to the Lordship of Christ, there are some different conclusions. For example, a leader is one who ministers; a leader *serves* through the gifts of the Holy Spirit, not in terms of prowess, not in terms of accomplishments or acquired knowledge, but in terms of what God is doing through his or her life. Leadership in the church is servanthood.

In the past fifteen years an interesting development has been taking place within mission-sponsored pastoral training. The trend, theological education by extension (TEE), has been an encouragement, although one wonders about the direction it is going at present. (It has become, for some missions, an excuse for sending more missionaries to do jobs that really should be done by national persons. I have nothing against sending out missionaries, but I am very uneasy about missionaries who replicate American institutional forms and values without even a dim consciousness of the damage they do.) One of the most valuable outcomes of the TEE movement is the question it has raised about how broadly distributed the benefits of theological education ought to be. This is an important question. It leads us in the direction of broadening access to theological education. It is unwise for any seminary—whether missionary or in the United States—to focus exclusively on a small number of people. First, the seminary ought to include in its teaching ministries (and some seminaries do) both clergy and lay persons (so long as that nonbiblical distinction holds). A seminary ought to make its expertise broadly available to the people of God. Second, with reference to the people who are being trained in a seminary, the emphasis should be on those who are in church leadership more than those who think they might be. In Third World situations, especially in theological education by extension, one sees how much more vital educational ministries become if they are focused on people who are already in leadership roles in the church. In other words, the theological education by extension models that seem most promising and most faithful to the church are focused on functioning pastors, not on pre-pastors. The educational institution should not be in the business of *creating* preachers, ministers and church leadership people, but of *equipping* leadership people. To serve the church, education should be broadly committed to equipping the saints in the roles, tasks and ministries to which they are called.

If theological education is going to devote itself exclusively to providing magic bags of merit for the relatively select few, and then impose those selected few on the churches with a take-them-or-leave-them attitude, then the church has lost something important. If this is what theological education is to be, the ground work is laid for a model of leadership that will become easily tyrannical.

Tyrants

Who are the tyrants? In simplest terms, a tyrant is a leader who aspires. Admittedly, this is less a definition than it is a harsh criterion. A leader who aspires tends to misuse others; such a leader attempts to manage things by manipulating events. This aspiration to leadership was exactly what Jesus was dealing with in Matthew 20, when the dear mother was deeply concerned about where her sons would be when they sat down in the glorious Kingdom. Jesus firmly explained that the value system of God's Kingdom is not like the value system that her question was expressing. A fundamental clash in value systems was evident: "You don't know what you're asking." In other words, she was not on the wavelength of the Kingdom of God. In the Kingdom of God aspirations to leadership are not valued unless they arise from commitment to servanthood. In the North American frame of mind I'm afraid the commitment to servanthood is seen quite often as a sort of apprenticeship. If you are willing to clean toilets for three weeks, God's people will see that you are willing to be a servant, glorify you, and make you a leader. Such thinking is wholly inconsistent with the Scriptural view of leadership. Our Lord taught that Christian servanthood is a servanthood of a low order for life. Not as an apprenticeship, but for life. "And after this the glorification," said the Apostle Paul in Philippians. After what? After the crucifixion, after the giving of one's life, *then* the glorification. Make no mistake, *anyone who aspires to leadership within the Christian community is essentially a tyrant.*

Tyranny can also be seen in a person's accepting privilege and the separate distinction that comes from privileged status. Sooner or later a tyrant comes to believe in his or her own worthiness (the "divine right"). This vulnerability is not confined to kings and dictators. Pastors and congregational persons are easily ensnared also. Any of the people of God who aspire to leadership, who accept privileges and the distinctiveness based upon what they see as their own merit, are in our midst as tyrants. "Whoever wants to become great among you must be your servant" (Matthew 20:26) is less an invitation to sign up as a leader than it is an action test that we can apply to ourselves when we hear the call to leadership tasks within the body of Christ.

Servants

Who are the servants? Servants are those who share and thus lead. Servants are those who give and thus receive. Servants bear one another's burdens. How can leaders discipline themselves to be servants? Becoming a servant on the do-it-yourself basis can become a big problem for the Christian. It is only by God's transforming work that we get far enough from the human tendency to dominate. We must examine our motives as individuals and we must examine the motives of institutions. Certainly as institutional faculty and administrators, we should examine our so-called "professional" motives.

Are we motivated to serve or are we motivated to dominate? So easily comes the answer, "Of course we're motivated to serve." Then comes the next question: is that the way we are living or do we slide toward a posture of domination? Do we rejoice in servanthood, or do we bear the burden of servanthood? It requires the grace of God to remain faithful to the servant role.

Leaders should ask God for grace to trust the people of God. Through contacts with pastors in various conferences and workshops, I'm impressed how little trust there is, especially from the pastorate toward the laity. Instead of trust, the tendency is to say "*they*," "*them*," "*their* problems," "*they* give me these problems," *they*-us, *they*-us. Greater and greater is the distinction between *them*, the laity, and *us*, the clergy. The church's programs are for *them*—doing things for *them*. I wonder . . . wouldn't it be better to do things *with* them?

Another suggestion: leaders should get in tune with the work of the Holy Spirit in the congregation. Let the gifts of the Spirit be recognized *in all* and *for all*. Perhaps pastors experience an occupational anxiety: if people discover that the gifts of God to the church are widely distributed, the pastor will be out of a job and then his children will be hungry. Is it anxiety or just plain pride? People easily pick up the nonverbal signals that the pastor sends: he's got to do it all and he's got to do it his way, after all, that's his responsibility, that's the pastor's job.

The remedy lies in accepting the breadth and variety of the works of the Holy Spirit. Where exciting things are happening, quite often the pastor is an important part of it—but not necessarily the spark plug or the steering wheel. If leaders can keep clear of rank and privilege, which are vanity, their ministry will be more pleasing to God and more edifying for the saints.

Jesus Christ has provided a set of evaluative criteria for leadership that each of us can use in self-evaluation, and by which we should evaluate every institution. In the first 12 verses of Matthew 23, Jesus describes for his disciples what had gone wrong in the synagogue. He presents the list of factors as a set of warnings about what should be avoided in the church. Clearer understanding of the secular origin of faulty leadership can come from a look at the history of pre-Christian Greek culture and philosophy. In this light, Matthew 23:1-12 reveals not the Old Testament synagogue, which the church improves upon, but a faulted synagogue, gone wrong because of the introduction of Greek (Hellenistic) models of leadership education.

HELLENISTIC INFLUENCES—THEN AND NOW

Prior to the time of Christ, the Greek (Hellenistic) culture had developed social models and definitional concepts that can be seen deeply entrenched in the church today. The Hellenists made their move toward Judaism in the time of Christ; He warned against it explicitly. Even so, it seems evident that the Greek model of school and schooling, which in turn shaped the relationship of leaders and followers— the dominant social configuration of western people—has become the characteristic human relationship within the church.

What are the characteristics of the Greek concepts of school and schooling? First of all, hierarchy is basic. There are those who *know* and there are those who *need to know*. Our church buildings are monuments to the pre-Christian proposition that the source is a person and that the masses are receivers. In the New Testament the church is people. Today it is a building to which people go to hear—to learn, to get information—about the things of God.

Social distance and its artifacts are a second characteristic of the Greek assumptions about human relationships. Yes, social distance is more than social circumstances and relational characteristics; it creates and thrives on its artifacts. A lectern is such an artifact; a platform is such an artifact. A public address system, sitting below in order to look up to authority, robes for the elite, all these common artifacts facilitate the superior/inferior relationship that we accept toward one another. It is a relationship in which one gives and others receive. This assumption found its way into modern times, especially in the distinction between the educated and the "uneducated."

The third characteristic of the Greek model of school and schooling is one-way communication: from the authority to those who are assumed to be in need of hearing. Obviously we all share in a common vulnerability to these criticisms. To a greater or lesser extent, we are each a product of the very things we're talking about. We conform very nicely because we have been brought up in it. I speak, you listen; I write, you read. It is a hard pattern to alter. But today the new emphasis on dialogue and sharing remind us that deliberation and exchange were characteristic of the human transactions of the Old Testament times, when God's people saw him as speaking both to and *with* them.

The fourth characteristic of the Greek model has to do with social privilege and how one gains social privilege. Education is essentially a social privilege. One gains further social privilege through educational competition. Education is a matter of competitively acquiring and proving one's worth and ability, by demonstrating it in meritocratic sorts of ways. This too, is inherently Hellenistic and thus Pre-Christian.

Beyond the assumptions about relationships and about communication, the faulted Greek concept of knowledge and its implications for human development are seen today in the church. Three particulars illustrate the problem.

1. *Knowledge as a commodity.* Knowledge is somewhere out there. It is to be appropriated, it is to be acquired and brought in. It exists "out there" and it is to be reached out and grasped. It is a commodity to be bought and sold, to be captured and hoarded.

2. *Learning as acquisition.* Learning, itself, is a task through which one reaches out selectively and acquires. The learner must be induced through various kinds of motivation to reach out systematically. The purpose of the teacher is to give motivation, direction and guidance in the reaching-out process. The Greek assumptions are in sharp contrast with Hebrew concepts of knowledge. In the latter, learning develops from within, as one applies himself in such a way that God reveals through inner light one's experience.

3. *Knowing as the basis of doing.* In the Hellenistic exalting of intellect and rationality, the concern for acting on one's knowledge was assumed to be unimportant; it was seen as virtually automatic or even irrelevant. What one *knows* was the important matter. Therefore, the matter of concern about action, and especially evaluating in terms of *doing*, was somewhat alien. Evaluating for the knowing was assumed to cover it all. Think of the academic approach to testing even today, for example: it is usually preoccupied with what one *knows*, in the sense of recall of information. It is very Greek and not very functional.

The teachings of Christ suggest relatively little emphasis on testing of knowledge. He screens people not on what they know but on what they do. This same priority is seen in the Epistles. In the book of James, there is a corrective teaching which suggests that the emphasis on *doing* was in danger of being lost. What was the cause of this apparent shift away from Christ's "follow Me . . . , "walk . . . , "do . . . "? Was it because of the Hebrew influence? Hardly. The Hebrew philosophy was very much an integration of knowing and doing—learning through doing; it was the integration of life itself. Instead, the shift James warns against was in the Greek philosophical outlook. Whereas the Hebrew argued for the inseparability of knowing and doing, the Hellenistic view valued *knowing* over doing. These social models crashed into the church early and have survived the Reformation.

One of the truisms in education is that people tend to treat others as they themselves have been treated. If teachers and administrators relate to theological students in a certain way, it is likely that the students will relate to the people of God in their parishes the same way. What relationships are thus propagated by theological education? What sort of authority structure is being exemplified? What sorts of powers of life-and-death, success-or-failure are held over students? What sort of community exists? All of these patterns become models for the church. Because of the importance Christians have placed on formal education, the Greek model and its associated views of learning and knowledge have been imprinted on the church down through the centuries.

Schooling has served the church reasonably well. God has elected to use it. Nevertheless, it is possible that we are at a point when another facet of the reforming work of God is about to become manifested. If so, will it not likely alter the educational approaches to leadership development in the church?

CONCLUSION

Jesus warned against the secular model of leadership. Nevertheless, it invaded the church even as it had invaded the synagogue. The Pharisees did it first, having seated themselves in the seat of Moses (Matthew 23:2). It is the picture of an incursion, an invasion, an intrusion, or a usurpation. If all these Pharisees and teachers of the Law were Jewish people, why shouldn't they be free to take their places in the seat of Moses? Because their approach and their values were less Hebrew than Greek. They wanted things to be crisply rational and structural in the Greek way that was sweeping the western Mediterranean at that time. It was *the* way, the *in* way, the faddish way to do things—to think Greek!

At the time of Christ the invasion of the synagogue was well advanced. In the early centuries of the church, it happened to Christianity—exactly as Jesus warned his disciples about so clearly.

Leadership for the church is to be *non-tyrannical servanthood*, evaluated in light of the teachings of our Lord. Let us therefore accept the evaluative criteria of Matthew 23:3-12. Verse 3: Let us reconcile word and deed. Verse 4: Let us not be delegative but participatory. Verse 5: Let us seek no exalted status. Verse 6: Let us accept no special privilege. Verse 7: Let us take no pride from secular recognition. Verse 8: Let us reject titles of authority, preferring instead a simple relationship as brothers. Verse 9: Let us develop *real* relationships, not artificial and titular relationships. Verse 10: Let us share with all God's people the recognition of one master. Verse 11: Let us relate as servants to the needs of others. And verse 12: Let us live in humble lifestyle.

Let us accept leadership as spiritual gifts: "It was he who gave some to be apostles, some to be prophets, some to be evangelists, and some to be pastors and teachers, to prepare God's people for works of service, so that the body of Christ may be built up" (Ephesians 4:11-12).

Let us reflect the mind of Christ: "whoever wants to become great among you must be your servant, and whoever wants to be first must be your slave—just as the Son of Man did not come to be served, but to serve, and to give his life as a ransom for many" (Matthew 20:26-28).

Chapter Three _____

Evaluating Metaphors of Education

Ted W. Ward

What education is and how it can be used properly are matters too important to be left vague. Education suffers from over popularity. Everyone has experienced it in one or many of its forms. Indeed, everyone "knows" what it is; education is commonplace. Self-appointed experts on education are everywhere. Small wonder then that so many ill-advised assaults on the human spirit are passed off as worthy educational ventures.

Three essentially different metaphors of education account for most of the thinking, planning and operation of formal education. Each of these ways of conceptualizing education should be evaluated in terms of the Christian concern for spiritual development.

IS TRUE EDUCATION MERELY INTELLECTUAL?

Christianity is in large measure a rational religion. Spiritual development does not exclude any of the aspects of human personhood. Even the physical is an object of God's redemption (Romans 8:11, 23; Philippians 3:21). And surely the intellectual is not rejected, for the Word of God in two ways testifies to God's valuing of human under-

_____

Ted Ward, "Evaluating Metaphors of Education: Part 3, Metaphors of Spiritual Reality," *Bibliotheca Sacra* 139 (556) (1982): 291-301. All rights reserved. Reprinted by permission. This was the third article in a series based on the author's W. H. Griffith Thomas Memorial Lectures at Dallas Theological Seminary, February 9-12, 1982.

standing: a) it is a readable documentation and b) it explicitly says, "I would not have you to be ignorant." To know God is a matter of experiential fellowship and communion based essentially on His revelation of Himself to humanity through the special revelation of the written Word. Even the Lord's self-identification as "the Word made flesh" (John 1:14) was made known to man by the explicit information of the written Word. These matters are made "knowable" through the mystery of God, Jesus Christ the Redeemer, whose work on man's behalf can be grasped intellectually as textual information, confirmed within him by the ministry of the Holy Spirit, and acted out in functional life as believers identify themselves with Christ in walk and conversation (Colossians 2; 3). Thus it should be seen that education which is concerned only with intellectual development or in which the acquisition of information is a compulsive priority is less than Christian.

Contemporary secular society, especially in the Western world, is profoundly influenced by rationalism and its roots in Hellenistic philosophy. The highest view of knowledge is that of clarified information. In contrast, the Hebrew cultural and religious roots of Christianity point toward true knowledge as that which is acted on. The Christian outcome of education, therefore, should not be the Greek-like satisfaction with clarified concepts. Instead the biblical concern for obedience—acting on truth—should be the central purpose of education and of life. It is not enough to argue that obedience requires knowing. The issue is that knowing, in Christianity, cannot be defined apart from doing. Both John and Paul are sensitive to the tendency to divide creed from deed, quite likely entering the early church from Greek philosophy and educational traditions (Romans 6:4; 1 Corinthians 3; Galatians 5:10-13; Ephesians 2:10; 5:2; Philippians 3:12-16; Colossians 2:6; 1 Thessalonians. 2 :1-12 ; 1 John 1:6-7 ; 2 John 6; 3 John 4). Their warnings are needed today as surely as in the first-century church.

WHAT IS THE PLACE OF EDUCATIONAL INSTITUTIONS?

It is entirely possible that Christianity in North America and Western Europe may have overemphasized formal education. Surely if access to Christian higher education were highly correlated with the development of the church of Jesus Christ, the United States would now be the most Christianized nation in history.

Evangelical Christianity has available today an unprecedented network of institutions of theological education, pastoral development, intellectual stimulation through literature, vocational training,

Bible study, and "liberal arts" foundational learning. So what happens? There must be some slippage somewhere. Could it be that Christian colleges and seminaries are giving academic credit for the wrong things? In the quest for excellence, Christian higher education may have become intoxicated with the intellectual snobberies so glorified in worldly academia. Much of today's institutional Christian education is off on a head-trip. The service motive is subordinated to intellectual goals. And service, when subordinated to anything, withers and dies. So long as "practical experience" is stultified by treating it as a poor cousin of intellectual learning, so long as "Christian service assignments" are weekend outings divorced from distinct and relevant dialogue with one's "academic learnings," and so long as theological education is seen as preparatory to (rather than simultaneous with) ministry, a weak linkage will continue between education and the development of the church.

In the past decade we evangelicals have been urged to think of Christianity and its institutions, especially the more conservative ones, as riding a crest of popularity and growth. If this view were altogether accurate, one could expect unprecedented strength and vitality in churches and dramatic influence on society at large. Increased enrollment in theological education is one evidence of the much-touted growth. A close look reveals certain changes of procedure but not significant differences in the net effects. For example, continuing education is becoming popular. Though the "preparatory" posture still holds at the core of things, the idea of advanced formal education for in-service development is becoming almost too popular.

More and more pastors are getting doctoral degrees. But what is the logic of it all? What does it mean? In what ways is the church affected? Should not learning be a lifelong affair? Does it really require the carrot-and-stick approach to motivate it? Does it really need to be punctuated by one degree after another?

The time has come to raise the question of how much formal education is too much. Many metaphors of "the good life" carry the notion that "more is better." Surely education, especially formal education, is in this category. So goes American thought.

Getting is its own end. One need not ask why. Could the American obsession with getting, gaining, collecting and accumulating be the reason evangelicals do not evaluate ways and means more carefully? Whether the question is how many degrees one needs to be considered educated or how large a church enrollment ought to be, it does not follow that more is better.

The American church is on the ragged edge of having too many pastors with doctoral degrees. The current trend toward more and more theology degrees is good news and bad news. It is good news, of course, whenever people are motivated to develop the talents and resources with which God has endowed them. But it is bad news when pastors in the competitive quest for degrees so easily get caught up in proud prestige-seeking and lofty intellectualism that will isolate them from the people they claim to serve. When Jesus' teaching about leadership and education in Matthew 23:1-12 is ignored, the result is again the pomp of the Pharisees and scribes.

Some of the motives for continuing education are less than Christian. Some pastors seek power and privilege through the secular medium of formal education. (Formal education is often highly reflective of non-Christian values and interpersonal relationships even when used in the service of the church, as in a seminary or a Christian college.) The trouble lies in two sources: a) the difficulty of keeping the Lord's model of humility and servanthood at the fore and b) the wrong choice of metaphor of education. The resulting experiences often tend toward alienation rather than the building of Christian communities.

THE METAPHOR OF FILLING

The practice of Christian education, with a few exceptions, is ambivalent, inconsistent and even erratic about what education is. Is it competitive or cooperative? Is it for all God's people or for an elite? Is it to prepare for *future* ministry or to facilitate an ongoing ministry? Education means several different things, some of which are contradictory; educational efforts often malfunction. There is no question about sincerity and hope; the root of the problem lies more in unexamined and unevaluated metaphors of education.

Consider two of the most common metaphors: education as *filling* a container and education as a *manufacturing* process. These two are closely related, though they use different symbolism. They are both faulty.

One of the key problems in both of these concepts of education is their rooting in a *tabula rasa* view of childhood. Worse yet this view of the learner as an empty slate to be written on by "those who know" is even applied to the teaching of adults. The result is high-cost "kiddie-schools" with larger chairs and less interesting teachers.

The learner is more acted on than active. The learner, especially in the "filling" metaphor, is essentially a blank page to be written on by those doing the educating. This orientation demeans the image of God shared in each person and it encourages a passive receptivity, ultimately lacking in creativity and skills of evaluation.

In the "manufacturing" metaphor the learner is assumed to have characteristics which the machinery must chip off and grind down. Irregularities and peculiarities in the learner—the "raw material"—are usually regarded as a nuisance. The system could be so much more efficient if everyone were exactly alike, it argues. This metaphor makes a teacher preoccupied with "the system" and its gadgetry. The learner is an object—something to be shaped and molded.

Teachers who think of education in terms of filling a container are rarely concerned with individual differences of background, interest or aspiration. The *content* is the thing. Most learning can be reduced to questions and answers; recall of information is the evidence of becoming educated; tests are good indicators of "success" or "failure"; grading can be objective. The more the teacher knows, the better the teacher is. Learning is essentially painful, but it is such good discipline! Such thinking leads to teaching that is little more than cognitive dumping.

Underlining the severity of dumping information and expectations on the learner—a process for which he prefers the metaphor "molding," Scheffler points out that "the one choosing the mold is wholly responsible for the result" (Scheffler 1960, 51).

Unfortunately those who dump and mold rarely see it that way. Dumpers tend to blame the students when the dump-out misses the bucket.

THE METAPHOR OF MANUFACTURING

On the other hand, teachers who see education in terms of the manufacturing metaphor are usually aware that they have to accept responsibility for whether or not any learning is taking place. These teachers—or pastors, or parents—see themselves as creating the machinery that will turn out the product. Many people with degrees in education operate within this model. Their key mistake is in taking to themselves too much responsibility for direction and control. Their strategies and educational devices are often overpowering. Rather than inviting learners into a shared relationship, they expect them to submit themselves to being "processed." The learners often interact and become more active in the whole experience than is possible in the filling metaphor, but the goals are usually firmly fixed. The goals (often stated as "behavioral objectives") are in the system, not in the learner's experiences or interaction with the learning system.

This writer at one period of his career accepted this metaphor of education. He saw it as substantially preferable to the filling metaphor, and it encouraged learners to decide for themselves the worthiness of the outcomes it promised.

At that time, a dozen or so years ago, TEE (Theological Education by Extension) caught on. As a consulting technologist for TEE, this writer saw two problems emerge. First, in the hands of compulsive people, programmed instruction and allied instructional technologies were used simply as more powerful ways to fulfill the old motives of cognitive dumping. I had pleaded for integrative seminars as the connecting link between the cognitive input experiences and the practical service tasks, but the technology of teaching became an end in itself for many in the TEE field (Ward and Rowen 1972, 17-27).

Second, the historical moment in which TEE emerged was marked by rapid nationalization of the church's educational institutions in the developing world. TEE promised to be an ideal vehicle to further the transition. TEE programs could put pastoral development education closer to the real fields of service, get theological education out of its preparatory preoccupation, and more readily employ local pastor-teachers as the delivery agents to help other pastors (Ward 1974, 246-58). Before 1975 it became clear that these desirable outcomes were being systematically frustrated. North American mission boards were recruiting more and more green seminary graduates as TEE missionaries, using the persuasive pitch, "you really don't need much experience to be able to teach in TEE programs. After all, the materials do it for you." The result was the largest influx of new missionaries since the post–World War II missionary boom. Thus faded the hopes of moving institutional education into more appropriate forms for the development of the Third World church (Ward 1977, 79-85). (This writer still believes in theological education by extension, and thanks God that in many places it is fulfilling some of the earlier hopes.)

THE METAPHOR OF LIFE-WALK

A preferred metaphor of education is to see it as *a life-walk to be shared*. Some analysts have called it the "travel" metaphor. Kliebard says it so well:

> The curriculum is a route over which students will travel under the leadership of an experienced guide and companion. Each traveler will be affected differently by the journey since its effect is at least as much a function of the predilections, intelligence, interests and intent of the traveler as it is of the contours of the route. This variability is not only inevitable, but won-

drous and desirable. Therefore, no effort is made to anticipate the exact nature of the effect on the traveler; but a great effort is made to plot the route so that the journey will be as rich, as fascinating and as memorable as possible. (Kliebard 1972, 404)

Kliebard's metaphor of education as "travel" is based on an earlier and more simple time. (It is not useful to visualize trains, buses, airplanes, and automobiles—or even sailboats or canoes.) What is in mind is the walk, purposeful yet subject to the thousand-and-one revelations that emerge as the trail unfolds to meet the pilgrim's step.

Such a vision of education does not suggest wandering, though it allows for exploring. It does not imply lack of purpose though it recognizes that *being* is even more important than *going*. This view of teaching and learning suggests a destination, though it implies that the experiences of going there are as important as the arrival.

Thus Christians have much to embrace in this metaphor of education. Jesus used it extensively. It fulfills the biblical teachings about human relationship, authority, and the inalienable sovereignty of God. All through the Scriptures God's people are seen as strangers and sojourners, walking together with God in the lead. We are pilgrims in a life-walk. Ours is not to "finish our education" and "settle down." (These are awful metaphors of human fulfillment.)

Christians are to learn, to develop and to experience the continuing of God's work begun in them (Philippians 1:6). "Marching to Zion," yes; their mission, however, is along that very line of march. They are not to avoid the needs of fallen humanity to the left and right of the path. Nor should they travel in lock-step. They learn through encountering life's realities as they discover God providing according to their needs, including the need for knowledge and wisdom.

As companions in the way, Christians have each other; some are gifted to teach and to help. They all interrelate; they are an interdependent community. Having one Teacher, one Father, one Leader, they are all brothers (Matthew 23:8-10).

Strangely, people think they understand something simply because they have seen it done so often. Teaching is like that. The study of education is often misunderstood. Many people view professional education as a sort of pretense. After all, "anyone can teach," it is argued. And some who have been trained to teach do not seem to do it very well. Thus those who study education are merely indulging in an exaggerated form of common sense.

The reduction of teaching and learning to a set of commonplaces creates a further misunderstanding. Among those who apply to the graduate school of education at Michigan State University are some educators whose focus is on techniques and technology. A concern for techniques and technology is not wrong, but the overemphasis on machinery and tactics can and does eclipse the issues of reason and faith which are much more important to the professional study of education. The field of Christian education, especially so-called "church education," can also be criticized for these two problems: reductionism and overemphasis on technology.

Within education in the service of the church—from Sunday Schools to seminaries—it is common, even popular, to "know nothing" about education, nothing beyond the immediate doing of one's own thing. But being an educator is a matter of stewardship. Whether it is listening to others or lecturing about one's subject of expertise or dealing with the complexities of a four-year-old's world-and-life view, educational issues and concerns as well as specific knowledge and understanding of teaching and learning are part of responsible ministry.

THEOLOGICAL EDUCATION

The following are some questions on theological education to think about.

1. Is theological education still being modeled on 19th century medical education? By 1900 medical education had become a very long preparatory education full of lectures but lacking hands-on experience. A substantial transition toward the clinical context and toward patient-centered learning was triggered by the 1906 Report of Abraham Flexner's study of medical education (sponsored by the Carnegie Foundation). Some old-guard medical educators had argued then that if medical education were to become patient-centered it would lose its emphasis on foundational science. By no means has this happened. Nor would any theological education need to sacrifice its Bible-centeredness if it focused more on the people of God. The church and Jesus Christ's building of His church is what ministry is all about. No inherent conflict exists between the centrality of the Scriptures and the need to deal with real people. Education can enhance the one through involvement with the other.

2. Is the church of Jesus Christ well served by pastors who are concerned only with the right handling of the Word of God and who lack substantial knowledge of the realities of their time? Sensitive awareness of the needs and the conditions of people is an essential part of the ministry, as exemplified by the Lord.

3. Are the intellectual roots of present-day theological education more Hellenistic or Hebrew? Are the metaphors of education it represents more a matter of cognitive filling, machining a product, or engaging in a life-walk? Is its view of development more mechanistic or more organic? Does its use of competition outweigh its advocacy of cooperation? Is its purpose communicated as winning and getting rewards, or as fulfilling the metaphors of salt and light? As one pastor has suggested, some seminaries are "turning out intellectual wizards and relational dwarfs."

4. To what extent are seminaries concerned about the persistent evidence that what is learned in an academic context, particularly the so-called "language skills," are often abandoned when the real context of ministry is encountered?

Nothing is more basic to pastoral responsibility than the spiritual development of God's people, the church. Pastors might delegate music-leading tasks or even some of the hand-shaking and the floor-sweeping, but they cannot give away their share of responsibility for the development of God's people. One of the grave ills in theological education is the isolation of the discipline of Christian education, compartmentalizing it into a distinct field, conceptually isolated from ministerial service. In many Bible colleges and seminaries, "Christian education" courses are avoided by prepastoral students.

The field of Christian education has been preoccupied with children at the expense of adult nurture and especially of parent development. No wonder churches have so many hurting parents, whose unpreparedness, anguish, and sense of inadequacy causes them to dump more and more responsibility on the church for the spiritual development of their children. The common pattern of Christian education in many churches falls far short of what God specified in the Scriptures.

The center of biblical Christian education should be in the home, anyway (Deuteronomy 6:4-9). In God's plan, parenting is a job for beginners. But God provides helps so that such a beginner—each new parent, whose tasks and responsibilities are enormously complex and demanding—is able to be prepared and competent. Parenting is no job for the unprepared, the self-taught, or casually knowledgeable dabblers. To be a prepared and developing parent requires a continuously open learning relationship with one's children. How ironic, by contrast, is the professor, teacher, Sunday school teacher—yes, even the pastor—whose role as a teacher of others is approached as a casual indulgence in matters of teaching and learning.

Arguments for knowledgeable responsibility in Christian education are heard more frequently today. For the most part they are widely accepted, especially within the Christian education field itself. But what follows from the repentance of past unconcerns and the conversion to a new life as a "real" educator is often equally disturbing. The transformation is too commonly marked by a shift into preoccupation about methods and materials. Few fields of education have seen such an emphasis on filmstrips, cassettes, programmed instruction, and various forms of video. The "awakened" Christian educator or pastor is a gullible buyer of all sorts of gimmicky methods and jazzy materials.

A teacher's purpose is to help people learn. A true educator is concerned about what and how people learn. In one way or another, every human being is a teacher; all teach each other, directly and indirectly. But to become an educator one learns, through practice and through various deliberate studies, a disciplined approach to making and sharing decisions about what should be learned. An educator is deeply concerned and professionally skilled in what makes for effective learning. An educator distinguishes between telling and teaching, between hearing and learning. A Christian educator should also distinguish between education that is satisfied with "measurable cognitive gains" and true education in which the incorporation of principles of God's truth facilitates spiritual development.

Such education, at its most practical level, is a life-walk to be shared by members of God's family in small groups and in larger communities.

References

Kliebard, Herbert M. 1972. Metaphorical roots of curriculum design. *Teachers College Record* 74: 404.

Scheffler, Israel. 1960. *The Language of Education*. Springfield, IL: Charles C. Thomas.

Ward, Ted, and Samuel F. Rowen. 1972. The significance of the extension seminary. *Evangelical Missions Quarterly* 9: 17-27.

Ward, Ted. 1974. Theological education by extension: Much more than a fad. *Theological Education* 10: 246-58.

_____. 1977. Types of TEE. *Evangelical Missions Quarterly* 13: 79-85.

SECTION II_____

NEW DIRECTIONS
IN THEOLOGICAL EDUCATION

_____

Direction in Theological Education

A View for the Twenty-First Century

ROBERT W. FERRIS

The capacity of theological schools to contour the faith and life of the church is beyond dispute. As seed beds of the church's leadership, seminaries shape the lives, hearts, and minds of those who shape the church. In an age when ideological and social change assumes dramatic proportions, at the threshold of a new millennium that promises the church both opportunities and threats unprecedented in recent centuries, preoccupation with conserving models and strategies of the past is a sure path to irrelevance. (Not that the gospel ever is irrelevant, but our witness and worship may be.)

At times it seems the church is changing all around us, and at other times it seems nothing has changed—indeed, that change is the church's greatest need. The emergence of virile "younger churches" in Asia, Africa, and Latin America as centers of church growth and as sending bases for international missions is cause for celebration. It is also a challenge to the lassitude and decline of many churches in the West. A relative few Western congregations have attained "megachurch" status, often employing innovative—and sometimes dubious—approaches to ministry, but the church as a whole remains stagnant.

It is reasonable to argue that the most accessible (although not the easiest) way toward significant revitalization of the church's life and witness is through renewal of theological education. Fundamental reorientation of the congregational life of the church presumes a fundamental reorientation of its leadership—and first, of the institutions that train them. Despite growing discussion of the need for renewal in theological education, however, institutional inertia has been overwhelming in all but a few unique and isolated cases.

In this section, five authors look at theological education and look to the future.

Yau-Man Siew offers a trans-Pacific perspective on Western theological education. He reviews the dangers to Asian churches of unthinking replication of Western educational models, he surveys problems inherent in Western theological education, and he calls for recentering Asian theological education in the Asian church. The challenge he offers is equally relevant to educators in Africa and Latin America—and in the West.

Mark Young recognizes that change in theological education must entail a rethinking of theological curricula. By insightful analysis, Young organizes the myriad of curricular planning variables into a series of planning grids. Thus he provides a schema for identifying and examining the effects of interdependent curriculum planning decisions. He alerts us, as well, to implications of theological understandings and commitments for theological curricula. Although his orientation is intercultural, his insights and schema are as pertinent to Western institutions as they are to others.

Lois McKinney's contribution to this collection presents a noticeable change of pace. In contrast to Mark Young's close analysis and tight logic, McKinney assumes an autobiographical and personal touch. She invites her readers to observe as she examines her own heart, applies the truth of God's Word, and experiences God's healing. As we observe her pilgrimage, she examines the impediments—and path—to meaningful community within our theological schools. Along the way we realize that significant change in theological education must begin with individual teachers and administrators—perhaps with ourselves.

Samuel F. Rowen argues that the inadequacies of present theological education structures are rooted in a misperception of its center and focus. Rather than understanding theological formation as the end of seminary training, Rowen challenges his readers to enlarge their vision. To achieve contemporary relevance and to serve well the church of the twenty-first century, theological education must be instrumental to the *missio Dei*.

Robert W. Ferris challenges the structure and practice of North American theological education and provides an implicit warning to Asian, African, and Latin American churches that would mimic it. By examining the task of theology and the role of theological schools, he identifies where and how so many Western seminaries have lost their way. He concludes that intentional integration of theology and ministry is essential to authentic theological education.

Certain themes recur throughout this section: the crying need for renewal in theological education; the essential place of integrity in contextual sensitivity, curriculum planning, community building, and mission; the interculturalness of all theological education, with the attendant opportunity and necessity to learn from one another; the absolute necessity of submitting our educational structures and strategies to the scrutiny of the Word of God.

The burden of these authors, however, is not theological education alone. Renewal in theological education is viewed as instrumental to renewal and revitalization of the church of Jesus Christ—today and into the twenty-first century. Even so, come quickly Lord Jesus. Maranatha!

*Chapter Four*_____

Theological Education in Asia
An Indigenous Agenda for Renewal

Yau-Man Siew

One characteristic of the modern era is the linking of people everywhere into global networks. With cheaper and safer travel, people cross national boundaries and carry ideas and products to distant markets. An important effect of this globalization for Asian theological education is that many Asian scholars go to the West for graduate studies and return to occupy key faculty positions (Conn 1979, 318). While this can bring about healthy cross-fertilization, a blind copying of the Western models of training,[1] including wholesale adoption of curricula and philosophies without thoughtful critique or recognition of contextual differences, is disastrous.

This chapter examines this phenomenon and proposes a different agenda for renewal. First, it outlines the consequences of blindly copying Western models. Second, it discusses specific issues and problems inherent in the Western model, which Asian theological institutions must be wary of emulating. Third, the chapter addresses educational philosophy. Effective renewal is founded on a cogent indigenous philosophy of theological education based on sound biblical and theological principles. The last section raises questions pertinent to a more relevant model of training.

CONSEQUENCES OF UNCRITICAL IMPORTATION
OF WESTERN MODELS

A major weakness of the uncritical acceptance of Western models for ministry education is their irrelevance to Asia's unique and diversified social contexts. Asian scholar Bong Rin Ro provides a sharp critique:

> Western evangelical theological schools emphasize the inerrancy of Scripture and orthodox theology versus liberal and neo-orthodox theologies. But these are not major issues in Asia. Rather, the prevalent areas of concern are poverty, suffering, injustice, communism and non-Christian religions (Ro 1990, 55).

Emilio Núñez, of Latin America, points out another consequence of a blind copying of Western models: it results in a dependency that kills initiative and creativity among indigenous efforts. Copying the West yields curricula insensitive to contextual needs, curricula which produce decontextualized thinkers and theologians (Núñez 1988, 76). A cursory survey of the past five years of the *Asia Journal of Theology* produces few articles on critical Asian issues apart from a handful on ecumenism, feminism, pluralism, or Islamization. The more pressing challenges presented by communalism, ethnic violence, poverty and suffering, corruption, materialism, urbanization, and modernization are virtually absent. Asian scholars must develop their theological agenda from the Asian church and its contexts if they want to be true to their theological task.

A third consequence of uncritical importation of Western models is that it maintains a vestige of imperialism that Asian churches can ill afford in an era of widespread nationalism. In a survey of theological education in Taiwan, Jonathan Chao, President of Christ College in Taipei, laments that one college received all its missionary lecturers from Asbury Seminary and sent all its scholars to the same seminary, while another preferred Westminster or Calvin.

> Such theological loyalty doubtlessly perpetuates conflicting branches of Western theological thought and extends American and European theological battlefields to Taiwan. Is this not theological imperialism? When will our Western friends grant us our theological freedom and independence? (Chao 1972, 9).

Perhaps the greatest blind spot in such thoughtless copying of Western models is in some Asians' undue fascination with Western gadgets and technology. This mindset, fostered by Hollywood and Disneyland, is fed by the movement of urbanized Asian societies toward secularism and rationalism. Paul Stevens, academic dean of Regent College, asks the daunting question: "How is it, knowing the church in the West is in decline, that Third World denominations are so hungry to get the sort of ministerial training the West offers?" (Stevens 1992, 8; cf. Conn 1979, 318-20).

In the history of theological education, the ambiguity of the present moment is tragically ironic: a Western theological degree is a *sine qua non* for aspiring Christian leaders in the developing world at the very moment when those responsible for that education are least sure of the integrity of the enterprise (Stevens 1992, 7).

ISSUES AND PROBLEMS INHERENT IN WESTERN MODELS

Western theological education is facing a crisis of identity and mission. Many doubt its viability and relevance to the church. When delegates to a 1992 "Gospel and Our Culture" meeting in Chicago drew up a list of concerns facing the future of the North American church, one-fourth of those present expressed uneasiness with the current nature of theological education.

A major weakness of the Western model is the fracturing of theological education into a plurality of disciplines, each with its own method (Farley 1983). This leads to hyper-specializations, eliminates faculty responsibility for integration, and fosters area fiefdoms and entrenched political structures resistant to change. Yet, when the old "theological encyclopedia" approach is replaced by a "theory-practice encyclopedia," theological education turns into mere pragmatics and technology. Edward Farley recommends that we reclaim *theologia* as the "unity, subject matter and end of clergy education" (Farley 1983, ix-xi).

While it is true that the goal of theological education is the development of theological understanding, Farley neglects the larger categories of the church's ministry and mission (Fiorenza 1988, 90). Moreover, he does not start from or interact with the authority of revelation. Christopher Duraisingh notes perceptively that "Farley's habitus model is still mired in a paradigm that is essentially individualistic" (Duraisingh 1992, 39).

A second weakness of the Western model is its strong church-school dichotomy, with the attendant problem of integrating theory with praxis. Although, historically, theological institutions were products and servants of the church, Western seminaries pursue a theological agenda independent from the church. Thus, churches often criticize the seminary for doing theology that is irrelevant to their historical and immediate needs. Christopher Walters-Bugbee notes that it is,

little wonder, then, that theology has acquired such a sour reputation among the laity of late; held captive so long by academia, it now appears to many entirely superfluous to the common life of faith, an enterprise reserved exclusively for the few hardy souls who find pleasure in batting around words like "phenomenology" over breakfast (Walters-Bugbee 1981, 1157).

In Canada, Keith Clifford notes that seminaries are most concerned with their relationships with the universities, which control government funding, and with the Association of Theological Schools (ATS), which controls accreditation (Clifford 1990, 3). Often overlooked is the central role of the ecology and environment of ministerial education to any understanding of theory-practice integration. When seminaries covet comparison with universities for status reasons, they become subject to the university's norms. Thus, they unwittingly subscribe to the tenure and promotions criteria that traditionally have emphasized research and publication over field work and clinical experience (Hopkins 1981; cf. Hill 1986, 176).

The church-school dichotomy has produced discontent even within the confines of the seminary. Michael Griffiths, Professor of Mission at Regent College, scathingly attacks seminaries for teaching as though they aim to produce scholars, and for choosing professors solely on academic standing without regard to ministry criteria. As a result, students who need "street credibility" to influence evangelism and church growth are taught by scholars with "library credibility," who relate better to books than to people in the midst of life (Griffiths 1990, 11-12).

Perhaps the greatest drawback of the church-school dichotomy is that theological education takes on the individualistic mentality of Western culture, rather than the community model of Scripture (Ward and Rowen 1972, 21-22; cf. Donovan 1991, 86-90). Theological training assumes a theory of individual conversion and vocation unrelated to community. Students are selected and trained apart from their supporting community, then placed in communities that do not know them, may not like them, and often do not find them suitable.

This approach contrasts sharply with the biblical model of commissioned leadership (Acts 6:3; 13:1-3). The sacraments testify to the community nature of the church. Baptism is not so much an individual decision as a public incorporation into community. The Eucharist is not just for private devotion but a community meal that signifies the sign and bond of unity (1 Cor. 10:16). Beyond being unbiblical, however, Western individualism is especially unsuited to Asian cultures, which highly value family and community.

A third weakness of the Western model concerns pedagogy. Western theological institutions embrace the ancient Greek model of schooling, apparently without awareness of its inherent problems.

Schooling stresses the primacy of the intellect and sees all educational life as integrated in cognition. Thus, it is not uncommon to find intense scholarly debates in seminaries about theories of justification without a parallel concern for holiness of life or Christian vocation.

Ivan Illich (1971) notes that the school as an institution has wrongly equated teaching with learning. He recommends that we adopt a "de-schooled" frame of mind and recognize schooling as only one way a society learns. Experience, culture, history, and reflection are just as legitimate, if not more effective.

Another pedagogical weakness is Western theological education's inadequate understanding of how theory relates to practice. The theory-to-practice, study-followed-by-field-education approach, although widely deemed deficient, still undergirds most seminary teaching and learning. Students amass large quantities of notes "for future ministry use." Linda Cannell and Walter Liefeld note perceptively that quantity of information does not equal quality education. Students would learn much more and would develop critical, lifelong learning habits if "we taught them to reflect rather than regurgitate" (Cannell and Liefeld 1991, 23).

Ward and Rowen drew on research from the field of professional training to propose a rail-fence metaphor for integrating cognitive instruction with field experience in theological education (Ward and Rowen 1972, 23-27). Although they call for a dynamic interaction between theory and experience within a community of reflection, their metaphor is rigid.

A more dynamic metaphor is that of a boomerang. The twisting of the boomerang (communal reflection), which represents the dynamic interaction between cognitive knowledge and field experience, is essential for movement (insight). A successful launch depends on an angle of throw (theological foundations), which takes account wind conditions (context).

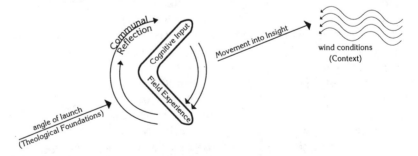

Fig. 1. The Boomerang Metaphor of Integrated Learning.

Such a view of learning calls for a new set of teaching skills among seminary professors. Success depends less on mastery of content than on the quality of classroom climate, group processes, and the needs and intellectual backgrounds of students. The teacher becomes a facilitator rather than only an expert, and encourages learners to see themselves as enabling each others' learning through a process of reflection, challenge, and problem solving.[2]

TOWARD AN INDIGENOUS PHILOSOPHY OF THEOLOGICAL EDUCATION

Although it is not wrong to borrow ideas from the West, we must undergird our models with a cogent philosophy of training. It is not enough to make cosmetic changes to a model if it is to be relevant to specific needs. Chao calls for innovation rather than renovation.

> This kind of rethinking, although by no means new, implies that any attempt to "improve" the present form of theological education is not enough. What we need is not renovation, but innovation. The whole philosophy and structure of theological education has to be completely reshaped (Chao 1976, 202).

A cogent philosophy of theological education comes from a biblical understanding of the gospel, the theology of the church, and the mission and task of theology. Duraisingh notes that the major weakness of Western models is their neglect of the vital aspects of ecclesiology and mission. He calls for reaffirmation of the apostolate as the singular *raison d'être* of the church. Mission is not one among many functions of the church, the church is a function in God's mission. If the church is the instrument and expression of the kingdom (proclamation and embodiment of the gospel), then the goal of theological education is to "form" people in congregations so that they can participate in God's local and global mission (Duraisingh 1992, 33-34).

In a similar vein African scholar Orville Nyblade notes that the purpose of theological education, in its simplest form, is to enable Christians to do theology. If the church is a community of believers who reflect upon the meaning of their faith and go out to serve in accordance with conclusions reached in their reflections, then theological education should facilitate this task. Thus, theological education exists for the purpose of doing theology; it should not be re-served to an elite (Nyblade 1991, 42-43).

John Stott suggests that a biblical doctrine of the church attests to its dual character of "holy worldliness." The church is a community called out to worship God (1 Pet. 2:5, 9), and is sent back to witness and serve (John 17:18; 20:21). Thus, it simultaneously is "holy" (distinct from the world) and "worldly" (immersed in the life of the world). This dual character of the church lies at the heart of its theological task. For Stott, to do theology is to practice "double-listening," to the Word and to the world (Stott 1992, 24-29). In this sense, the church theologizes as it critically reflects upon Christian praxis in the light of God's Word.

In sum, an indigenous philosophy of theological education must undergird any Asian model of training. A cogent philosophy must interact with a biblical understanding of the gospel, ecclesiology, mission, and the task of theology. The purpose of theological education is not to train in theological abstractions for respectable scholarship but to "form" people in the church to participate effectively in God's local and global mission. Theological education should enable Christians to do theology. To the extent that Asian theological education is not equipping Asian churches to critique, inform, and transform their contexts and cultures in fulfillment of the *missio Dei*, it has failed its crucial task.

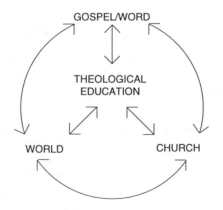

*Fig. 2. A Biblical Philosophy of Theological Education
(adapted from Kinsler and Emery 1991).*

ASPECTS OF A MORE RELEVANT MODEL FOR ASIA

What are some aspects of a more relevant model of training? Núñez proposes three important questions every wise theological educator must ask (Núñez 1988, 73).

1) Whom Do We Want to Educate Theologically?

Presently, theological education in Asia is limited to relatively young students who have given themselves to "full-time" ministry. While we should not discourage commitment among our youth, one questions the wisdom of regularly commissioning youthful leaders in societies that value experience and age. Moreover, if the church is the whole people of God, with each member equally responsible for embodiment and proclamation of the kingdom (1 Pet. 2:9-10), then theological education should be available for all willing learners in the church.

Walter Wright, president of Regent College, after a recent visit to Singapore, Malaysia, and Hong Kong, reported that the critical shortage of "full-time" pastors there may question the immediate relevance of Regent's laity emphasis (Wright 1992). Yet, even if we could train enough full-time pastors, Asian churches may not be able to support them. If we truly believe in the "priesthood of all believers," then theological education should equip lay ministers who already shoulder significant leadership responsibilities in their churches. Since it is difficult for Asian leaders to leave their jobs (due to loss of seniority, or even employment), we must find more innovative ways to bring theological education to the marketplace. In this light, TEE assumes critical relevance (cf. Ward and Rowen 1972).

2) For Whom and for What Do We Want to Educate Them?

Western theological education, sadly, has become the prodigal of the church. This has resulted in a serious loss of mission and is the root of many theory-praxis problems. One, the church-school dichotomy, is the greatest setback of Western theological education. Just as medical schools exist for the health of a country, and military academies exist for the safety of a nation, so seminaries are products of the church and exist for the mission of the church.

If seminaries exist for the church, what is the nature of ministry to which we should train our students? Ross Kinsler and James Emory, pioneers of TEE in Guatemala, note that Ephesians 4:11-16 provides essential guidelines for church ministry that every theological educator will do well to heed (Kinsler and Emery 1991, 3, 35). God has distributed various gifts (and ministries) among his people; these are not centered in one ordained pastor (v. 11). The primary task of ministers is equipping (enabling, mobilizing, training), and they are to equip the body so that the members are the primary agents of ministry (v. 12a). The goal of ministry is body development for world service (vs. 12b-13). This is the only effective protection against spiritual infancy and false doctrines (v. 14). Finally, growth results from the development of individual parts (vs. 15-16).

In this light, the church and its ministry is both the focus of, and the most appropriate context for, theological training. Theological education should be intimately related to the discovery and development of spiritual gifts (cf. Padilla 1988). This means that church-based models are more than just a good idea (cf. Ferris 1990, 119-26). Such a locus and focus of training necessitates a review of contemporary evaluation criteria, which are largely summative and norm-referenced. Since ministerial education includes professional skills development, assessment should be formative and criteria-based.

3) How Do We Want to Educate Them?

"Creative teaching" is the least important factor, and "theological grounding" is the most important, according to seminary professors of the Asia Theological Association, indicated in the ICAA Manifesto on Renewal of Evangelical Theological Education (Ferris 1990, 39). This is sad, because relevant educational approaches are foundational to the effective conveyance of Christian truth. If we limit ourselves to the lecture method, we must not be surprised when the ministries of our graduates are marked by ineffectiveness. Recent educational theory emphasizes the critical importance of integrating theory and practice in the context of reflection. If we ignore this insight, we will continue to reap the bitter fruit of ineffectiveness. Thus we see that renewal begins with the faculty. Key questions for self-examination include: What is our commitment to effective teaching? Do we value research and writing skills more highly than teaching skills? What kinds of faculty development programs do we promote, and why?

CONCLUSION

The church is both local and global. Theological education should make use of the rich diversity within the universal church in its struggle to be faithful. A model limited to local perspectives is parochial, blind to its own shortcomings, and ignorant of the insights and wisdom of the wider church. Yet, an imported model suffers from irrelevance and insensitivity to local needs. This agenda for renewal calls the Asian church to develop an indigenous philosophy of theological education based on a biblical understanding of gospel, church, mission, and the task of theology. Only then will we be able to differentiate the strengths from the weakness of any model, including our own.

Notes

1. Although there are slight differences in emphasis, in this chapter "the Western model" of theological education refers generally to one characterized by a clear church-school dichotomy and a curriculum divided into four distinct domains: biblical studies, theology, church history, and practical theology. This model has virtually become sacrosanct and is found in almost every seminary catalogue, whether Protestant or Catholic, liberal or conservative, in North America.

2. See Christensen, Garvin, and Sweet (1991). The Harvard Business School has adopted the discussion method for all its courses. This excellent book contains personal reflections of these professors who changed from lecturing to the discussion method. The book outlines helpful foundations to discussion learning.

Works Cited

Cannell, L. M., and W. L. Liefeld. 1991. The contemporary context of theological education: A consideration of the multiple demands on theological educators. *Crux* 27, no. 4 (December), 19-27.

Chao, J. 1972. Foreign missions and theological education. *Evangelical Missions Quarterly* 9, no. 1 (Fall), 1-16.

_____. 1976. Education and leadership, in *The New Face of Evangelicalism: An International Symposium on the Lausanne Covenant*, ed. C. René Padilla. Downers Grove, Ill.: InterVarsity Press.

Christensen, C. R., D. A. Garvin, and A. Sweet. 1991. *Education for Judgment: The Artistry of Discussion Leadership*. Boston, Mass.: Harvard Business School Press.

Clifford, N. K. 1990. Universities, churches and theological colleges in English-speaking Canada: Some current sources of tension. *Studies in Religion/Sciences Religieuses* 19, no. 1, 3-16.

Conn, H. M. 1979. Theological education and the search for excellence. *Westminster Theological Journal* 41, no. 2 (Spring), 311-63.

Donovan, V. 1991. *Christianity Rediscovered*. Maryknoll, N.Y.: Orbis Books.

Duraisingh, C. 1992. Ministerial formation for mission: Implications for theological education. *International Review of Mission* 81, no. 1 (January), 33-45.

Farley, E. 1983. *Theologia: The Fragmentation and Unity of Theological Education*. Philadelphia: Fortress Press.

Ferris, R. W. 1990. *Renewal in Theological Education: Strategies for Change.* Wheaton, Ill.: The Billy Graham Center.

Fiorenza, E. S. 1988. Thinking theologically about theological education. *Theological Education* 24, Supplement II (Spring), 89-119.

Griffiths, M. 1990. Theological education need not be irrelevant. *Vox Evangelica* 20, 7-19.

Hopkins, D. 1981. It is true what they say about theory and practice. Unpublished paper presented at the Conference of the Western Canadian Association for Student Teaching, Vancouver, British Columbia, Canada, March 13, 1981.

Hill, B. V. 1986. Theological education: Is it out of practice? *Evangelical Review of Theology* 10, no. 2 (April), 174-82.

Illich, I. 1971. *Deschooling Society.* New York: Harper & Row.

Kinsler R., and J. Emory. 1991. *Opting for Change.* Geneva: Programme on Theological Education, World Council of Churches.

Núñez E. A. 1988. The problem of curriculum. In *New Alternatives in Theological Education.* Ed. C. R. Padilla. Oxford: Regnum Books, 73-87.

Nyblade, O. 1991. Curriculum development in theological education. *Africa Theological Journal* 20, no. 1, 43-53.

Padilla, C. R., ed. *New Alternatives in Theological Education.* Oxford: Regnum Books, 73-87.

Ro, B. R. 1990. Training Asians in Asia: From dream to reality. *Evangelical Review of Theology* 14, no. 1 (January), 50-56.

Stevens, R. P. 1992. Marketing the faith: A reflection on the importing and exporting of Western theological education. *Crux* 8 no. 2 (June), 6-18.

Stott, J. 1992. *The Contemporary Christian: Applying God's Word to Today's World.* Downers Grove, Ill.: InterVarsity Press.

Walters-Bugbee, C. 1981. Across the great divide: Seminaries and the local church. *The Christian Century* 98, 1154-59.

Ward T., and S. F. Rowen. 1972. The significance of the extension seminary. *Evangelical Missions Quarterly* 9, no. 1 (Fall), 17-27.

Wright, W. 1992. [Untitled President's Report]. *Regent World* (Summer).

Chapter Five

Planning Theological Education in Mission Settings

A Context-Sensitive Approach

MARK YOUNG

_____

The question of appropriate forms of theological education compels us to consider the interdependence of three primary issues in educational planning: 1) philosophical commitments about theological education (mission, convictions, and values), 2) the form of a given program of theological education, and 3) the dynamics of the program's unique social context. Unfortunately, many educational endeavors in mission contexts have been started with no serious consideration given to these issues. Program planners have tended to adopt educational forms from respected theological schools in their homeland. Uncritical intercultural adoption of any educational form almost invariably contributes to the inappropriateness of that program. Theological education programs must be context-sensitive; that is, they must be created in response to the unique conditions in given settings.

Claiming biblical authenticity for any contemporary form of theological education because it allegedly replicates the training models of Jesus or Paul is hermeneutically dangerous and philosophically naive. Our best-intentioned efforts cannot recreate the unique social, political, geographical, economic, psychological, climatic, religious, cultural, historical, and interpersonal forces that compelled Jesus to teach his disciples as he did. A careful analysis of Scripture can lead to biblically based convictions about theological education, but we may not claim that any contemporary expression of those convictions is necessarily biblical (Bosch 1992, 23).

The purpose of this chapter is threefold: first, to identify and explain the primary variables in forms of theological education; second, to describe the interdependence of decisions made with respect to the primary variables; and third, to propose three tests for evaluating the appropriateness of given forms of theological education for particular settings.

VARIABLES IN FORMS

Planners must make literally hundreds of decisions when designing a theological education program. The interdependence of these decisions creates a seemingly unmanageable number of potential variables in the planning process. Most of these decisions, however, can be grouped and analyzed on four planning grids: stakeholders, structures, curriculum, and pedagogy. Each grid has two axes; movement along these axes represents variations in program form. The grids are used to show how decision-making relates to program variables and to identify potential problems in planning.

The Stakeholders Grid

The Stakeholders Grid (Figure 1), with the axes of Resource Provision and Governance, reflects the relationships among parties holding vested interests in the success of an educational program. It focuses on issues of responsibility and accountability for the resources needed to establish and operate the program.

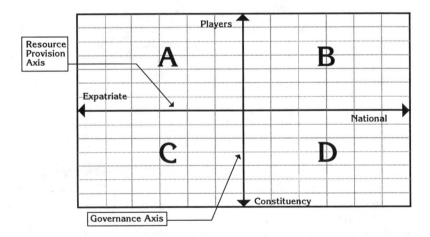

Fig. 1. Stakeholders Grid.

The Axis of Resource Provision

The ongoing provision of resources needed to establish, develop, and operate an educational endeavor must be a primary concern of educational planners from the beginning of the planning process. Although needs will vary according to the decisions reached on the other planning grids, most educational programs require (at least) human, fiscal, and material resources.

The poles of the Resource Provision axis, designated "expatriate" and "national," represent exclusive sources of program resources. At one extreme (the expatriate pole) the educational program is resourced solely from outside the group the program intends to serve. At the other extreme (the national pole) human, fiscal, and material resources are locally provided by the program's beneficiaries.

Many educational programs in mission contexts begin with an extreme expatriate profile but hope to move toward a national profile over time. Facilitating this transition, however, is problematic and may be unrealistic. A more practical model includes the shared provision of resources by national and expatriate stakeholders. Shared resource provision also accurately reflects the dynamic interdependency within the body of Christ.

Program development should proceed only upon a realistic appraisal of available and potentially available resources. In other words, "Don't design what you cannot afford."

If national or shared resourcing is a desired characteristic of the program, initial resources (human, fiscal, and material) must be utilized to develop a national resource pool. Although expatriate start-up resources typically are allotted for faculty and facilities, it may be just as legitimate to hire someone to work on developing a local funding base. The pace of faculty and facilities development should proceed only according to resourcing agreements worked out between expatriate and national stakeholders.

The Axis of Governance

Issues represented by the Governance axis may be illustrated by asking, "Who feels ultimate responsibility for the success of the program?" and "To whom are the program planners and leaders ultimately accountable?" Responsibility and accountability for the utilization of program resources interplay significantly with issues of resourcing. Many potential problems arise when those providing resources are not proportionately involved in providing oversight and accountability for the utilization of those resources.

One pole of the Governance axis, designated "players," represents internal responsibility and accountability for utilization of resources; that is, the planners, staff, and faculty provide governance functions.

The opposite pole represents involvement of the constituency in leadership of the program. Typically this is achieved through representative individuals selected by the larger constituency to promote its interests.

Of particular concern are programs with governance structures that are solely internal. Lack of accountability to the program's constituency allows planners and leaders to develop educational forms and goals that are prime candidates for irrelevance. Constituency involvement in governance often supplies the dose of contextual reality that all educational planners and leaders need in order to design and maintain appropriate forms of theological education.

Another potentially serious mistake is to commit governance to those not involved in providing resources for the program. In order to avoid irresponsibility, leaders need the sharpening brought about by the pressures of providing resources and bearing the consequences for decisions made. Too often educational programs have failed, and relationships soured, through an imbalance between resource provision and governance. Both expatriates and nationals must realize that resource provision carries the right to govern in the minds of most North Americans, but that this may not follow in the thinking of many others around the world.

The Structures Grid

The Structures Grid (Figure 2) reflects the identity and scope of influence of an educational program. The grid contains the axes of Mode and Accessibility.

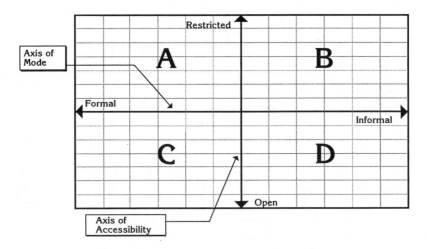

Fig. 2. Structures Grid.

The Axis of Mode

Modes of theological education may be conceptualized along a continuum with three markers: formal, nonformal, and informal. Mode primarily relates to two characteristics of an educational program: 1) its relationship to a culture's social system of education, and 2) the degree of intentionality in its programming.

Social systems of education. In most countries around the world the operative assumption of a social system of education is that the completion of a given level indicates an individual has developed needed competence, either for beginning the next level of training or for taking on particular social tasks. Educational programs that function fully within the established social system of education in a given country are defined as formal; those that operate outside the social system are either nonformal or informal.

Because a society expects certain competencies to be present after completing designated levels of schooling, most systems of education incorporate standards for formal programs. In some cases accreditation agencies have been formed by educational institutions as self-policing organizations. Generally, however, accreditation procedures are established and policed by government ministries.

If recognition through an accrediting body is desired, theological education programs can expect to be held to the same set of faculty, resource, and curricular standards used for other schools in their society. Whether a graduate is competent for ministry is not an issue in accreditation by most government ministries; competence is assumed when criteria transferred from other professional fields have been met. The question the church must ask is, "Can we afford to make that assumption?"

Intentionality in programming. The second factor present in educational mode is the degree of intentionality and planning in the training program. If an educational program is carefully and intentionally planned, it is considered either formal or nonformal. At the opposite end of the Mode axis, informal teaching and learning occur without significant planning or intentionality. Whereas formal and nonformal programs are characterized by planned lists of courses designed to accomplish specified objectives, informal learning occurs spontaneously. Although informal education has identifiable goals (for example, to pass on cultural and family values, to model wisdom), no particular learning events are planned or artificially created by the "teacher."

Three markers: formal, nonformal, informal. When programs are analyzed with respect to social recognition and intentionality in programming, one of three designations can be applied: formal, nonformal, or informal.

a) A formal mode of theological education relates fully to the social system of education, thereby seeking societal recognition of its programs and graduates. Curricular and institutional characteristics conform to the standards established by the social system's accrediting bodies. Teaching and learning events in a formal program are characterized by a high degree of planning and intentionality; in fact, they generally are limited to encounters pre-planned in the program.

b) A nonformal mode of theological education is characterized by an intentionally planned program that is not integrated into the dominant social system of education. By not adopting the recognized social system of education, nonformal programs may be undervalued by the constituency they seek to serve and may suffer from a lack of credibility in the society at large. Recognition of a program's value must be earned through its effectiveness in serving the church and through the quality of its graduates' lives and ministries. Examples of nonformal programs of theological education are plentiful in mission contexts; they include continuing education seminars, teacher-training courses, and discipleship programs. Strictly speaking theological schools that are accredited by regional associations but not recognized within their governmentally validated systems of education are nonformal education programs.

c) An informal mode of theological education occurs in the context of natural relationships between teacher and learner. An informal approach to theological education has no relationship to the social system of education in a given context, nor does it seek recognition on the basis of its identity in the social system. Teaching and learning occur spontaneously as teacher and learner engage in tasks of life and ministry, then critically reflect upon their experiences. Examples include mentor and disciple relationships and unstructured apprenticeships.

The Axis of Accessibility
The axis of Accessibility contains at least three issues related to the conditions for student participation in a program: entry requirements, cost, and location. At one pole is the restricted-access program, which provides training for a limited number of potential leaders; at the other pole one finds open-access programs, accessible to all who aspire to the leadership roles the program is designed to address.

Entry requirements for programs of theological education vary greatly. Unfortunately, many programs focus on an applicant's academic accomplishments. When scholastic requirements are considered exclusively, more important issues for church leadership, such as calling to ministry, godly character, personal maturity, ecclesiastical endorsement, and emotional stability, may be undervalued or overlooked.

The cost of theological education may sharply restrict participation. Cost issues include more than the amount paid for fees and materials or given in exchange for housing and board. Educational programs that prohibit or limit opportunities for work may cost the student's extended family substantially in lost productivity and income.

"Location" relates to the physical aspects of a program. At one extreme is the highly localized program in which all teaching and learning events take place in a single location; the opposite approach establishes multiple teaching sites scattered among the constituency. Strengths of highly localized programs include (1) controlled teaching and learning environments, (2) concentrated library and material resources, (3) centralized administrative functions, and (4) a recognized presence in a community. Criteria for accreditation traditionally favor localized programs. Weaknesses of localized programs of theological education may include (1) separation of learning from students' natural ministry contexts, (2) limited access to those living at a distance from the program's location, and (3) a parochialism that limits teaching content and methods to those most appropriate in the localized setting.

Highly accessible programs of theological education utilize multiple locations determined by the convenience of participating students and the accomplishment of program goals. The strengths and weaknesses of scattered sites are the opposite of those of localized programs.

The Curriculum Grid

Through its two axes the Curriculum Grid (Figure 3) reflects concern for the content and goal of theological education. It examines what will be taught and for what reasons, as well as the kinds of leadership needs a program will attempt to address.

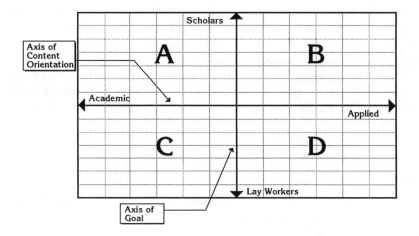

Fig. 3. Curriculum Grid.

The Axis of Content Orientation

The axis of Content Orientation speaks to the way knowledge is viewed. Its two poles describe the much discussed dichotomy between theory and practice, a dichotomy present in theological education at least since a university model for educating church leadership was adopted in Berlin in the early 1800s. According to David Kelsey, the Berlin model "is bipolar: it stresses the interconnected importance of two quite different enterprises—Wissenschaft or orderly, disciplined critical research on the one hand, and 'professional' education for ministry on the other" (Kelsey 1993, 12).

The names assigned to the poles of the axis—"Academic" and "Applied"—sometimes are used to designate types of knowledge. Rather than supporting the common misconception that certain subjects are more academic and others more practical, however, the nomenclature intends to focus two orientations toward knowledge. To state the issue another way, the axis of Content Orientation probes the motivations, goals, and rationale for teaching and learning.

An academic orientation to knowledge views learning as an end in itself; the accumulation of knowledge is the primary objective of teaching and learning. Since an academic orientation to knowledge seemingly provides a pure motivation for scholarship, questions of rationale for research may be undervalued. If we believe in human depravity, however, motivation always is clouded by self-interest. The accumulation of knowledge, if viewed as an end in itself, may be accomplished for purely selfish motives of power, protection, and prestige (cf. Cahn 1986). Thus, an academic orientation to knowledge may result in (1) heavy dependence upon jargon that limits access to the ideas of a field to "insiders," (2) an arrogant intellectual smugness that places concerns of scholarship beyond the reach of the program's constituency, and (3) self-serving scholarship. Unfortunately theological schools are not immune to these characteristics. Even worse, an academic orientation to knowledge has led to the trivialization of theology in much of North American theological education.

The opposite end of the Content Orientation axis, designated "Applied," represents an approach that views learning as a means to serving others, especially those outside the academic community. In theological education an applied orientation to knowledge is driven by leadership needs within the church. Research questions are motivated by a desire to understand and resolve the factors contributing to identified needs.

An applied orientation to learning, research, and scholarship should in no way be considered inferior to, or less rigorous than, an academic orientation. It is, however, more complex. The problems of ministry seldom are as tidy as those of academia. For that very reason teachers in theological education programs may be tempted to adopt an academic orientation to theology and exegesis rather than to pursue vigorously an applied orientation focused on meeting leadership needs. Unfortunately, although most North American seminaries have mission statements that affirm service and ministry, the primary orientation to knowledge exhibited by some instructors is academic. While paying lip service to the greater needs of the church and mission, faculty members retreat to the safe and secure world of self-serving scholarship.

The Axis of Goal

The Goal axis identifies the church leadership needs a given program will attempt to meet. Although leadership needs can be defined both quantitatively and qualitatively, the poles of the axis—"Scholars" and "Lay Workers"—reflect a bias toward qualitative definition. For each role identified, planners should define a list of traits needed to fulfill that role effectively.

Although quantitative needs assessment will not be addressed here, there is a direct correlation between the kinds of leaders needed and the number needed. Simply put, the church needs more able Sunday school teachers than seminary professors. Unfortunately, educational planning and resource allocation often proceed without consideration to quantitative leadership needs.

The Goal axis contains six categories of leadership needs that should be addressed by some form of theological education. One pole represents the need for theological scholars; the other pole represents the need for church lay workers, those involved bivocationally in evangelism, edification, and everything else vocational leaders either can not or will not do. Working from the foundation of the lay worker, Table 1 identifies specific leadership needs and concomitant educational program needs (McKinney 1987).

Unfortunately, many theological education programs suffer from a dire lack of focus with respect to goals and a much too optimistic view of what a given program can accomplish. It is virtually impossible for any program adequately to educate leaders across the spectrum of roles represented on the Goal axis. Without a clearly defined goal that responds to a specific leadership need, curricular choices often are made from a vague sense of what "ought" to be included in theological education.

Leadership Need	Educational Program Characteristics
Lay leaders—see description above	Widely accessible programs at appropriate educational levels; broad spiritual-growth content focus; applied orientation to content; nonformal and informal modes
Leaders of small congregations—people God uses to hold small groups of believers together; almost exclusively bivocational in ministry	Widely accessible programs with specific ministry content focus; applied orientation to content; nonformal and informal modes
Evangelists/missionaries—people God uses to penetrate new areas of society with the gospel; may be vocational in ministry	Widely accessible programs with specific ministry, content focus; applied orientation to content; nonformal and informal modes
Leaders of large congregations—people God uses to pastor larger groups of believers; often vocational in ministry	Programs with some measure of credibility in the subculture for educating leaders for this role; specific ministry content focus; applied orientation to content; nonformal, informal, and formal modes
Leaders of associations of churches and parachurch ministries—people God uses to provide specialized ministry and services to churches; often vocational in ministry	Programs with credibility in the subculture for educating leaders for this role; applied orientation to content with specialized administrative ministry focus; nonformal and formal modes
Scholars—people God uses to propagate and develop the church's understanding of theology; often vocationally engaged in teaching ministry	Programs with credibility in the subculture for educating leaders for this role; applied orientation to content with specialized discipline focus; formal mode

Table 1. Qualitative Leadership Needs Assessment.

Some may argue that the Curriculum Grid is incomplete without consideration of the content of courses. The concern is legitimate, but program content can be determined only after planning decisions regarding content orientation and educational goals have been made.

The Pedagogy Grid

The Stakeholders Grid and Structures Grid address the questions, Who? and For whom?, while the Curriculum Grid resolves issues of What? and Why? The Pedagogy Grid (Figure 4) completes our consideration of planning variables in theological education by examining the question How? It deals with the dynamics of teaching style and the nature of teacher-student relations.

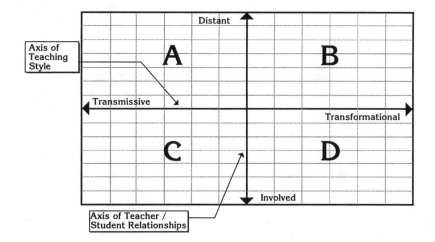

Fig. 4. Pedagogy Grid.

The Axis of Teaching Style

Most teachers, consciously or subconsciously, conceptualize the teaching and learning process through the use of metaphor (Postman and Weingartner 1969, 82-83). Because so much of cognition is experientially based and stimulated, we naturally construct mental images of abstract concepts (Postman 1985). These metaphors form visual constructs through which we associate, interpret, and organize thought. They dominate and delimit our consideration of experience and phenomena. Because one's metaphor of teaching and learning interacts with fundamental issues such as the nature of knowledge and the nature of persons, it impinges directly on the way pedagogical decisions most naturally are made. Two contrasting metaphors are represented by the poles on the axis of Teaching Style.

The transmission metaphor. Transmission metaphors conceptualize teaching and learning as a unidirectional act whereby the teacher transmits knowledge to the minds of passive learners. One popular transmission metaphor is the "bucket filler"—the teacher is one who must fill students with knowledge. The students are perceived as passive recipients of the information poured into their minds by the teacher (Postman and Weingartner 1969, 82-83). In an alternative image of educational transmission, Paulo Freire's banking metaphor, the teacher deposits knowledge into passively receptive students (Freire 1985, 57-74).

Transmission metaphors of education assume that learners understand information the same way it was understood by the teacher. Such an assumption is very dangerous (cf. Smith 1992, 50-63). No learning is passive. If the transmission metaphor includes an active role for the learner, it can promote certain kinds of learning, largely limited to the cognitive domain (cf. Joyce and Weil 1986, 23-138; also Habermas and Issler 1992, 112-13).

The transmission metaphor has been dominant in theological education in Europe and North America. Two emphases in conservative evangelical Christianity tend to predispose teachers to the transmission metaphor: 1) emphasis on proclamation as an overarching concept of ministry, and 2) emphasis on orthodoxy, conserving "the faith once delivered." Both emphases are legitimate and should be retained. The transmission metaphor serves them well, if the active role of the learner is not naively overlooked, if teaching methods that stimulate creativity and independent thinking are not ignored.

The discovery metaphor. Whereas transmission metaphors focus on the teacher's role, discovery metaphors emphasize the learner as one who develops new understandings through exploration. In the discovery metaphor the teacher functions as a guide, one who facilitates the learning process by creating opportunities for interaction with new information and stimuli. To the degree that the discovery metaphor emphasizes the role of the learner as an active participant in teaching and learning, it affords powerful insight for the development of theological education. Church leaders need to construct their own theological convictions, beliefs formed through critical consideration of biblical truth, theological ideas, and their ministry context.

Given the domination of the transmission metaphor in theological education, there is little wonder that the development of indigenous theologies in non-Western societies has been couched in an atmosphere of struggle. Because the discovery metaphor emphasizes the role of the learner in constructing ideas and convictions, control-oriented teachers fear it. The discovery metaphor downplays control and emphasizes reflection; it trusts the student—and the working of the Spirit in the student's life—more than the speaking or writing skills of the teacher.

The Axis of Teacher-Student Relationships
The degree to which a teacher is involved in the life of a student is the primary concern of the second axis on the Pedagogy Grid. On a broader level this axis deals with priority in the teaching and learning event.

At one pole of the axis is the aloof teacher, who maintains a comfortable distance from involvement in the lives of students. The aloof teacher is concerned with presenting the knowledge accumulated in personal study; student learning is a secondary concern. Professional research and writing are assigned priority over student counseling or discipleship. In some settings, research is considered more important than the task of teaching.

At the opposite end of the axis is the involved teacher, who attempts to know and understand, as well as is possible, those whom he or she is teaching. Learning is the highest priority. Lowman (1995) describes the masterful teacher as one who generates intellectual excitement through clarity and skill at presenting information and who creates excellent interpersonal rapport.

The involved teacher also seeks out other times and places for contact with students. Not content with being available to meet with students, the involved teacher actively pursues fellowship with students in settings outside of the normal teaching and learning environment. Such contacts allow the teacher to broaden the range of teaching and learning events; it creates opportunities for interaction at a deeper, more personal level than is possible in the controlled, public environment of the classroom.

There is no doubt that the involved teacher has chosen a more difficult path than the aloof teacher. Involvement in the lives of others demands self-sacrifice and risk. People are more personally threatening than books; involvement in the lives of students will make the teacher aware of a range of needs in students' lives that demand intervention. Many professional educators feel incompetent when faced with personal need. Such feelings cause insecurity and the desire to retreat to the relative safety of the study.

APPROPRIATENESS AND FORMS

The form of a theological education program is determined by the dozens of planning decisions represented in the four grids presented above. The appropriateness of any form is based on three factors: 1) the integrity of the form with respect to the interdependence of the planning decisions; 2) the consistency of the form with fundamental issues of mission, theological convictions, and educational values; and 3) the relevance of the form to specific needs, limitations, and opportunities in its setting.

Form Integrity

The planning grids provide a tool by which the educational planner can identify and evaluate primary choices to be made when designing a theological education program. Each axis of a grid represents a range of characteristics for the decision made about the primary issue associated with that axis. By locating the intended characteristics of the decisions at some point on the axes, the planner can plot the intersect point of the decisions made on the issues represented.

Using the Stakeholders Grid as an example, if the program is (or will be) dependent upon expatriate resources, that decision should be plotted to the left of the vertical center line on the Provision of Resources axis. The distance from the center of the grid should reflect the degree of dependence upon expatriate provision of resources. If the program will be primarily governed by internal players, that decision should be plotted on the Governance axis above the horizontal center line of the grid. The relationship between these two decisions can then be plotted on the grid as an intersect point of the two decisions. Figure 5 illustrates this example.

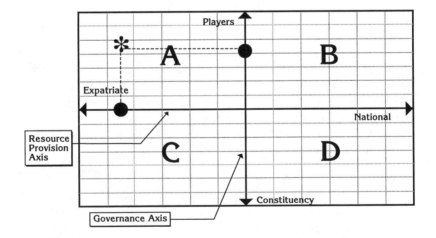

Fig. 5. Stakeholders Grid (with intersection of decisions in quadrant A).

A natural affinity between the poles of the axes can be found in quadrants A and D of each grid. For example, with respect to the

Curriculum Grid, programs that have a goal of developing scholars will most often be characterized by a more academic orientation to content. When the relationship between decisions made relative to each axis is plotted in quadrants B and C, planners face greater challenges in making the form of the program appropriate. For example, a program characterized by an academic orientation to knowledge that is focused upon meeting the need of more lay workers for the church (decisions plotted in quadrant C) probably will be ineffective. Such a program may suffer from a lack of form integrity.

The four planning grids also should be used in combination with one another to assess the overall integrity of an educational form. A program wherein the primary decisions are plotted in the same quadrant on all four grids displays the greatest degree of form integrity. The greater the number of quadrants within which decisions are plotted, the greater the potential for diminished form integrity. The form integrity of programs plotted in two quadrants is not necessarily at risk if the quadrants are not diagonal to one another (for example, A and D). A program characterized by decisions plotted in three or four quadrants can be expected to exhibit a low degree of form integrity.

Form Consistency

Because of the impossibility of re-creating the world of the Bible we have argued that contemporary forms of theological education should not be termed biblical. Nevertheless, we wholeheartedly affirm that fundamental issues of mission, convictions, and values in theological education should be resolved theologically. Before any educational planning decisions are reached, theological positions held with respect to mission, convictions, and values must be clarified. Any form of education that is inconsistent with the articulated theological positions must be considered inappropriate. Thus, even if a given program of theological education has integrity (as defined by the planning grids), it is inappropriate if decisions taken are inconsistent with positions on theological issues.

Examples of the interplay of form and theology in these three areas include:

a) *Mission*: A form of theological education characterized by restricted access on the basis of cost, location, and denominational affiliation is inconsistent with a stated mission to contribute to the development of leadership among the poor in a given society.

b) *Convictions*: A form of theological education that denies nationals a role in resource provision and governance is inconsistent with a theological conviction affirming the interdependence of members of the body of Christ.

c) *Values*: A form of theological education that does not encourage teacher involvement in the lives of students is inconsistent with a theological value placed on the role of interpersonal relationships in developing leaders.

Form Relevance

Although a form of theological education may have integrity and may be consistent, it also must be relevant to the specific needs, limitations, and opportunities found in a given context. Neither the decisions reached on the planning grids nor the positions taken on the fundamental issues are accomplished in a cultural vacuum. Given the nature of educational planning and theologizing, it is unlikely that a form of theological education could be characterized by planning integrity and fundamental consistency, and yet not be characterized by some degree of relevance to its context.

In order to evaluate a form's contextual relevance it is helpful to categorize the needs, limitations, and opportunities that each individual context presents to the planner. Four categories may be proposed: 1) socioeconomic and sociopolitical, 2) sociocultural and sociohistorical, 3) psychosocial, and 4) ecclesiastical. Each category contains a set of interrelated issues and questions that must be considered by the educational planner if a given form of theological education is to have any chance of being appropriate to its context.

Table 2 offers a series of sample issues and questions that need to be considered in most settings. The table is written generally; planners must formulate the questions specifically for their context. The table is not exhaustive, but it is designed to represent the kinds of realities planners must consider.

CONCLUSION

In this chapter we have attempted to describe a reasonable approach to designing appropriate forms of theological education in mission contexts. Unfortunately, the appropriateness of the form of a program of theological education will be known only after it has served the church for a number of years. The responsibility of planners and leaders is to design programs on the basis of sound theological positions, with sensitivity to the integrity and relevance of decisions that define a given form of theological education. To the degree that a program of theological education contributes to the glory of the eternal

King and the expansion of his church's presence on earth, we enter into a privileged task. Let us pray and plan with that truth in mind.

Contextual Reality	Issues	Questions
Socioeconomic and sociopolitical	Financial possibilities	Can students afford the program?
	Financing possibilities	Can the church afford the program?
	Economically determined lifestyle patterns	How much time does daily life allow for non-economic activity?
	Legal possibilities	Must the program gain legal status to operate?
	Relationship to dominant powers	What authorities must be satisfied to allow the program to exist and operate?
Sociocultural and sociohistorical	Credibility	What constitutes credible leadership education for the constituency?
	Attitude toward education	How is education viewed in the subculture?
	Educational experiences of students	What types and level of education are available for potential students?
Psychosocial	Sins of society	What are the predominant sins of the subculture?
	Student motivations	What are possible inappropriate motivations for entering theological studies?
	Student expectations	What constitutes a credible learning experience for students?
	Learning style	How do students most effectively learn?
Ecclesiastical	Leadership role	How do church members view the role of the leader?
	Leadership style	What is the most commonly adopted style of leadership in the subculture?
	Power structures	Who will have ultimate control of the program?

Table 2. Form Relevance.

Works Cited

Bosch, David. 1992. *Transforming Mission: Paradigm Shifts in Theology of Mission.* Maryknoll, N.Y.: Orbis Books.

Cahn, Steven M. 1986. *Saints and Scamps: Ethics in Academia.* Totowa, N.J.: Rowman & Littlefield.

Farley, Edward. 1983. *Theologia: The Fragmentation and Unity of Theological Education.* Philadelphia: Fortress Press.

Freire, Paulo. 1985. *Pedagogy of the Oppressed.* New York: Continuum.

Habermas, Ronald, and Klaus Issler. 1992. *Teaching for Reconciliation: Foundations and Practice of Christian Educational Ministry.* Grand Rapids: Baker Book House.

Joyce, Bruce, and Marsha Weil. 1986. *Models of Teaching.* 3rd. ed. Englewood Cliffs, N.J.: Prentice-Hall.

Kelsey, David. 1993. *Between Athens and Berlin: The Theological Education Debate.* Grand Rapids: Eerdmans.

Lowman, Joseph. 1995. *Mastering the Techniques of Teaching.* 2d ed. San Francisco: Jossey-Bass Publishers.

McKinney, Lois. 1987. *Educational Planning for Cross-cultural Ministry.* An extension course manual. Wheaton, Ill.: Wheaton Graduate School.

Postman, Neil. 1985. *Amusing Ourselves to Death: Public Discourse in the Age of Show Business.* New York: Penguin Books.

Postman, Neil, and Charles Weingartner. 1969. *Teaching as a Subversive Activity.* New York: Penguin Books.

Smith, Donald K. 1992. *Creating Understanding: A Handbook for Christian Communication Across Cultural Landscapes.* Grand Rapids: Zondervan.

Chapter Six _____

From Loneliness Toward Solitude and Community

A Seminary Professor's Journey[1]

Lois McKinney

_____

I am a seminary professor. The journey I am sharing is within a seminary context. It is the latest stage of a four-decade sojourn in educational and intercultural ministry. Over and over, across these years, Jesus Christ has filled the void of loneliness. My hope is that the experiential and subjective elements of this journey will enhance its objectivity rather than destroy it. Approaching a topic with both the heart and the mind, from both -emic and -etic perspectives, is within the best tradition of ethnographic writing (Spradley 1980, 56-58).

The journey from loneliness toward solitude and community is developmental. There are "already" and "not yet" elements in the moments and movements along the way.[2] My deep conviction is that renewal in our seminaries can and will occur as we allow moments of loneliness to move us toward solitude with God and community with one another.

THE MOMENT OF LONELINESS

A seminary professor's role often is lonely. We value collegiality and interdisciplinary reflection. We want scholarly conversations with faculty members outside our own department. We would like to bring

our distinctive disciplinary perspectives into broader academic debates. We wish we could know one another in more than superficial
ways. We want to be a caring community of brothers and sisters in
Christ. Yet much of the time, in many of our schools, we find ourselves trapped by loneliness.

Where does loneliness come from? What are some of the factors
that contribute to it? Let me suggest several possible sources.

A primary source of loneliness within a seminary community is
competitiveness. We seminary professors all too often find ourselves
comparing our accomplishments; counting our publications; and
vying with one another for promotions, tenure, sabbaticals, and
awards. These competitive behaviors can pit us against one another
and create a climate in which isolation and loneliness take root.

Another potential source of loneliness is excessive disciplinary
specialization. Our faculties are made up of academic specialists and
subject-matter experts. We spend far more time pursuing our own
research interests than we do in talking to one another and exploring
the commonalties and diversities of our disciplines. We seldom listen to one another long enough or hard enough to break out of our
disciplinary isolation.

For some of us, loneliness may result from an unwillingness to be
vulnerable. We become so expert at wearing our masks and hiding
our limitations that we trap ourselves in a cycle of fear. We cannot
risk community, because community calls for vulnerability. Vulnerability means that our colleagues will discover how little we really
know. When they discover how little we know, we fear they will no
longer respect us and we will lose our credibility. Our lack of openness and vulnerability erects defensive walls around us, isolating us
into lonely, private worlds.

For many of us, busyness creates loneliness. We seem to believe
that if we drive ourselves hard enough, and keep ourselves busy
enough, we can drown out the inner cry for collegiality. We some-
how convince ourselves that if we work seventy-hour weeks, we can
ignore our need to be a part of a community.

Institutional structures also contribute to loneliness. Traditional
education thrives on hierarchy and clear chains of command. The
faculty report to department heads, department heads report to the
dean, the dean reports to a vice-president, the vice president reports
to the president, and the president reports to the board. There also
are informal hierarchies through which junior faculty members ac-
cede to senior faculty, students defer to teachers and, in some cases,
women are subordinated to men.

An unfortunate result of these kinds of hierarchical structures is
the divisions they can create among the "we's" and "they's, the "us's"

and "them's." They can separate administrators from faculty, faculty from students, and women from men. A perfect climate is created for stereotyping, prejudice, discrimination, and abuse of power. When those in positions of authority protect their power base, the end result can be a distorted seminary community where, in the language of Paulo Freire, the Brazilian educator, even teaching and learning will flow down from the "oppressor" to the "oppressed" (Freire 1972, 27-56).

One further factor that contributes to loneliness in seminary life needs to be mentioned. We relate to one another in simplex roles within a single context. We know one another in dyadic, role-based relationships, such as those between student and professor, professor and colleague, or professor and dean. These roles contrast with multiplex roles through which people share a variety of relationships. In such relationships two professors might be professional colleagues, next-door neighbors, golfing partners, members of the same church, and parents of children who play together (Hiebert 1983, 148-150).

In some seminary contexts, multiplex relationships are extremely rare. Contact between students and faculty often is limited to the classroom, chapel, fixed office hours, and perhaps a brief chat between classes. Among faculty, relationships may include prayer meetings, committee meetings, infrequent social activities, and quick greetings as we pass in the corridors. We seldom relate to each other within the broader contexts that make up our lives. It is possible to be together for several years in an academic setting without getting to know one another in more than superficial ways.

The portrait I have painted of loneliness in our seminaries is admittedly overdrawn. In all of our institutions, we can point to encouraging expressions of community. In some of our schools, community may even be a dominant theme. Yet, even in the most communal of our institutions, powerful centrifugal forces still spin us away from one another into lonely, isolated orbits.

THE JOURNEY TOWARD SOLITUDE AND COMMUNITY

How can we break out of the isolation of seminary life? How can the destructive moment of loneliness be transformed into a movement toward solitude with God and community with one another?

The movement begins when we recognize the sources of loneliness and the negative values they reflect. When these sources of loneliness—competitiveness, excessive disciplinary specialization, a fear of vulnerability, busyness, hierarchical structures, and the limited, simplex roles through which we relate to one another—are examined more closely, we recognize that they grow out of negative, culturally based values, which can and must be transformed by the Word of God. Only then can genuine community occur.

Competition is endemic to our society. Some of us have internalized its values of individualism, striving, succeeding, and winning. Positive values such as team building, cooperation, and learning from one another are easily lost in our competitive struggle to get to the top (Joyce and Weil 1996, 67-70).

Excessive disciplinary specialization can be equally destructive. It can lead to self-absorption, turf protecting, and an obsession with academic recognition. It also can keep us from integrating our particular disciplines into the broader frameworks of God's truth (Holmes 1985, 11-17).

When vulnerability is seen as a weakness rather than a strength, communal values can be eroded even further. We can succumb to feelings of inadequacy and fears of rejection. We can feel threatened by possibilities of openness, accountability, or corporate guidance (Lingenfelter and Mayers 1986, 105-16).

Busyness grows out of task orientation and time orientation (Lingenfelter and Mayers 1986, 37-51, 81-94). It can keep us from valuing people. It can make us see time as a commodity to be used rather than a kairos moment to be enjoyed (McConnell 1983, 61-70). It can lead to obsessive-compulsive workaholism. It can confuse our priorities and crowd out our leisure.

The power-based values implicit in hierarchical structures can be especially devastating. They can tempt persons in positions of authority to be domineering and controlling—perhaps even abusive (cf. Johnson and VanVonderen 1991). They can negate biblical values associated with submission and servanthood (Foster 1988, 110-40).

Fragmenting relationships into simplex roles makes it exceedingly difficult to practice Christian community. Knowing our colleagues only at work is not the same as knowing them in multiple contexts. The corporate disciplines—confession, worship, guidance, and celebration—can be practiced best among believers who share the multiple roles and complexities of their lives together (Foster 1988, 143-201).

From Loneliness Toward Solitude

We cannot move beyond loneliness until we have identified its sources and recognized its underlying values. In this process, value recognition is more than an intellectual exercise. It becomes an act of confession. We begin to see individualism, striving for success, turf protecting, excessive busyness, and questing for power for what they are. They are expressions of self-centeredness, pride, fear, and greed—sins of the heart that have isolated us and our institutions into lonely, private worlds. We long for forgiveness; we long to be freed. We cry out to God.

In solitude with God, our voices are stilled. We listen to God's voice, and we respond to God's Word. We are reminded of our Lord's example when he washed his disciples' feet (John 13:1-20). It was time for Jesus to leave this world and go to the Father (v. 1). He was on his way to the cross. Judas would betray him. The other disciples would desert him. At that moment, he took off his outer robe—the trappings of status, rank, privilege, position—wrapped himself with a slave's towel, and performed the most menial of tasks for those he was serving (v. 4).

Then we remember the day Jesus visited Mary and Martha (Luke 10:38-42). He was taking time to be with his friends. Mary was sitting at the Lord's feet listening to what he was saying. Martha was busy with household tasks; she wanted Mary to help her. Jesus gently rebuked Martha's busyness and her mixed up priorities: "Martha, Martha . . . you are worried and upset about many things, but only one thing is needed. Mary has chosen what is better, and it will not be taken away from her" (vv. 41-42).

As we listen to God speak through his Word in ways like these, our hearts respond in silence, obedience, humility, and contrition. God breaks our stubborn will and brings down our haughty pride, calms our fears, and fills our hearts with love. We are in solitude with God, and we know we are not alone.

From Solitude Toward Community

Community born out of solitude with God frees us from competitiveness and disciplinary self-absorption so that we can share with one another, learn from one another, and encourage one another. We no longer are afraid to be vulnerable. We are able to trust our colleagues and to share caring, mentoring relationships with them. We no longer are controlled by our busyness and heavy workloads. We make time to celebrate with one another, enjoy one another, and worship with one another. Institutional and societal norms no longer control us. We have recognized the negative values they reflect, and we have begun our journey toward community. It is a long and difficult journey, to be sure, but it also is a journey of hope. We believe that people can be changed, structures can be transformed, and institutions can be renewed so that, speaking the truth in love, we will in all things grow up into him who is the Head, that is, Christ. From him the whole body, joined and held together by every supporting ligament, grows and builds itself up in love, as each part does its work (Eph. 4:15-16).

Notes

1. The development of this essay began with a panel presentation by the author on April 29, 1994, during a North Chicago Theological Institute course, "Praying the Loneliness: The Movement from Loneliness to Solitude."

2. *Moments* are defined in this essay as strategic points in time that offer both danger and opportunity. *Movements* are the growth that occurs in both persons and communities as the moments are being redeemed (cf. Groome 1991, 146-48).

Works Cited

Foster, R. J. 1988. *Celebration of Discipline: The Path to Spiritual Growth*. Revised ed. HarperSanFrancisco.

Freire, P. 1972. *Pedagogy of the Oppressed*. New York: Herder and Herder.

Hiebert, P. G. 1983. *Cultural Anthropology*. Grand Rapids: Baker.

Holmes, A., ed. 1985. *The Making of a Christian Mind: A Christian World View and the Academic Enterprise*. Downers Grove, Ill.: InterVarsity Press.

Groome, T. H. 1991. *Sharing Faith: A Comprehensive Approach to Religious Education and Pastoral Ministry*. San Francisco: Harper & Row.

Johnson, D., and J. VanVonderen. 1991. *The Subtle Power of Spiritual Abuse*. Minneapolis: Bethany House Publishers.

Joyce, B., and M. Weil. 1996. *Models of Teaching*, 5th ed. Boston: Allyn and Bacon.

Lingenfelter, S. G., and M. K. Mayers. 1986. *Ministering Cross-Culturally: An Incarnational Model for Personal Relationships*. Grand Rapids: Baker.

McConnell, W. 1983. *The Gift of Time*. Downers Grove, Ill.: InterVarsity Press.

Spradley, J. P. 1980. *Participant Observation*. New York: Holt, Rinehart and Winston.

Chapter Seven _____

Missiology and the Coherence of Theological Education

SAMUEL F. ROWEN

_____

What makes theological education cohere? What is the center that holds the theological curriculum together? This question has been with us for a long time. Many attempts have been made to answer the question. A quick review of the journal *Theological Education* will reveal that at least once a decade the issues related to the theological curriculum are revisited. Seminaries constantly involve themselves in revising the course of study in order to improve the education of Christian workers. There is little evidence that the theological curriculum will change fundamentally in the near future. This prognosis is made in spite of the tremendous amount of energy that is being focused on institutional change. Change will occur, but change does not necessarily mean improvement.

I reflect upon my own experience in theological education as a student. The seminary I attended had a tradition rooted primarily in Europe, with adjustments made to adapt to life in the New World. The president actually was the president of the faculty. Each Saturday morning the faculty would gather to listen to, interact with, and challenge a paper written by a faculty member. This truly was a theological community. I recall being impressed as a student by how knowledgeable the Old Testament professors were in church history and systematic theology; the systematic theology professor discussed at length an issue in exegetical theology with his colleagues before putting his thoughts into print.

Then the revolution occurred. A new way of organizing the seminary was introduced by the accrediting association. The president became the president of the seminary. A different person became the vice-president of academic affairs or dean of the faculty. Thus a model was introduced that leads, in a society bent toward adversarial relationships, to conflict between administration and faculty—conflict that did not exist in the same way before. Previously conflict was possible between the faculty and the board, but the faculty remained the primary driver in the institution. Now the seminary exists as a tripartite entity—board, administration, and faculty.

I recently asked the president of an evangelical theological seminary, "If I were to give you a 'magic wand,' in what ways would you change your institution?" Knowing that he had been frustrated recently, I waited for the answer. He responded without hesitation, "I would reduce the present number of departments so that we had only three departments." It was then that I knew the revolution had been completed. The coherence of theological education is "modern scientific management theory."[1]

A number of years ago I was asked to assist in facilitating a meeting of the presidents, academic deans, and denominational representatives of seven theological seminaries of the Reformed tradition. The purpose of the gathering was to discuss the status of theological education and to explore ways of mutual cooperation. The discussions took the course of the problematic nature of the present situation. As the discussion progressed the president of one seminary penned the following words:

> Say, how does the minister function out there?
> Is he climbing a wall? Is he tearing his hair?
> What problems look large? What forces look
>   sinister?
> To the poor harried soul who is known as a
>   minister.
> Will someone please tell him what he should do
> When he finds that his halo is coming askew?
> The young people think that his sermons are dead
> The older ones say he's too easily led.
> The ladies aid questions the depth of his piety
> And he's not quite in step with the John Birch
>   Society.
> His wife wants the freedom to be a whole person
> And one gossip swears that she heard him a-
>   cursing.

Say, what is the trouble with old what's-his-name?
If he's such a numbskull just who is to blame?
The answer to who manufactured this fool
It's that gang at Reformed Theological School.

(Rowen 1990, 95)

In 1983 Edward Farley, in *Theologia: The Fragmentation and Unity of Theological Education*, focused on issues of the reform of theological education. He sees the basic problem as theological in nature. *Theologia*, for Farley, is a form of sapiential knowledge (*habitus*), a salvific knowledge of God. The disappearance of theology as the unity, subject matter, and the end of clergy education is the root of the current crisis in theological education. "This disappearance is responsible more than anything else for the problematic character of that education as a course of study" (Farley 1983, ix).

The eighteenth and nineteenth centuries produced a large body of literature on the encyclopedia of theological education. During this period there was much reflection on the nature of theology. Largely absent from these writings, however, is an awareness of the tremendous shift from the Middle Ages and Reformation understanding of theology as a *habitus*, "an act of practical knowledge having the primary character of wisdom, to theology used as a generic term for the cluster of disciplines" (Farley 1983, 81).

It is to this discussion, the nature of theology and theological education, that I now turn to address the topic in the title of this chapter. It is a discussion that has been facilitated by the seminal writings of Farley. The following quotations will illustrate the nature of the problem:

The Christian faith is intrinsically missionary. It is not the only persuasion that is missionary. Rather, it shares this characteristic with several other religions, notably Islam and Buddhism, and also with a variety of ideologies, such as Marxism. A distinctive element of missionary religions, in contrast to missionary ideologies, is that they all hold to some great "unveiling" of ultimate truth believed to be of universal import (Bosch 1991, 9).

Contemporary New Testament scholars are affirming what the systematic theologian Martin Kahler said over eight decades ago: Mission is "the mother of all theology." Theology, said Kahler, began as "an accompanying manifestation of the Christian mission" and not as a "luxury of the world-dominating church." The New Testament writers were not scholars who had the leisure to research the evidence before they put pen to paper. Rather, they wrote in the context of an "emergency situation" of church which, because of its missionary encounter with the world, was forced to theologize (Bosch 1991, 16).

If we turn to architecture for an analogy we may say that theological education in the United States has never had a Gropius, or a Wright, or a Harrison, or a Saarinen. That is, we have never had a new statement, a genuinely creative response by men who are ruthlessly determined to push beyond the inheritance of the past (Wagoner 1965, 90).

Great confusion prevails in some quarters about theological education. What, it is asked, is the meaning of this ministry? For what purpose are we educating? The situation in some circles of theological education seems to be similar to the one found among certain foreign missionaries and sponsors of foreign mission. They know that what they are doing is important, but an understanding of the strategy of their work, a relatively precise and definite understanding of its meaning is lacking (Niebuhr 1954, 120).

Karl Barth describes the ethics of the New Testament as a downward pull, the pull from the heights to the depths, from riches to poverty, from victory to defeat, from triumph to suffering, from life to death. . . . How can Yale University which seems to encourage everything except a downward pull, look at itself as an institution which sends its people out into the world to serve? Doesn't Yale University instill within its students the desire to move upward from weakness to power, from poverty to wealth, from ignorance to knowledge, from servant to master (Williams 1978, 67).

Farley suggests the center or coherence of theological education is *theologia*. I suggest the center of theological education is *missiologia*. It is in an understanding of the *missio Dei* that we find the coherence of all theological disciplines and the purpose of the theological educational enterprise.

Missiologia gives coherence to all the theological disciplines. Paul employs a military metaphor. He concludes the task is one in which "we demolish arguments and every pretension that sets itself up against the knowledge of God, and we take captive every thought to make it obedient to Christ" (2 Cor. 10:5). Lenski, the Lutheran commentator, says mission entails taking captive thought systems and rendering them obedient to Christ.

The *missio Dei* does not apply only to work done at the missionary edges of cultural boundaries or in the pastoral, educational, and diaconal work of the church. It also happens when a scholar writes a commentary. A scholar is pushing back the borders of understanding and reclaiming the territory for the Lord to whom it rightly belongs. The scholar is taking captive diverse human thoughts so that they will be obedient to Christ. The writers of the New Testament took words and ideas with pagan meanings and filled them with new meaning. In these transformations the words and ideas became vehicles of the revelation of God. Teaching, scholarship, spiritual formation, and practical experience are all missiological tasks (Lenski 1937, 1208).

To this discussion I bring what is always an enjoyable experience—the writing of a former student. Elias dos Santos Medeiros (1992), a Brazilian missiologist, puts forth in his dissertation a proposition that I believe all those engaged in theological education must seriously consider.

Medeiros, in his quest to understand the place of missiology in the theological curriculum, first discusses the nature of theology. He finds a great deal of support for his thesis in the works of Abraham Kuyper. Medeiros criticizes missiologists for not dialoguing with theologians at this deeper level of the nature of theology itself. He maintains that it is for this reason that missiology has remained outside the mainstream of the theological curriculum.

Abraham Kuyper, the nineteenth-century Dutch theologian, was an important contributor to the discussions on the theological encyclopedia. He was concerned that theology would have a place within the context of the other disciplines in the university. He was searching for what he called the *principium theologiae*. Kuyper concluded that the knowledge of God in theology was different from the kind of knowledge in the other disciplines. In biology he maintained that the object of study, for example, the animal, did not actively contribute to the knowledge of the inquirer. By contrast the knowledge gained in theology, a knowledge of God, is obtained because the object of study is active in making himself known. God actively communicates this knowledge in creation and the redemptive revelation in Scripture.

Medeiros says that there is a "missiological motion" in God in which he is making himself known. God is on a mission and the mission is to make his glory known throughout all the earth. The only knowledge of God we have is the knowledge of a God who is on a mission. Therefore, he suggests the term *principium missiologiae*, a term he maintains Kuyper would embrace.

THEOLOGICAL EDUCATION—*QUO VADIS?*

Why is it that there seems to be little substantive change in theological education even though much attention and energy is directed to renewal and reform? Part of the problem may lie in the nature of the language we use to discuss the issue. By *renewal* we speak of bringing new life to what already exists. Some things should not be renewed; they should be left to die. It is true that resurrection can bring new life to the old, but only in the radical sense of what is "sown in dishonor is raised in honor." To seek the resurrection of theological education is to look for some radically new form.

The second word we use often is *reform*. This word implies a different form. Many attempts at reform have resulted merely in rearrangement. It is the same house, but the furniture has been put in different places. One only needs to look at attempts at curriculum reform to see that in essence it is the same product placed in different boxes with different labels and a different order on the shelf. A close examination of the contents, however, reveals it essentially is what was there in the old boxes.

There can be no curriculum reform without a different center. Theological education, as Farley has noted, has been dominated by the concept of the theological encyclopedia. Schliermacher was the first to develop the categories that have become the orthodoxy of curricular design and development for theological education. He did cause a reform in theological education, because he offered a new center. In his attempt to respond to the challenges of the Enlightenment, he placed humanity and its experience of God in the center. It has been a traditional critique of Schliermacher that he developed an anthropology rather than a theology.

As we enter the twenty-first century we are confronted with a significant shift at the core of Western civilization. We are transitioning to the post-Enlightenment or postmodern world. What more appropriate time to begin seeking the reform of theological education by setting aside some of the assumptions that have characterized the development of theological curriculum. The center for a new formation will come by placing God and God's mission in the center.

There are two primary implications for the reform of theological education:

   1. Each division or department of the theological institution must begin by discerning the missiological implications of each discipline. None can be exempt if it is to justify its inclusion.

2. The issues of spiritual formation must be seen in their missiological perspective. Spirituality is not simply a matter of inwardness as articulated in many writings on the spiritual disciplines. There also is the outward dimension of spirituality. There is no place for a dichotomy between heart and mind or between mind and service. We need to develop what Bosch calls a "spirituality of the road" (Bosch 1979).

A simple example will give insight into the direction that needs to be taken. The study of the biblical languages of Greek and Hebrew have a missiological dimension as well as implications for spiritual formation. Language is more than grammar, vocabulary, and syntax. Language is the way a particular people view the world. In this case it is the world view of the people of biblical times as reflected in their language. Learning the biblical languages in this manner opens one up to understand how language functions as the doorway to a person or culture interacting with the world. This is the point of entry for the communication of the gospel to people of every culture.

One of the ways in which spiritual formation is viewed is to have "the mind of Christ." Language studied as a reflection of world view, not merely as a technical task, allows a person empathetically to enter into another person's world. It is the old saying that a person who gains a second language gains a second soul. This is one of the characteristics of Christ who, in the incarnation, entered the world of human experience to the extent that he is able to empathize even with the fallenness of human experience (Heb. 4:15). The study of language can be a means of developing the Christlike quality of empathy. Language studied this way can be a means of preparing students to minister the gospel incarnationally.

Mission has been peripheral to the theological curriculum because it has been peripheral to the church. Mission has been relegated to the preaching of the gospel to pagans where the church did not exist. The reconversion of neopagans is called evangelization (cf. Verkuyl 1978). It is this definition that has kept mission at the edge of the church and not at its center. "We are in need of a missiological agenda for theology, rather than just a theological agenda for mission . . . ; for theology, rightly understood, has no reason to exist other than critically to accompany the *missio Dei*" (Bosch 1991, 494).

Missiology cannot be understood only as a subdiscipline within the field of practical theology. It is at the very center of the entire theological education enterprise. The training of a pastor is to prepare him or her for engagement in the mission of God in the world. The training of a missionary is to prepare him or her for engagement in the mission of God in the world. The training of a theological and biblical scholar is to prepare him or her for engagement in the mission of God in the world. Missiology is both a subdiscipline in the area of practical theology or diaconal studies and also the coherence and center of theological education.

The reform of theological education will become renewed and energized when it discovers its missiological center. The time has come for serious dialogue between theologians and missiologists. Missiological perspectives can provide significant insight to the task of reforming the theological curriculum.

Note

1. For an analysis of the ways in which management theory has affected education in North America, see Edward Callahan (1964).

Works Cited

Bosch, D. 1979. *A Spirituality of the Road*. Scottdale, Penn.: Herald Press.
_____. 1991. *Transforming Mission: Paradigm Shifts in Theology of Mission*. Maryknoll, N.Y.: Orbis Books.
_____. 1995. *Believing in the Future: Toward a Missiology of Western Culture*. Valley Forge, Penn.: Trinity Press International.
Callahan, E. 1964. *Education and the Cult of Efficiency*. Chicago: University of Chicago Press.
Farley, E. 1983. *Theologia: The Fragmentation and Unity of Theological Education*. Philadelphia: Fortress Press.
Lenski, R. C. H. 1937. *The Interpretation of 1 and 2 Corinthians*. Minneapolis: Augsburg Publishing House.
Niebuhr, H. R. 1954. The survey of theological education. In *The Nineteenth Biennial Meeting of the American Association of Theologial Schools, Bulletin 21*.
Niebuhr, H. R., et al. 1956. *The Purpose of the Church and Its Ministry: Reflections on the Aims of Theological Education*. New York: Harper and Brothers.
Rowen, S. 1990. Theological education since World War II: The American experience. In *Practical Theology and the Ministry of the Church: 1952-1984*, edited by H. M. Conn, 91-106. Phillipsburgh, N.J.: Presbyterian and Reformed Publishing Co.
Santos Medeiros, E. dos. 1992. *Missiology as an Academic Discipline in Theological Education*. Unpublished doctor of missiology dissertation, Reformed Theological Seminary, Jackson, Mississippi.
Verkuyl, J. 1978. *Contemporary Missiology: An Introduction*. Grand Rapids: Eerdmans.
Wagoner, W. D. 1965. A model for theological education, *Theological Education*, 1, no. 2 (Spring), 90-95.
Williams, C. 1978. Purpose in a university divinity school, *Theological Education*, 14, no. 2 (Spring), 67-73.

Chapter Eight _____

The Role of Theology in Theological Education

ROBERT W. FERRIS

Throughout this century theological educators have vacillated between an uneasy acceptance of the incumbent approach to ministry education and periodic reviews of the nature of their craft and calling. Despite shifts in secular culture and theological rhetoric, seminary curricula at the end of the twentieth century retain a recognizable continuity with that of the first North American seminary, founded in 1803. This curricular conservatism, and the assumptions on which it is founded, has been examined in major studies of American ministry education published in 1934 (Brown and May) and in 1956 (Niebuhr).

Currently, the nature and shape of ministry education are under review again. This round, which has been the most sustained and has produced by far the most extensive literature, was launched in 1983 by the publication of Edward Farley's *Theologia*. David Kelsey articulated the driving question of the current debate, however, when he asked, "What's theological about the theological school?" (Kelsey 1992).

Kelsey raises a fair—and important—question, one to which evangelicals owe a response. A biblical response to Kelsey's question, furthermore, can resolve ambiguities that contribute to dissatisfaction with current models of seminary education and that diminish the effectiveness of our theological schools. Before grappling with the role of theology in theological education, however, we must clarify the task of theology and the role of theological education in the church.

101

THE TASK OF THEOLOGY

Central to any discussion of the education of the church's leadership is our understanding of the task of theology as a discipline field. Farley (1983) argues that *theologia*—the knowledge of God—was the task of theological education until the early eighteenth century.

With the spread of Enlightenment thinking in Europe, this deductive (predominantly Platonic) approach to theological studies was challenged by the inductive (Aristotelian) methods that were proving so productive in the natural sciences. Thus, the attention of theologians shifted from *theologia* to theological science—or, more specifically, to theological encyclopedia, the rational distinction and affiliation of theological disciplines (Farley 1983, 49).

When challenge was raised to including a chair of theology among the professorships in the University of Berlin, Friedrich Schleiermacher argued that theology pursues a historically situated scientific method in establishing theological truth (Hough and Cobb 1985, 2). This argument for theology as science drew deeply from the streams of the encyclopedia movement, and Schleiermacher's *Brief Outline on the Study of Theology* (1811) unleashed a flood of theological encyclopedias within European theology (Farley 1983, 73).

Antedating Schleiermacher and with growing strength following him, the encyclopedia movement set forth a fourfold curriculum for theological studies. Bible, church history, dogmatics, and practical theology defined the curriculum for clergy education in Germany, in the rest of Europe, and in North America.

Schleiermacher's casting of *theology-as-science*,[1] combined with this fourfold distinction of discipline fields, has engendered two devastating effects within theological education. Farley (1983) contends that the fundamental flaw in clergy education today is a fragmentation of theological studies. Rigorous pursuit of the four discipline fields has left theological education without a unifying center. With ongoing scholarly investment, furthermore, the disciplines continue to fragment into ever more discrete specialty fields. It is no secret that biblical and theological scholars orient themselves much more toward members of other faculties who share their specialty field than to colleagues on their own faculty. As a result, theological students are left to invent unifying theories of their own or, more commonly, to live in a fragmented world of theological disciplines and understandings.

A second destructive result of viewing theology as science Farley terms "surfeiting." Farley describes this effect in unmistakable terms.

In disciplines whose subject matter is more or less fixed—for example, an ancient text—and in disciplines where there has been a surfeit of investigation, there is still a moving horizon of inquiry, but the focus is always on new methods to interpret that more or less fixed material. A book of an ancient canon or a famous literary figure from the past can be psychoanalyzed, deconstructed, psychohistoricized, structuralized, and phenomenologized. But the neomethodologies give scope only to a kind of artificial ingenuity whose subtleties grow more implausible with each new analysis (Farley 1988, 49).

When a specialty field is surfeited, scholars have only two lines of recourse: They can pursue ever finer strains of minutia, or they can apply new hermeneutics to the study of their fixed subject matter. Both avenues of research serve only the interests of the scholarly guild; practically, they are sterile. Yet this effect of the pursuit of theology-as-science is everywhere evident in American theological societies and seminaries at the end of the twentieth century.

The pursuit of theology-as-science—as its own, self-justifying end—cannot avoid the twin consequences of fragmentation and surfeiting. If theological studies are to recover wholeness and significance, another conceptualization of its task must be recognized.

Within historic orthodoxy and contemporary evangelicalism, an alternative understanding of theology's task emphasizes the articulation and ordering of biblical truth. As a revelational faith, biblical Christianity proclaims a message from God. The clear and orderly presentation of that message has been seen as the task of the theological sciences. Thus Erickson defines theology as,

> that discipline which strives to give a coherent statement of the doctrines of the Christian faith, based primarily upon the Scriptures, placed in the context of culture in general, worded in a contemporary idiom, and related to issues of life (Erickson 1983, 21).

Most evangelicals endorse this emphasis on message—"the doctrines of the Christian faith"—and conceive the task of theology (at least in part) as providing a coherent statement of this message. Revelation as inscripturated in the Bible, however, is not rationally ordered; much of the Bible is narrative history. While this history, and the message it bears, is consistent, it is not systematic. Herein lies the task of *theology-as-message*: to provide a clear and orderly presentation of the revealed message, primarily in the biblical text.

That God chose to set revelation in history rather than in creed or theological disposition, however, should not be overlooked. Since human rationality has its origins in God, God certainly could have revealed and inspired the ultimate statement of divine truth, rationally ordered and indisputably clear. That he did not, that he chose instead to give us a history of revelation, reflects God's intention that truth should be situated in life.

The pursuit of theology-as-message does not preclude situating truth, clarified and ordered, in life. Too often however, evangelical theologians have lost their way, producing works that obscure truth rather than clarifying the divine message. When we seek truth in abstraction, rather than truth in life, the goal of theology-as-message is forfeited even as the task is pursued. This should not amaze us, since pursuit of truth in abstraction, whether orthodox or heterodox, is indistinguishable from Schleiermacher's promotion of theology-as-science. In both cases theology becomes an end in itself, a self-justifying activity.

The solution to this tendency, clearly, is to reassert the biblical primacy of truth in life. As we clarify and order the biblical message, our theological task never is complete until we have specified the implications of the truth we handle for our lives and the lives of our students or readers.

A third understanding of the task of theology begins with the life situation of the reader. The role of the theologian, thus, is to bring to the biblical text questions arising from the social-historical context in order to determine the Christian response to that context. While liberation theologians have been the most explicit in advocating an understanding of *theology-as-engagement*, this view of the theologian's task neither originated with liberation theology nor does it require the Marxist assumptions characteristic of that movement. Indeed, orthodox and evangelical Christians always have brought to the authoritative Scriptures questions of truth, morality, and spirituality. As orthodox Christians brought questions to the Bible and found there the guidance they sought, communities have been ordered, governments have been established, legal codes have been framed, principles of Christian living have been clarified, and churches have been organized.

The modern missionary movement has sensitized us to the critical role of cultural assumptions and perspective. Although the biblical message does not change from culture to culture, the questions brought to the Bible by persons from different cultures vary widely. Contextualization, therefore, entails pursuit of theology-as-engagement, bringing to the Bible the questions that arise within a specific cultural context, and articulating the Bible's answers in ways which communicate within that culture. The differences among our Western theologies, Asian theologies, African theologies, and Latin theologies lie not in the *source* of the answers we proclaim—otherwise our theologies would not be Christian!—but in the questions we bring.

In Titus 1:9, Paul stipulates that a church leader "must hold firmly to the trustworthy message as it has been taught, so that he can encourage others by sound doctrine and refute those who oppose it." Here, too, we see that the proper task of theology is clarification and articulation of the biblical message ("encourage others by sound doctrine") and engagement with challenges arising from the sociocultural context ("refute those who oppose it [truth]"). Thus, biblical and theological studies are rigorously pursued, but always with an eye to shaping character and equipping for ministry.

Whereas theology-as-science has proven to be misleading and sterile, evangelicals find both theology-as-message and theology-as-engagement to be fruitful and necessary understandings of theology's task. The theologian must listen to the Bible to clarify and order the expression of its message so that its implications for life and godliness are clear. Theologians also must listen to the historical-social cultures in which they live. The theologian must take to the Scriptures the questions of truth, morality, justice, and spirituality that arise from our cultures in order to declare God's authoritative truth to our communities. Thus, theology-as-message and theology-as-engagement are twin aspects of an evangelical understanding of theology's task.

THE ROLE OF THEOLOGICAL EDUCATION IN THE CHURCH

If evangelical theological education in America currently reflects tragic confusion about the task of theology, our understanding of the role of theological education in the church is similarly fractured. The first American seminaries were established for the preparation of clergy, and contemporary seminaries without exception continue to profess that purpose. Nevertheless, Niebuhr's proposal that the theological school be viewed as an "intellectual center of the church's life" (1956, 107; cf. Gustafson 1988) is widely embraced by seminary faculties. Unfortunately, a tension between the intellectual and the equipping functions of seminary training commonly exists in our theological schools. Some even reserve the term *theological education* for the intellectual functions, while assigning the designation *ministry education* to the less prestigious task of clergy preparation (Dyrness 1993, 42).

Niebuhr's suggestion that *the theological school* functions *as an intellectual center of the church* can be useful or destructive, depending on one's understanding of the task of theology. When this view is wedded with the pursuit of theology-as-science, the seminary is indistinguishable from a graduate school of religion, spinning out and testing theological theories of negligible interest or significance to the church or to church leadership. Indeed, some evangelical seminaries today owe their irrelevance directly to this combination of understandings.

Theological education need not be irrelevant, however, even when the seminary is seen as an intellectual center of the church. When seminary faculties focus their efforts on the pursuit of theology-as-message and theology-as-engagement, the intellectual contribution of the theological school sustains and feeds the church and its leadership. Instead of occupying itself with arcane interests unique to the guild, attention is directed toward re-articulating the biblical message in contemporary language and idioms. Instead of re-arguing debates of the past or dignifying unbiblical scholarly proposals with serious response, effort is directed toward an apologetic engagement of sociocultural realities and the spirit of our age. Our seminaries serve well as intellectual centers of the church when focus is given to contemporary communication of the biblical message and sensible apologetic challenge to unbiblical assumptions in our culture.

Even more central to an understanding of the role of theological education, however, is a proper appreciation of *the seminary as the church's center for clergy education.* It has become expected in some quarters to decry the distinction between clergy and laity in the church. It is not necessary to defend clerical dominance or lay passivity, however, to acknowledge the functional importance of recognized leadership within the church. Acts and the epistles, especially the pastorals, make clear that a vigorous, recognized leadership functioned within the apostolic church.

The passage most often cited to support the ministry of all believers is Ephesians 4:11-12:

> It was he [Christ] who gave some to be apostles, some to be prophets, some to be evangelists, and some to be pastors and teachers, to prepare God's people for works of service, so that the body of Christ may be built up.

Clearly, the work of ministry belongs to the saints—all those whom Christ has made holy. The gifts of the risen Christ to his church are individuals; apostles, prophets, evangelists, and pastor-teachers are mentioned, but the list may not be exhaustive. In the light of this list (as well as the New Testament evidence mentioned above), it is difficult to conceive a case against the exercise of church leadership.

As significant as the existence of leaders within the church is the role designated for these special individuals. Their task, as given by the risen Christ, is to "equip" the saints. The term used (*katartismas*) means "to set in order" or "to prepare for use." Church leaders do not assign or distribute spiritual gifts to believers, this is the work of the Holy Spirit (1 Cor. 12:7-11). Gifting alone, however, does not prepare believers to employ their gifts in the practice of ministry. The missing element is equipping; church leaders must "equip the saints for the work of ministry." Effective service—building up the body of Christ—is the combined effect of the Spirit's gifting, the church leaders' equipping, and the saints' labor in ministry. Thus, church leaders are equippers who prepare Christians to use their spiritual gifts in ministries to the congregation and to the non-Christian community, both local and global.

The focus here is the leaders' role in equipping believers for fruitful service. We might ask, however, about the equippers themselves. If the saints are gifted, yet require equipping to be effective, it is reasonable (by analogy) to recognize that equippers also must be equipped for their equipping ministry. It is the Word, the inspired Scriptures, that God uses to shape our lives and to minister through us to others. Knowledge of the Scriptures, however, is not a spiritual gift. Neither is the most gifted teacher-discipler exempt from learning how his or her equipping gifts are most effectively used. Equippers themselves need to be equipped. This is the role of the seminary as the church's center for clergy education.

The seminary's role as intellectual center of the church is integral to its role as center for clergy education, and vice versa. As seminary faculty interpret the biblical message to our age and engage the issues of our culture with biblical challenge and response, church leaders are provided models for the use of Scripture within their own ministries. The task of theology does not exhaust the task of the seminary; equipping has other dimensions which must be pursued, as well. Positioning theology (understood as message and engagement) within clergy education, however, restores clarity and focus to the task of theological education.

First and foremost, then, the seminary is the church's center for clergy education, equipping those God has chosen and gifted to equip his saints. An essential aspect of this equipping task is careful instruction in theology—not losing itself in pursuit of scholarship for its own sake, but interpreting the Christian message into our sociocultural context and exposing unbiblical assumptions and dogmas of our age. In doing so, the seminary functions as an intellectual center of the church, but always within the larger context of clergy education.

THEOLOGY AND THEOLOGICAL EDUCATION TODAY

When our inquiry into the role of theology in theological education shifts from theology to observation, we find two distinct models extant among evangelical seminaries in America at the end of the twentieth century. Some embrace the task of *equipping the church's leadership as the seminary's central mission*. Without minimizing their role as the church's intellectual center, these seminaries focus attention and energy on equipping church leaders.

The faculties of these seminaries embrace a holistic understanding of their task. Since the biblical qualifications for congregational leadership emphasize Christian character and ministry effectiveness (skills), curricular priorities are given similar weighting. Attention to biblical and theological studies is not diminished in these seminaries, but it is directed toward equipping for ministry leadership.

These seminaries recognize that character cannot be taught; it develops when the truth of God's Word is met by obedient faith in the life of the believer. Although ministry skills may be taught, the dynamic of effective ministry never resides in human expertise. Only as the Spirit of God empowers the Word of God are spiritual victories won; the most skillful minister is only a channel through whom God's power flows. Nevertheless, accurate knowledge of biblical truth is requisite before God can convey that truth to others through us.

The alternative model champions *theological education as distinct from equipping for ministry*. Emphasis is placed on the theological school as the intellectual center of the church, not with a wholesome focus on theology-as-message and theology-as-engagement, but as a home for theology-as-science—for theological studies as ends in themselves. Because the seminary's role as center for clergy education cannot be totally ignored, the commitment and engagement of the faculty is torn in two directions. In some cases this schizophrenia regarding task and mission is institutionalized by dividing the seminary into two discrete units—a school of theology and a school of missions. This is a troubling—and troublesome—development.

As we have seen above, when the task of the seminary is identified with theology as an end in itself, theological education cannot avoid the twin consequences of fragmentation and surfeiting. To retain wholeness and significance, theology must be pursued in the context of ministry—in interpretation of the biblical message and in dialogue with non-Christian elements of our culture. Focus on ministry provides a needed discipline on the pursuit of theology. Creation of a school of theology separate from a school of missions liberates biblical and theological scholars from this essential discipline.

Surprisingly, perhaps, separation of a school of missions from a school of theology can be equally harmful to the ministry and missiological disciplines. Freed from the constraints of careful engagement with the biblical text, instruction for church and mission leadership tends to emphasize strategy and methods. Often this leads to an uncritical dependence on the social sciences. The social sciences bring helpful perspective to equipping for ministry when their assumptions and findings are biblically tested. This biblical scrutiny is easily slighted, however, when theological and missiological faculties are structurally insulated in separate schools. The ministry and missiological disciplines suffer when they are undisciplined by careful biblical and theological studies.

Institutional structures may facilitate or hinder the integration of theology and ministry, but they also can be deceiving. Within seminaries divided between a school of theology and a school of missions, either or both units may seek to pursue an integrated model of theological education. A school of theology may intentionally locate theology within a context of ministry, or a school of missions may intentionally focus the theological foundations of ministry. Similarly, ample evidence exists that an undivided seminary structure is no guarantee of an active and productive integration of theology and ministry. An undivided seminary structure offers a more natural context for realizing curricular integration, but intentionality is crucial.

When intentionally and actively pursued, a focused commitment to equipping the church's leadership avoids the pitfalls of isolation. By placing theology within the context of ministry education, the unity of the seminary's task is preserved. Theology, rigorously pursued as message and engagement, is disciplined by its focus on ministry and by its ongoing dialogue with ministerial studies. Likewise, studies in ministry and missions are informed and disciplined by their ongoing dialogue with biblical and theological studies. Theology and missiology never occur in separation; constant dialogue is maintained. When this dialogue is interrupted, whatever its confessional stance, theological education is less than Christian.

CONCLUSION

We now are able to address directly Kelsey's question, "What's theological about the theological school?" Our answer is, everything! Theology is central to the mission and task of the theological school, not because theology is pursued as an end in itself, but because every aspect of the seminary's larger task—equipping for ministry—is theologically informed. Locating theology within the context of equipping for ministry affords a useful wall against pursuit of theology-as-science while, at the same time, counteracting dangerous tendencies toward over-dependence on social sciences in ministry and missiological training.

Intentional integration of theology and ministry in theological education is both biblical and prudent. Isolation of theological and ministry studies distorts our understanding of our task, with destructive effect on the church and its leadership. Theological educators, in America and around the world, need to preserve, pursue, and exploit this biblical integration.

Note

1. In adopting the term *theology-as-science*, I do not intend to question all of the qualities associated with scientific activity. The quest for an overarching understanding of the discipline field and commitment to rigorous pursuit of appropriate tasks clearly are legitimate and important. My focus, rather, is on the self-justifying assumptions which often attend scientific research. It is theology pursued as an end in itself that is in view here. It is true that Schleiermacher's case for a chair of theology at the University of Berlin also turned on an argument for the professional preparation of clergy for the state church. The churchward orientation implied in this assertion, however, is barely evidenced in the ensuing development of German theology. Today, for many on our Western seminaries faculties, the pursuit of theology-as-science—theology as its own, self-justifying end—has thoroughly overwhelmed any engagement with communicating Christian truth in the realities of parish ministry.

Works Cited

Brown, W. A., and M. A. May. 1934. *The Education of American Ministers.* 4 vols. New York: Institute of Social and Religious Research.

Dyrness, W. A. 1993. Review of *Renewal in Theological Education: Strategies for Change,* by R. W. Ferris. *International Bulletin of Missionary Research* 17, no. 1 (January): 41-42.

Erickson, M. J. 1983. *Christian Theology.* Grand Rapids: Baker Book House.

Farley, E. 1983. *Theologia: The Fragmentation and Unity of Theological Education.* Philadelphia: Fortress Press.

_____. 1988. *The Fragility of Knowledge: Theological Education in the Church and the University.* Philadelphia: Fortress Press.

Gustafson, J. 1988. Reflections on the literature on theological education published between 1955-1985. *Theological Education* 24, Supplement 2, 9-86.

Hough, J. C., Jr., and J. B. Cobb, Jr. 1985. *Christian Identity and Theological Education.* Chico, Cal.: Scholars Press.

Kelsey, D. H. 1992. *To Understand God Truly: What's Theological About a Theological School?* Louisville, Ky.: Westminster/John Knox Press.

Niebuhr, H. R. 1956. *The Purpose of the Church and Its Ministry: Reflections on the Aims of Theological Education.* New York: Harper & Brothers.

Schleiermacher, F. 1811. *Kurze Darstellung des theologischen Studiums zum Behuf Einleitender Vorlesungen.* Berlin. Translated as *Brief Outline on the Study of Theology.* T. Tice, trans. Richmond, Va.: John Knox Press, 1966.

SECTION III

GLOBAL MISSION
IN CHANGING TIMES

Global Mission in Changing Times

STEPHEN T. HOKE

Pioneer. Leader. Co-worker. Servant.
Apostle. Church Planter. Partner. Mentor.
Innovator-Change Agent. Team Worker. Helper. Encourager-Facilitator.

These words capture some of the externally induced role-shifts that have radically reshaped missionary profiles over the last fifty years. Theology has narrowed and then broadened. Methods have multiplied. Values have shifted and some have disintegrated. But overwhelmingly, change has been the single contextual constant in global mission.

We have witnessed the rise and decline of crusade evangelism. We have viewed the emergence and sophistication of electronic media from short-wave radio to the cassette player, the ubiquitous television set, and the VCR. We have seen the proliferation of Bible translations from one predominant English text to over two thousand translations among sixty-seven hundred different language groups. We have witnessed the generational movements from pioneering, institution building, consolidation, and retrenchment toward networking and renewal. And we have seen splintered evangelistic efforts now merged into carefully planned and integrated evangelistic initiatives among unreached peoples. As the world has changed, the way we do missions has changed along with it.

But missions has often been slow to keep abreast of both global and local changes. When wars wreaked havoc across continents, our efforts in Christian relief were slow, scattered, and ineffectual. When

115

worldwide waves of refugees lapped at our shores, we struggled to rescue and rehabilitate them into our culture. When natural disasters and global political and climactic shifts threatened Africa and Asia, the Western church was in remedial biblical grade school learning the lessons of biblical developmentalism in order to be able to respond as Jesus would to facilitate long-term, sustainable holistic development efforts.

Our contextualization efforts have also been decades behind. Our first institutions, whether educational or medical, looked remarkably similar to those in Nashville, Chicago, and Boston. That was the only way we knew to do medicine, missions, and education. Our churches too often bore the names, architecture, and worship forms of our churches in Seattle, Sioux City, and Savannah. Our messages were crafted more in the cultures of our North American communities and in reaction to our issues and needs than they were adapted to the immediate physical and spiritual needs of host villages, barrios, or urban neighborhoods. We were blind to the "flaw of the excluded middle" in our own world view. Too often we were ill-equipped to wage global spiritual warfare with principalities and powers. Ministry was often delivered to the poor rather than being incarnated among them. Too often we lived safely in compounds in the suburbs instead of alongside the people we came to love. Our ministries were dichotomized and prioritized instead of biblically integrated and holistic.

Most recently, when geopolitical walls crumbled overnight in regions for which we had prayed for generations, our individualistic, triumphalistic, and segmented approaches created scenes of mass confusion in which we trampled our own in the stampede to help. Mishandled sheep lay strewn across the countryside as careless and unwitting pseudo-shepherds offered quick fixes to complex generational and multi-ethnic dilemmas. The Western mission movement once more became known for its *blitzkrieg* slash-and-burn tactics followed by rapid retreats from areas that did not yield overnight to our outdated, out-of-touch, and misdirected frontal attacks.

Yet—in spite of all our misguided and ill-prepared efforts—there have been notable examples of appropriate adaptation, sensitive contextualization, and proactive developmental ministry. Bible translation efforts have laid the foundation for transforming cultures through sensitive cultural analysis and relationship building. Church planting has crossed bridges of God to follow indigenous cultural patterns of multiplication. Theological education has extended itself into more natural delivery systems that are nonformal and easily adaptable to cultural learning styles and geographical challenges.

Missions has rediscovered the social sciences as a ministry resource and, in the process, has recovered for itself a more biblical and developmental approach to fulfilling the Great Commission and Great Commandment in tandem. Evangelism has discovered appropriate cultural equivalents to communicate the Good News in local idioms and images that capture the hearts and imagination of whole peoples. Telling the gospel has moved from unidirectional proclaiming on street corners to contextualized storytelling in homes and community groups.

The chapters in this section reflect different dimensions of the dynamic change taking place in the mission context at the end of the twentieth century. A special focus is placed on the adaptive role of the missionary as educator and facilitator. More appropriate responses to changing contexts are described. A fundamental heart-transformation in the way we do mission is assumed: a turning from external to internal issues and a move toward a biblically-based, inside-out approach of working with people as God created them—his masterpieces, co-workers with him in the fulfillment in this "story of his glory."

In her article, "Considering the Contexts of Twenty-First-Century Missions," Lynn Joesting Day focuses our attention on the currently developing global trends that challenge time-worn mission paradigms. As nations, people groups, families and individuals seek to design their personal truths about life and creatively assemble convenient belief systems, Christians must learn how to respond meaningfully to micro-pockets rather than only national needs. Our missionary response must increasingly emerge from three strong commitments—to understand the significance of emerging global trends; to retire paradigms, programs and individuals whose "insightful light and salty significance no longer relate to the world's changing life contexts"; and to worship in honest humility the living Lord who promises us abundant life. Certainly the stories in the book of Acts will bring great hope and comfort to the adventurous life promised twenty-first-century Christians.

As a long-term missionary in Africa, Jim Plueddemann saw firsthand the need to think through the integration of theory and practice in course and curriculum design and for theological education. From his current perspective as a mission executive, he views much of the current thinking on visionary leadership as autocratic, task-oriented and behavioristic. In "Visionary Planning for World Missions" he proposes a balanced participatory approach that is thoroughly congruent with biblical values as it seeks to stimulate creative planning from the bottom up.

Mission educators seeking to be effective in multicultural settings must be sensitive to both the value bases and delivery systems that will facilitate the holistic learning. In his chapter, "Research in Missiological Curriculum and Instruction," Edgar Elliston suggests that a biblical rationale for research in education and missions arises out of the educational dimensions of the Great Commission and the appeal to communicate effectively to the *panta ta ethne* (nations). In order to keep the curriculum relevant and effective, educational research is needed in each community and with each generation as developmental changes occur. The educator enters a situation asking questions about the condition of the people in the present and what their condition could be in the future. The gap between these two answers provides an arena for research to inform both perspectives to take (theory) and appropriate decisions to make (evaluation) in the development of missiological curriculum and instruction.

J. Allen Thompson has committed his life to initiating church-planting movements around the world. "Training Church Planters: A Competency-Based Learning Model" describes an approach to the preparation of leaders who understand and are able to interact with the dynamics of expanding church movements, not just to copy the programmatic models of others. His article focuses on the preparation of a specific type of Christian leader—the church planter who starts a church with the goal of producing other churches. And he outlines how.

Mission is global. We are living in radically changing times. I trust that the challenges raised by the authors in this section will clarify our vision and commitments as we enter the twenty-first century.

*Chapter Nine*_____

Considering the Contexts of Twenty-First Century Missions

Lynn Joesting Day

_____

That sentimental ditty "love makes the world go round" must no longer be true. Today we wonder why fast-paced "love" makes us dizzy, as myriads of people, events, and technologies spin wildly about us. Even the most securely grounded Christians cannot help but suffer some "stop the world, I want to get off" panic attacks due to the unrelenting change constantly barraging us.

Missionary sages are especially aware of the tension. They are the men and women persistently working in field assignments, administering missionary agencies, or teaching in Christian colleges and seminaries—people doing their best to respond to radically changing world scenes. They know that success paradigms of even fewer than ten years ago may fail to reach their mark today. We live in a world where nations, people groups, families, and individuals seek to discover their own definitions of truth and invent new "realities" for their lives.

Global appeals of cyberspace escapism, economic gluttony, violent outbursts, and unlimited indulgences mesmerize people deeply hungry for a sense of personal significance and particular value in today's world. Our missionary response to these peoples must emerge from three strong commitments. First, we must understand the significance of past and currently emerging societal and global trends as the contexts in which Christ's redemptive love is learned. Second, we must retire all paradigms, programs, and individuals whose insightful light and salty significance no longer relate to the world's changing life contexts. And, finally, we must return to the Lord in honest humility, prepared with the knowledge of the signs of the times but peacefully awaiting the anointing of his Spirit for the adventures ahead. He calls us his friends. He yearns to take us into the best life of all, a walk of total integrity with Christ in a world hungry for such integrity.

UNDERSTANDING THE SIGNS OF THE AGE

As for all Christians, missions-focused leaders must find sane ways to be informed and in touch with the times. With God's leading we are to be involved in but not subservient to the godlike powers often ascribed to astonishing information, technology, and social change. We are to assess the trends and understand their significance in order to help guide them to the Lord's purposes.

This is nothing new. The Christian commission has always been to envision boldly and then to enact God's plans. The book of Acts narrates fascinating stories of the first-century adventures with Christ in the clashes between Roman political and Hebrew religious and cultural powers. Our world is not that different today in terms of global turmoil. Toffler (1981) metaphorically defines this age as an information-based "third wave" era crashing against vestiges of industrial and agricultural age waves still sloshing about the globe.

Our turbulent finale to the second millennium amazingly resembles first-century turmoil, when long-established religious, cultural, and political paradigms were totally shaken. Imagine the panic of a devout Jew in that day: "What's this about a Messiah having come from God up there in Galilee today? . . . Why does this man talk with women and children and sinners so comfortably yet brazenly rebuke our temple priests? Oh, yes! Now I've met Jesus. I see and understand. Now I know for myself about him and I, too, believe. . . . But, what do you mean I have to associate with Gentiles and be willing to share our thousands of years of faith and traditions with them? What right do *they* have to jump in with unsolicited ideas about how to observe *our* faith? I know my Jewish traditions were inadequate, but they were comfortable. And, yes, Jesus is the fulfillment of our faith, but do all these changes have to be so painful?"

Would it be hard, here at the end of the twentieth century, to write a parallel analogy? It might go something like this: "I used to think all Christians were simple-minded right wingers until Glenna insisted on praying, loving, and teaching me into faith. I never knew the deep joy of knowing Christ, or that life circumstances can't shake his realities. The Bible is fascinating and a huge comfort for me. But I'm only comfortable talking about Jesus in church. What's this about having to love purple-haired kids with nose rings who refuse to work at anything? Please don't add guitars or change our Sunday worship services just to reach them; it's the one chance a week I have to be still and enjoy a holy worship service. No, I don't have time to help start a Saturday chores program for the neighborhood shut-ins. Oh, Lord, forgive my self-centered attitude; I've been frazzled and lost your focus."

By God's grace we will respond meaningfully to the astounding changes we face. Undoubtedly, like the first-century Hebrew Christians, we need to open our eyes and ears to what is happening, and not just let it float by us. Some of us need to be there for elementary school children who murder for the thrill of it, others for adults ridiculing Christianity without a clue about its tenets, and still others to bring Christ's peace to terrified citizens of countries slipping into total anarchy.

Mission visionaries increasingly realize that many nineteenth- and twentieth-century (primarily Western) assumptions about learning, leadership development, group processes, economic development, and quantitatively derived success measures and the like are about as helpful today as steam-powered locomotives would be in downtown Tokyo. Yet habits persist, especially when left unattended. We need to reexamine standing assumptions about theological education and community development models in light of a number of emerging global trends.

RESPONDING TO TWENTY-FIRST CENTURY REALITIES

For the most part, twenty-first-century missionaries will no longer have the luxury of focusing on just one language or culture group, challenging as that has always been. Instead, missionaries will be preparing for multi-ethnic and multi-lingual teamwork, learning how to model as well as encourage community life in Christ.

Effective missionary teams of the future will flow with changing job and ministry opportunities. Emotional ties will be strong but flexible as individual members or small groups within a tentmaking team accept short term work opportunities, furlough, or leave for new assignments. E-mail will be the blessing for maintaining close fellowship with one another, their home churches, and relatives. Yet the flip side of this technological blessing, especially when experiencing culture shock, will be the temptation to retreat to safe e-mail friendship and security blankets rather than persist in establishing work and social friendships with still uninterested host co-workers.

Although missionaries will face similar spiritual challenges to those of their predecessors, twenty-first-century paradigms will cause both their understanding of and their approach to missions work to differ. They will more fully understand problems defined in the Bible but not experienced or at least acknowledged by twentieth-century Western Christians. For example, Americans today are fascinated by male and female deities of ancient cultures (Babylonia, Greece, Rome, India). They may actively oppose Christian evangelism and community development involvements in Western countries or sharing the Christian message with well-educated but biblically illiterate adults (modern-day Nicodemas situations). They may ridicule believers for practicing and teaching Christ's basic morality messages.

The clamor for "black and white" responses to thorny issues will continue as careless church leaders offer self-righteous bandwagon and band-aid solutions. The media will promote instant gratification, self-righteousness, and call for immediate decisions on "Christian" responses to medical and other agonizing ethical problems.

Most likely there will be fewer "megamission" agencies as highly specialized, culture-specific organizations emerge. Organizations will be less hierarchical as industrial-age paradigms give way to laterally cooperative cross-cultural agency settings. We will see remarkably changing perceptions of the concepts of *work* and *missions*. Early twentieth-century concepts of the work ethic will be critically examined for their often inappropriate power and addictive characteristics.

Missionaries will on the whole be better educated, culturally aware, and thoughtfully prepared for their work. Many will earn their own keep and have greater say in missionary decisions of the smaller agencies. As "boomers" begin to face retirement decisions, some will likely start missionary agencies that focus on early retirement missions opportunities.

Individuals previously excluded from missions will be accepted and even valued for their unique life preparation to reach out to growing segments of the population—singles with children and individuals who have been divorced or married to divorced people.

Missionary agencies' structures, governance and funding will change as they offer more local-site autonomy. Missionary boarding schools may become a thing of the past. Armed with personal experience and the excellent materials available for home schooling today, missionaries in team settings will likely favor working together to educate their own children rather than sending them away to school.

Future missionaries must be better schooled in the historic evolution of major components of Christianity and Judaism from the acts of the apostles to the present, especially in the historic conflicts from within the church. Past teaching has polarized to a fault the personal works of key theologians and has been guilty of reductionism when defining doctrinal splits within Protestantism. Broad-based knowledge of the history of Christendom is necessary preparation for missionaries to confront the secular protagonists who so effectively discredit popular evangelical Christianity.

Dependence on U.S. resources has been perceived as entrapment in the past. Missions must intensify efforts to become free from dependence on Western financial resources. Contributions from the West will fall as fewer people affiliate with churches in the United States. The middle class will have to live with progressively less discretionary income. Tax deductions for Christian organizations will come under new critical review. Certainly strong elements within the United States will dissect the tax code as they continually seek to rid our society of any identification with Christian values. Funding, staffing, and culture will become increasingly international, with a greater Asian influence. No matter its monetary sources, sustainable development will become a hallmark issue if God's mission is to be non-sectarian, non-nationalistic—or, better put—global.

Access to instant communication will ameliorate one of the most difficult problems facing missions in the past. Teleconferencing will supplement but not replace international conferences. The overabundance of information, rather than its scarcity, will present a unique set of problems as it competes with real-time, here-and-now interpersonal needs. Missions, like everyone else, must learn to make sense of information overload and make appropriate choices.

Opposition to missions work will come from global as well as local groups. Even as Christians network by e-mail, so will those seeking to oppose the work. Paul of Tarsus experienced opposition just about everywhere he went; we will experience it too from many more locations without even having to enter those cities.

Old questions must be newly addressed: To whom are we accountable in our work? the local church? where we are located? the sending agency? our home church? Working in cross-cultural organizations, missionaries will more and more often be serving under the leadership of Christians from various contexts.

Increasingly, missions will tie into global sustainable environment issues. We will need to follow and respond to global trends of wealth and power, peace and culture. Anderson says it well in a book by the same title: *Reality Isn't What It Used to Be: Theatrical Politics, Ready-to-Wear Religion, Global Myths, Primitive Chic, and Other Wonders of the Postmodern World* (1991).

SO, WE KEEP IN MIND THAT . . .

Our task is to seek the Lord's visionary scenario for the future as we work to help influence and guide currently emerging trends around us toward that end. Love *does* make the world go round—Christ's sustaining love, that is. But as human enthusiasm for unexamined change faces no moral code restrictions, the world spins even further off kilter. The industrial age work ethic will not be enough (yes, it did once help). Agility with information tools will not work either, even though they will greatly help. Our job is similar to what Billy Graham's has been. We must now, in twenty-first-century ways, hang on to Christ with persistent integrity, without letting the times entice us to inappropriate gimmicks.

Works Cited

Anderson, Walter Truett. 1991. *Reality Isn't What It Used To Be: Theatrical Politics, Ready-to-Wear Religion, Global Myths, Primitive Chic, and Other Wonders of Postmodern World*. San Francisco: Harper & Row.

Toffler, Alvin. 1981. *The Third Wave*. New York: Bantam Books.

References

Anderson, Roland. 1992. *Globalization: Social Theory and Global Culture*. Thousand Oaks, Cal.: Sage.

Cetron, Marvin, and Owen Davis. 1989. *American Renaissance*. New York: St. Martin's Press.

Chandler, Russell. 1992. *Racing Toward 2001: The Forces Shaping America's Religious Future*. Grand Rapids: Zondervan Publishing.

Coates, Joseph, and Jennifer Jarratt, eds. 1992. *The Future: Trends into the Twenty-First Century*. The Annals of the American Academy of Political and Social Science (July).

Drucker, Peter. 1989. *The New Realities*. New York: Harper & Row.

King, Alexander, and Bertrand Schneider. 1991. *The First Global Revolution: A Report by the Council of the Club of Rome*. New York: Pantheon Books.

Migdal, Joel S. 1988. *Strong Societies and Weak States*. Princeton: Princeton University Press.

Moyers, Bill. 1989. *A World of Ideas*. New York: Doubleday.

_____ . 1990. *A World of Ideas II*. New York: Doubleday.

Olasky, Marvin. 1992. *The Tragedy of American Compassion*. Washington, D.C.: Regnery Gateway.

Thurow, Lester. 1992. *Head to Head*. New York: William Morrow & Co.

Wagar, W. Warren. 1991. *The Next Three Futures: Paradigms of Things to Come*. New York: Praeger.

Ward, Ted. 1984. *Living Overseas*. New York: The Free Press.

Woodiwiss, Anthony. 1993. *Postmodernity USA*. London: Sage.

Chapter Ten _____

Visionary Planning for World Mission

James E. Plueddemann

_____

In the last hundred years the church has sprouted and grown in every country in the world, expanding beyond anyone's predictions. Yet because of the population explosion, even though almost two billion people call themselves Christians, never since the creation of the world have there been more lost people. About four billion people desperately need to hear the Good News, and over a billion so-called Christians urgently need a vital growing relationship with Jesus.

PROBLEMS WITH PLANNING

Missionary vision is seeing the world through God's eyes. But vision is only the first step. People with vision also need a plan. Planning includes three steps: 1) analyzing the needs and opportunities, 2) setting visionary goals and 3) designing an action plan. A rekindled vision for the world must lead to visionary planning. Yet visionary planning is not easy. Churches are often distracted by the pain of their own hurting people, budget worries, and the challenge of keeping programs staffed, organized, and funded. Harried pastors might feel that the missions program is pushed by one ardent church committee working in competition with other committees. With so many local needs and programs, visionary missions planning is often neglected.

Visionary planning can be difficult for missionaries as well. As I write this article I am on the phone almost hourly with directors who are trying to evacuate over seventy missionaries from out-of-control violence in Liberia. This is the third time in the last six years these people have had to evacuate. When missionaries are ducking bullets, it is thoughtless to ask them for a visionary five-year plan.

METAPHORS OF PLANNING

Another obstacle to visionary planning is that we often have an inadequate mental picture of planning. Our understanding of missions is dominated by mental pictures or metaphors. These metaphors have a powerful influence on the theory and practice of missionary planning. Metaphors are often unconscious, or at least not clearly defined in our minds, yet these hidden pictures predispose us to be attracted to certain values and strategies for missionary planning. Our mental metaphors reflect our fundamental values.

The problem with hidden metaphors is that we tend to accept them uncritically, for reasons below the level of our awareness. Because metaphors influence us more than we know, our reasons for accepting or rejecting missionary strategy are largely unconscious. We are often controlled by metaphors that are inconsistent with a biblical view of missions. The dominant missionary planning metaphor is the behaviorist model of a machine. The second metaphor is an existentialist reaction to the behaviorist model that I call the wild-flower metaphor. I suggest that a developmental metaphor of pilgrimage is the best paradigm for visionary missionary planning.

The Missionary Machine (Behaviorist Model)

Many missionary planners see the world as a machine. They are dominated by the cult of efficiency. They view the missionary enterprise as accomplishing precise goals in a predicted time frame, with the least amount of money, and with the fewest missionaries. Because of their passion for precision and predictability, they set goals for things that easily can be counted. They wish to know exactly what the final result will look like, when it will be accomplished, and how much it will cost.

People who see the task of missions mechanistically tend to have a vision of something that is very big and easy to measure. They then set a long-range timetable with several short-range plans. For such people, "going into all the world and making disciples" is too vague. They say we must first precisely define "all the world" as quantifiable people groups, and "disciples" as those who have gone through a prescribed program. They would argue that the task is completed when a specific percentage of people are attending church. Success is measured on graph paper.

But when we aim only at what we can measure, we avoid the most important goals of character and holiness. As soon as we try to predict and quantify character and holiness, we are forced to become legalistic. Results of missions should be measured by spiritual qualities rather than by the mere quantity of buildings or people.

The Western world has been influenced by the philosophy of logical positivism, which argues that all meaning must be verifiable by empirical data. Behaviorism asserts that observable behavior is the only reality. But the apostle Paul commands us to "fix our eyes not on what is seen, but on what is unseen. For what is seen is temporary, but what is unseen is eternal" (2 Cor. 4:18). The mechanistic paradigm of planning promotes unhealthy practice and builds an inadequate theory of missiology. It forces one to aim for goals that can be accomplished in a specific time frame, such as by the year 2000. Mechanistic visionaries do not have real vision, even if they are aiming at big numbers.

Fortunately, most mechanistic missiological planners have a genuine love for the Lord and a deep passion for world missions. Even though their behaviorist paradigm makes it harder for them to focus on eternal results in the hearts of people, they have helped to compel genuine concern for the eternal destiny of the world. While I am bothered by their world view, I am challenged and encouraged by many "big thinkers" in missions.

The Missionary as a Wild Flower (Existentialist Model)

While the machine metaphor makes sense to people with an analytic personality, the wild-flower metaphor is attractive to the more intuitive types. While mechanistic planners have too little tolerance for ambiguity, wild-flower planners enjoy ambiguity. The former conceives of the missionary enterprise as a sophisticated assembly line, and the latter sees it as a seed to "bloom where it's planted." While the former think of church growth in terms of slide-rule analysis, some of the latter are intrigued by emotional signs and wonders.

Many wild-flower missionaries see planning as a waste of time. They say the world is too uncertain to permit goal-setting. They may be so embedded in the existential present that they have no time for future planning, and they may even assume such thinking is unspiritual.

If mechanistic missionaries have their day planned in fifteen-minute intervals, wild-flower missionaries seldom bother to plan anything. One is management by objectives, the other is management by interruption. The primary goal is to keep busy. There is often no visionary sense of direction.

Here is an example of Joe "Wild-Flower" Missionary. He sleeps in a bit longer than he planned and never does finish his quiet time. He decides to deliver a new copy of the Jesus film to a nearby village. Getting into his Land Rover, he notices that the tires need more air, and on his way to get the pump, he sees goats in his garden. While he's repairing the garden fence, the local carpenter walks by. They discuss the price of cement blocks for a project, and then a medical emergency requires Joe to take a patient to the clinic in the next town. And so his day goes, from one activity to the next with no sense of direction. People without vision often feel burned out and exhausted from so much meaningless activity. They run around in circles, and at the end of the day they wonder why they don't have more of a sense of fulfillment.

The Missionary as a Pilgrim (Developmental Model)

Pilgrims have a clear sense of direction, even though they aren't sure where the path may lead in the near future. In contrast to mechanistic missionaries, pilgrims have their eyes open to serendipitous possibilities. Pilgrims have a strong vision of God's blessing in this world and the next. Because pilgrims have a sense of direction and a clear endpoint, they are better able to decide if an event is an unfolding opportunity or a side-track interruption. Mechanistic vision focuses only on what can be predicted and counted. Wild-flower vision is too small and lacks focus. The pilgrim missionary is the true visionary. Pilgrim vision is like beauty. It is difficult to define, but we recognize it when we see it. Pilgrim planners ask three questions: 1) What is the challenge? 2) What is the vision? and 3) What are the action steps?

Pilgrim Challenge—Where Are We?

Pilgrims are visionary realists. They move deliberately and steadily in pursuit of a clear goal. As they press on, they are also aware of the swamps, valleys, and obstacles along the path. Pilgrim planners know they must understand their situation, needs, resources, and opportunities.

So how does the pilgrim metaphor influence planning? At home, a church wishing to be more mission-minded needs to analyze factors in its present situation such as current attitudes toward missions, awareness of needs, and faithfulness in praying and giving. Field missionaries need to assess thoughtfully their language ability, cultural awareness, and family needs. Missionary planning teams need to work with the national church to investigate unreached people groups, examine possible cultural reasons for resistance to the gospel, and assess the spiritual state of the church. Where is the church strong, and where are the areas of need? What are the challenges for theological education and opportunities for helping pastors? How politically stable is the country? What is the economic condition of the national church? How many theological schools are needed? What are the discipleship needs in the church?

When I am leading vision seminars, I ask missionaries to brainstorm about factors in the present situation that reflect opportunities and challenges for planning. We fill many flip-chart sheets and tape them to the walls. For example, if we were interested in reaching the Quechua people of Bolivia we would ask: How many Quechuas live in Bolivia? Where do they live? What is their world view? What are their fears and concerns? How many of them are Christians? How many Quechua churches are there? What opportunities do pastors have for learning? What is the evangelistic vision of these churches to reach the rest of their people? Are the Scriptures available in Quechua? What is the literacy level? What efforts has God blessed in the past?

Pilgrim Vision—Where Are We Going?

Pilgrim planners are driven by eternal vision. They have a vision of a holy church, without stain or wrinkle. They picture people from every nation, tribe, people, and language, singing the Hallelujah Chorus at the wedding feast of the Lamb. They can picture the kingdom of this world becoming the kingdom of our God. They are motivated by a picture of what individuals and society might become if God were to bless their ministry. The metaphor is developmental, in that the vision is for the full development of people and churches. Development is an inner process that has external (though unpredictable) indicators. The vision is not for mere behavior changes that can be predicted and controlled, but for holy lives that bring glory to God. It is a vision of the growth of the kingdom of God. I encourage our missionaries to pray humbly that the Lord will show them possible eternal results if God were to bless their ministry. I challenge them to ask the Lord for a sense of direction and for qualitative goals they can set by faith. I suggest they prayerfully write out the answer to the question, "If the Lord were to bless your ministry richly in the next five years, what might the results look like?"

I want missionaries to describe a picture of results in people and in the church. Too often missionaries limit their vision to mere programs. They have a vision for using radio, literature, or theological education by extension, and they define their vision by numbers and activities. While successful programs are good things, we need to force ourselves to ask, "What are the developments in the hearts of people and in the character of the church that will change the world and endure through eternity?" Such thinking leads to a big vision of what God could do to transform people and mature the church.

It is also good to reflect on more specific parts of the big vision. "If the Lord would bless your Sunday school class or your market evangelism, what might be the eternal results?" Missionary life puts strain on families. I encourage couples to reflect prayerfully on what their marriage might be if the Lord would richly bless them. How might a vision for Quechua ministry in Bolivia be expressed? I picture the Lord blessing this ministry and hundreds of thousands of Quechuas coming to Christ. I have a vision of what a difference the gospel might mean for family life and social systems. I see pastors who love the Lord, love people, and have the ability to teach what the Bible means in their cultural context. I see lay people actively involved in their churches and reaching out to their communities. I see Quechua missionaries crossing cultures for the sake of the gospel. The hopes and dreams go on and on.

Missionary life tends to squelch vision. It is easy to become so overwhelmed by culture shock, limited language ability, and the frustrations of heat and dust that dynamic vision seems like a distant dream. On the sending side, even the most mission-minded churches are within a few years of a dying vision. Both missionaries and sending churches urgently need a rekindled vision of how all of heaven and earth can be influenced by God's blessings to the nations. Such a vision will keep us going in a suffering world with courage, enthusiasm, and excitement.

Pilgrim Action-Steps—How Do We Get There?

Vision by itself is worthless. Vision needs feet and action steps. Pilgrims know they cannot merely sit on a hilltop and dream about heaven. They must get out the map, put on their shoes, and get going. Missionaries need to plan with national church leaders things they should be doing together that the Lord might bless to fulfill the vision. Pilgrim planners know there is no one sure method for reaching the vision, but since they have a strong sense of direction they have great creativity in working with different strategies. Since the vision is much bigger than the method, they won't get bogged down in using only one strategy. If showing the Jesus film seems to bring eternal results, they use it, but the film is the means, not the end.

Action steps must be related to the challenge (Where are we?). They must also relate to the vision (Where are we going?). For example, Bible translation might not be a necessary action step if there is already a good translation in Bolivian Quechua. But literacy classes might be an important action step. If the Lord shows us the need for reaching Quechua people in the mountains of Bolivia, we need to reflect on a vision of a vibrant Quechua church. We see hundreds of thousands of Quechuas coming to Christ and being discipled into churches. They sing indigenous Quechua songs, use an easy-to-understand Quechua Bible, and the church leadership is equipped to help the church grow toward maturity in Christ. Since the Quechuas live in hard-to-reach mountains, a missionary strategy might include partnering with the Quechua church to develop evangelistic radio. The mission might also recruit ethnomusicologists and train people who can begin a program of theological education by extension. The program grows out of the vision and is evaluated by how much it contributes to the hoped-for qualities in the Quechua people.

CONCLUSION

The missionary enterprise is in urgent need of a quiet, gracious revolution. There's a war going on between Satan and God. Yet too often we merely seek faddish methods that help us to be better assembly line workers or wild-flower tenders. Too often planning reflects a vision of mere outward change or massive programs, while neglecting the most important vision of heart changes in people's lives. The most urgent need is not for better methods but for pilgrim planners who realistically assess the challenge, ask the Lord for a picture of how he might bless his church, and then plan creative and flexible actions that God might use to fulfill his purposes.

*Chapter Eleven*_____

Research in Missiological Curriculum and Instruction

Edgar J. Elliston

Research to support missiological curriculum and instruction provides one important set of concerns for emerging theological education and leadership development for the church worldwide. This kind of research combines both the concerns of missiology and education for the well-being and obedience of the whole church.

RATIONALE FOR RESEARCH
IN MISSIOLOGICAL CURRICULUM AND INSTRUCTION

Missiological curriculum and instructional concerns grow out of the *missio Dei* as seen throughout Scripture and made explicitly clear in the Great Commission. The central command of the Great Commission as recorded in Matthew is to make disciples. Jesus' concern for instruction was evident from the outset of his ministry through the post-resurrection appearances. One can identify the curricular parts of the Great Commission by looking at the "as you go" and the "teaching to obey all things" participles. The clear central command of the Great Commission to "make disciples" carries an unmistakable instructional goal. The "all nations" statement underscores the missiological dimension of the Great Commission. Missiology among other concerns addresses the crossing of barriers with the Good News of the gospel of Jesus Christ. It carries an appeal to the *panta ta ethne* (all nations) to become learners or followers of Jesus Christ.

132

Missiological education aims at the facilitation of learning and obedience to this command.

In the (Hebrew scriptures) the issue of instruction plays a prominent role in the responsibilities of both the family and the Hebrew people. The instruction was not only intended for the children but for the nations around them.

The scriptures consistently focus on a holistic approach to the development of the person in community to serve God's purpose. Modern secular education typically identifies three areas for instruction: knowledge (cognitive development), skills (psycho-motor development), and attitudes (affective development). From a biblical perspective the first two of these instructional areas are very similar, but the third differs significantly. Biblically, the issue of affective development would much better be understood in spiritual and character formation leading to ministry formation. Certainly the focus is on relationships, but the values of integrity and character development clearly appear through the whole of God's revelation. The formation is not just for the individual's benefit, but for the broader purpose of fulfilling God's calling and plan. While some modern education appears to be focused on the individual and individualistic training, a biblical perspective places learners much more in a community perspective, both to learn and to serve. While this chapter aims at the issue of research, the foundational rationale for instruction is clear through Scripture.

Contemporary missiological and church-related concerns for curriculum and instruction grow out of these clear biblical and theological roots. The planning of curriculum and the instruction of God's people continue as great concerns to the church today. Whether one desires to instruct nonbelievers to lead them to Christ, to nurture believers, or to teach maturing believers how to participate in the *missio Dei*, Christians everywhere are and must be concerned about these issues.

To be effective in either the design of curriculum (that is, all that is planned for instruction) or the actual instruction itself, one must be informed. That information often must come from locally done research. A well-designed curriculum and instructional program for any given situation will not fit optimally in another situation without some adjustment. Curricular variables are never the same from one situation to another.[1] These differing variables always change the dynamics of the instruction and what is required for an optimally effective curriculum. Curricular variables interact dynamically.

One clear result of the interaction of these variables is the resulting modification of the curriculum. A change in any one of the variables will ripple through all the others. For example, a slight change in purpose will affect the content, selection of teachers and learners, and will likely affect all the other variables as well. A shift in the resources to be used may significantly affect the structure of the delivery systems, who may be employed to teach, the venue, learner selection, and so on. While the purpose may be the central driving variable, given a local situation any of the other variables may take a priority role, thus requiring curricular adjustment. If world view and cultural differences exist, major changes should be expected. What those changes should be can only be determined as one evaluates the local situation in the light of the revealed biblical values. Research then must continue both from a biblical and theological perspective and into the changing local contexts.

METHODOLOGICAL CONCERNS

Methodological concerns for the instruction, nurturing, and equipping of people to benefit from and participate in the *missio Dei* require attention in two major directions for research: *values* to be applied, and the *situation* in which they are to be applied. Educators typically rely on other disciplines to provide the substance or content to be taught, whether it is biblical knowledge, mathematics, history, biology, or some other subject area. Educators are concerned with the value bases and delivery systems that will facilitate the holistic learning that is expected from a biblical perspective.

The range of methodological concerns facing the missiological educator, then, includes values both from a biblical perspective and the existing values in the local situation. When the values and local situation are known, one can identify changes that need to be made through an educational process. When one looks at a person in community two questions must be asked: What is the condition of that person now?, and What should be the condition of that person in terms of knowledge, skills, and spiritual formation? The difference between the two answers provides the arena for the educator to work in instruction. The instructional questions include such concerns as what can be done with the person to best facilitate the change from where he or she is now to match the value-based goals of knowing, doing, and being.

Common journalistic questions serve to raise methodological concerns. Each of these questions must be answered in the light of the responses to the others to have a balanced integrated educational program.

Why?

Why should the content, skills, and formation be taught? Research into the local goals and purposes for the instruction is a recurring need. Reference to the *missio Dei* as it applies to the local context remains an essential part of the purpose for missiological education.

Who?

Who should teach? Who should learn? Who should make the decisions about the curriculum and instruction? Who is to be served by the learners? What are the characteristics, needs, interests, and perspectives of each of these constituencies? Answers to each of these questions will differ from one situation to another. Each difference requires an adjustment in the curriculum.

When?

When should the different issues be raised? The timing issue includes concerns about *when* in a person's relationship with the Lord (that is, the person's stage of spiritual, personal and ministry development), *when* in terms of administrative scheduling, and *when* in relation to community concerns. The when question must also be raised in terms of scheduling related to learning styles. Questions concerning the duration and sequence of the instruction demand local attention. *When* in terms of scheduling logistics of the individual, community and teaching agency requires research. Taken together, timing issues often call for significant adjustments to contextualize a curriculum.

What?

What should be taught? What needs to be learned? A missiological educator will raise these questions from the learner's perspective rather than just the perspective of the subject matter specialist. Concerns from both the learner's and curriculum developer's cultural perspectives always condition what should be taught. The question is, what should the learner be learning?, not, what should the teacher be teaching? Missiological education rests on several disciplines for perspectives, methods, and content that serve to provide an understanding of the *missio Dei*. This same set of disciplines serves as bases for equipping to serve in the *missio Dei*. Theology, history, philosophy, anthropology, sociology, education, leadership, geography, political science, linguistics, economics, and psychology all may contribute to the what and how of missiological education. The *what* should be informed by information from the learner, the community to be served, and the subject matter specialist, all the while being guided by a biblical and theological value base. The *what* of a missiological curriculum requires local information from a globalized perspective for both optimal appropriateness and effectiveness.

Where?

Venue questions raise issues about access and relevance of the learning. Where can the learner learn best? If the learner is not yet a believer, then the venue should be where he or she is. If the person is a new believer, then the instruction and nurture should occur in the community where it can be permanently established. If the person is being instructed as an emerging leader, the venue should be with the people being led, so that the knowledge, skills, and relationships can be established there. The leader should be developed within the projected sphere of influence where he or she is expected to exercise influence. If the focus is on equipping local leaders, then the venue should be local, in order to build or empower the interpersonal and community relationships that will occur. Similarly, regional leaders should be developed regionally. The three power bases of leadership should be considered in terms of the venue.[2] Occasionally, an outside venue may be indicated as the better place to learn, at least temporarily. However, to make wise and informed decisions, local information is needed. Broader venue research may serve decision-makers to make wise decisions about the optimal setting for a given set of learning objectives.

How?

How should instruction be delivered? How should the educational modes be balanced?[3] How should the complementary teacher-centered and learner-centered approaches to education be optimally balanced in the learning situation? How should the delivery system be administered? What technologies should be employed, and how should they be balanced? The appropriate balancing of technologies emerges as the curricular variables are locally considered. Questions of purpose, resources, who the learners are, instructor competencies, and learning styles are among the keys to unlock the growing puzzle of technologies. Availability of a technology is not the primary argument for its use. Again, the curricular variables mentioned above must be researched locally to contextualize the curriculum and instructional approach. The delivery methods should also be conditioned by the local learning styles. To answer these questions requires local, ongoing research informed by a globalized perspective.

How Much?

How much instruction is needed? How much should be offered? How much should it cost? What are the local resources? How much can or should they be used? Key value questions arise when looking at this set of questions. Answering the question of how much has parallels in agriculture and medicine. Illustrations could be given from other disciplines as well. A farmer will carefully test the soil and then review the nutritional needs of the crop to be planted before applying fertilizer. The gross amount of fertilizer will comprise a balance of the individual nutrients needed by the crop that will not be naturally replenished in the soil. A physician will prescribe a medication in a specific amount with the individual patient's condition in mind. In either case too much or too little treatment will be either ineffectual or dangerous.

Education similarly needs to be balanced with the person, the situation, and the task in mind. Not only do issues of purpose, content, and delivery methods require attention, but the balanced amounts of educational "carbohydrates, vitamins, fiber, proteins, fats, and minerals" require contextualized attention. Just as a farmer would not fertilize two fields the same way and a physician would not prescribe the same medicine for every patient, so education must give individualized attention.

Summary

From this brief overview, some broad methodological concerns begin to appear. Educational research is needed in each community, with each generation, and as developmental change occurs to keep the curriculum relevant and effective. Each of the broad communities identified (nonbelievers, new believers, and emerging leaders) changes over time and so requires somewhat different approaches in curriculum and instruction. Research is needed to inform both the perspectives to take (theory) and appropriate decisions to make (evaluation).

DISTINCTIVES

Research in missiological education, like missiological research in general, ranges across disciplinary lines. While some of the research subject matter in educational research is distinctive, the methods are not. Sociology, anthropology, history, theology, economics, political science, and leadership all may contribute. Surveys, interviews, grounded theory cycling through the data, unobtrusive observations, examination of historical archives, and other methods all contribute to missiological education research. However, missiological research has not as yet taken full advantage of the rigors of experimental methods. Much of the research that has been done over the past fifty years has been either descriptive research leading to theory formation or evaluative research that has aided in decision-making. Now that significant theory bases have been established, some of them would be greatly improved by the use of experiments to test and refine them.

Data Collection and Analysis

The data collection and analysis procedures for educational research resemble other forms of social research. Whether the primary methods are descriptive, experimental, or evaluative, the same concerns will be raised. However, to establish foundational assumptions, perspectives, and values, the hermeneutical and exegetical concerns of theology and philosophy are required.

Missiological researchers face the same basic concerns of describing the population, selecting an appropriate sample, and developing the means to elicit reliable and valid information as other researchers. Similar ethical questions apply. Questions of data analysis require prior planning in the data-collection stage to provide useful data whether one is examining archival materials, interviewing, administering questionnaires, or doing unobtrusive observation. The selection of the data-analysis procedures must always be closely linked with the data collection. One should pre-plan statistical procedures to summarize and facilitate analysis before the data have been collected.

The establishment of values for use in evaluative research requires the same kinds of research rigor and methods as in other methods. For missiological educators, the identification of values normally requires some biblical, theological, and philosophical foundations.

A significant methodological risk remains for the person doing research to undergird missiological education. That risk consists of the inappropriate balancing of theological and human-science perspectives. The theologian sees theology as the queen of the sciences and may assume a position of pride resulting in a know-it-all attitude from revealed truth. On the other hand, the social scientist sees empirical data that emerge from careful observation. This documented observation may lead to overconfidence and a denial of the less observable or replicable theological insight. Missiological educators—because of this concern to cross human and spiritual boundaries in participation in the *missio Dei*—must integrate both the theological and human-science perspectives to be both obedient and effective.

Validity and Reliability

All of the issues related to validity described in the first part of this chapter apply to the missiological educational concerns. The questions remain: Is the right information being collected? Are the values that are being selected the appropriate ones? Are the values being used truly biblical or are they just culturally adapted perceptions? Are the values from the local culture really from the local culture or are they projections from the researcher? The issues of construct validity, that is, valid theoretical explanations, are required for effective planning of curricula and the application of teaching methods. For example, to explain local learning styles inappropriately (invalidly) would result in wrong choices in terms of content, timing, selection of learners, selection of instructors, and formation activities. The whole delivery system would be inappropriately skewed.

A common mistake many make when moving into a new community or across a cultural boundary is to generalize about educational needs and planning too soon. One has an experience or an explanation and then makes an application to the whole community. While what was experienced or explained may have been true, it may not have been reliable. That is, if the same question or issue were raised again, the same experience or answer might not be forthcoming. One may discover inconsistent (unreliable) answers that require the questions to be changed (a validity question).

When treating foundational theological and philosophical issues, the issues of validity and reliability become more complex. Issues of truth arise. One's limitations in perceiving truth emerge. Often truth is held in a dialogical or paradoxical tension. For example, while evangelical Christians affirm the Trinity, they recognize that too much emphasis on either the unity or diversity of the Trinity leads to heresy. Too much emphasis on any member of the Trinity leads either to the neglect or abuse of appropriate action in the church.

The wise missiological educator who seeks to inform the educational and curricular issues at hand will treat these research issues from within the context being served. The complexities of establishing the world view and value bases both within the context and from a theological perspective will be noted. Whatever the educational issue, the problems of asking the right questions locally and eliciting the right information in consistent replicable ways present a serious challenge.

CONTRIBUTIONS TO MISSIOLOGY

The insights gained from answering the above questions are essential in the facilitation of two great tasks of the church: bringing people to Christ, and then bringing them up in Christ. Evangelism and nurture require education all along the way. Effective communication of the gospel across cultural boundaries requires attention to these educational issues.

None of the complementary academic disciplines is static. Each one is continually expanding and testing its theory base, whether it is theology, anthropology, sociology, economics, leadership, political science, or history. The experience and insights gained in curriculum design and instructing nonbelievers, new believers, and maturing believers serve to inform all of these disciplines. As each discipline is applied in missiology with these new insights, the study of and obedience to God's will in the *missio Dei* will be improved.

Notes

1. Some curricular variables include the following: purpose, content, control, costs, resources, delivery system, learner needs, learning style(s), instructional style(s), selection of learning experiences, selection of learners, selection of teachers, venue, timing, spiritual and community formation, community needs, evaluation, and so on. Further explanation of these variables can be found in J. Dudley Woodberry, Charles Van Engen, and Edgar J. Elliston, eds., *The Book, the Circle, and the Sandals* (Maryknoll, N.Y.: Orbis Books, 1996).

2. Power bases include spiritual power, personal/interpersonal power, and positional power.

3. Educational modes may include: 1) formal education that is highly structured, teacher-centered, theoretical, content-focused, certificate-oriented, long-term, stabilizing in terms of community standards, and resource intensive; 2) nonformal education that is highly structured, learner- and community-oriented, short-term, functional, and change-oriented; and, 3) informal education that is relationally based, not structured, acculturative, functional, and learner-oriented.

Chapter Twelve _____

Training Church Planters

A Competency-Based Learning Model

J. ALLEN THOMPSON

_____

More than two billion people around the globe are beyond the reach of the gospel. In the United States alone there are 120 million people unchurched and 40 million unevangelized. How will all these be reached? The most powerful and biblical method to carry the glorious gospel of God's grace to the heart of an individual is through the incarnational ministry of a local church.

God's plan for "filling the earth with his glory" is directly related to the kind of evangelism that results in the formation of reproducing Christian communities. McGavaran states emphatically that "the *essential task*, in a world where three-fourths of all men and women have yet to believe in Jesus Christ as God and only Savior, *is that of planting new churches*" (Hesselgrave 1980, 7). In the last two decades the Lord has focused the attention of many denominations and missionary agencies upon the primacy of church planting as the key to world evangelization. Numerous approaches for training church planters have emerged—from graduate courses in seminaries to field-based seminars for lay people in evangelization and cell-group formation. The results have been mixed. While thousands of people have been drawn into Christ's kingdom, many groups of new believers have remained immature and have lacked the impetus to penetrate their societies for Christ. What is needed is a "movement."

Among the educational tasks necessary to initiate a movement of church multiplication is the preparation of leaders who understand

141

and are able to interact with the dynamics of expanding church movements. Two key words in movement thinking are *momentum* and *multiplication*. Momentum is increased activity toward the goal. Multiplication is the replication of the main ingredients in the mix—in this case, disciples and effective leaders who will lead new churches. It is not enough to have exciting happenings that bind people together to fulfill a compelling vision. It is not enough to have many people coming to Christ. Powerful movements are the result of Spirit-anointed leaders; leaders who have the ability to form an interdependent ministering body out of a diverse mix of believers, leaders who specialize in selecting and training emerging leaders and instill in them the vision, skills, and motivation to "do it again."

This chapter focuses on the preparation of a specific type of Christian leader—the church planter who starts a church with the goal of producing other churches. Assumptions of leader training will be explored first, then a competency-based model of training will be explained, and finally a case study of training in a North American denominational setting will be presented.

TRAINING ASSUMPTIONS

The following five assumptions form the basis for the theory of leader training advocated in this chapter. Assumptions establish an ideational map of reality and form a set of key perspectives to guide trainers. Each assumption must be explored carefully to determine its implications for educational practice in a given context.

1. *Training by itself does not produce leaders*. God directs and superintends the development of leaders through life experiences. Training is only a means. Training is usually associated with the "technological side of education in which content, skill, and attitude development is focused on an application in a specific context" (Elliston and Kauffman 1993, 16). In this sense, training produces skills that are repeatable in a given situation. Education is broader and prepares the person as a whole for unpredictable situations. Christian leaders are formed by God through a variety of experiences including various modes of education: formal, nonformal, and informal.

While training alone does not produce a leader, it can enhance growth in a number of important directions of learning. This is called the value-added definition of quality. To the extent that the training adds value to the learner in terms of desired knowledge, desired characteristics, and desired skills, it can be described as offering transforming quality (Bergquist and Armstrong 1986, 2).

2. *Creational developmentalism*, a theory of learning that draws on the social sciences and affirms the biblical view of humankind and its maturation, provides principles for training at various stages of development. The Bible speaks of the nature of persons as created in the image of God and therefore with tremendous potential for good. While humankind has fallen and is therefore utterly bankrupt spiritually, God's story of redemption addresses the sinful nature with hope, since through Christ and the Cross God has set down a process for transforming people. This process is an incremental journey from birth until persons enter the presence of Christ (1 Cor. 13). Christian spiritual formation occurs across a series of phases where God uses all of life's processes to develop Christlikeness (Clinton 1988, 30).

Developmental theory supports the importance of personhood, human responsibility in development, and the interactive nature of growth. Developmentalists see growth in stages, look for evidences that accompany transformations from stage to stage, and understand the process as being lifelong with milestones representing fundamental change. Committed to wholism, developmentalists see all aspects of life influencing and interacting with each other.

3. *Learning principles apply universally and interculturally to the formation of church leaders.* Developmentalists hold that persons in all cultures progress in their development in a similar manner. The experiences of learning may vary widely as will the specific curricular design, but the principles of transformation remain constant (Elliston and Kauffman 1993, 3) Developmentalists have a particular view of human learning. They see learning as a matter of growing. On the other hand, the aquisitional view of learning sees learning as a matter of grasping and gaining. The assumption in the developmental view is that learning depends upon experience. The aquisitional view of learning, the apparent dominant paradigm in evangelical churches, depends on teaching. Figure 1 summarizes these comparisons.

The Developmental View	The Acquisitional View
•Learning is a matter of growing	•Learning is a matter of grasping and gaining
•Learning depends on experience	•Learning depends on teaching
•<u>Teaching</u> is a matter of sharing	•<u>Teaching</u> is a matter of leading
↓	↓
Emphasis—being	Emphasis—knowing

Figure 1. Comparisons Between the Developmental and Acquisitional View of Learning (Ward n.d.)

Principles drawn from Scripture supporting the developmental view of learning include the following:

- *Real life "experiential" learning.* Christ called the twelve disciples to be "with" him, sent them into ministry while being trained, and to equip them completely for the task (Mark 3:13-15).
- *Learning as process.* Jesus taught in parables, anticipating the teaching implications of stage theories of cognitive development.
- *Evaluation of learning.* Six principles, flowing out of Matthew 23:1-7, provide the evaluative criteria for educating in life: "The emphasis on knowing accompanied by the emphasis on doing; people are to help in identifying their own needs and should participate in goal-setting; teachers show by precept and example the value of doing nothing for self-glorification; traditions and symbols are to be evaluated against the criterion of servanthood; access to resources are to be shared as peers; and the whole environment is to reflect the unity of true community" (Ward n.d.).
- *Focus on growth.* The Pauline model utilizes principles of effective teaching and mentoring intended to bring maturity to followers. In Ephesus (Acts 19) Paul teaches in real life, combines the concepts of ministry and reflection, and utilizes peers as teacher-learners. As a teacher-mentor, Paul demonstrated concern for content (Ephesian epistle), facilitation of learners' needs (1 Timothy), and identification with learners in their learning pilgrimage (1 and 2 Timothy).

4. *Norms defining Christian leadership are found in Scripture.* Biblical standards for leaders give content and weight to the leadership profile and become the basis for evaluative criteria. To be a Christian leader means displaying the qualities specified in Scripture; it does not mean that leadership styles are expressed in a similar way in every setting or culture.

5. *Church planter leadership training is primarily focused toward adults* (persons who view themselves as responsible for their own lives). Therefore the assumptions of adult education are utilized in training. These assumptions are that as individuals mature:

a) their self-concept moves from one of being a dependent personality toward being a self-directed human being; b) they accumulate a growing reservoir of experiences that becomes an increasingly rich resource for learning; c) their readiness to learn becomes oriented increasingly to the developmental tasks of their social roles; and d) their time perspective changes from one of postponed application of knowledge to immediacy of application, and accordingly, their orientation toward learning shifts from one of subject-centeredness to one of performance-centeredness (Knowles 1980, 44-45).

COMPETENCY-BASED LEARNING DESIGN

The objective of church-planter training responds to the learners' needs, producing growth in knowledge, maturity in character development, and competence in ministry skills. Learners progressively grow in relationship to God as they explore the tensions between their experience, the Bible's teaching, and their individual response in obedience. A way to encourage this exploration is to apply the elements of competency-based learning. As a curricular model for the transformation process, competency-based learning seeks to develop competencies in persons at different stages of their maturation journey. Competencies encompass the development of the whole person: affect, understanding, character, and skill.

Four forces in educational thinking are strongly influencing the shift toward competency-based learning: (1) a new conception of the purpose of education from the transmission of knowledge to the producing of *competent* people; (2) a focus on learning instead of teaching; (3) the concept of lifelong learning as the organizing principle for all of education; and (4) a concern for developing new ways to deliver educational resources (Knowles 1980, 18-19).

A competency-based learning model is a flexible schema that provides a framework for learning in a variety of contexts. It differs from the content-transmission model, which relies on subject matter as the organizing principle. The competency-based model is directed by the natural process of each particular learning situation.

Four basic questions, depicted in Figure 2, form the basis for designing competency-based church-planter training.

The first question is, What competencies should church planters possess? This question focuses on the selection of the *outcomes* that the program will help students reach. The list of competencies is developed from research as to what a competent church planter looks like (Thompson 1995, 126). The second question is, What knowledge, skills, and attitudes do church planters currently possess? This question acknowledges that every potential leader already has been formed by informal and formal means and requires prescribed resources to meet his present developmental needs. The third question is, How can church planters participate in value-added experiences that contribute to the desired outcome? At issue here is the selection of the *learning activities* most appropriate for producing competent or high performing church planters. These may include learning contracts, mentoring, or specific training modules of instruction. The fourth question is, How will we know when church planters have changed—acquired new understandings, deepened their character, examined their attitudes, and sharpened their skills?

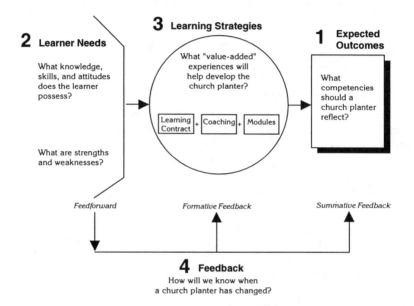

Figure 2. Church Planter Competency-Based Learning Process.

Developing Competency Profiles

The effectiveness of competency-based training programs is dependent on clearly articulated competencies. Church planters are called upon to *be* certain kinds of individuals and *do* specific tasks at predetermined levels of proficiency. The competency profile, a summary of the commonly held traits and abilities to do a specific task effectively, is the keystone of the training system. Like any keystone the church-planter profile is the most vulnerable point in the structure. Therefore, profiles are under constant review to be sure they are comprehensive in covering the complete range of traits and qualities needed and to be sure they are reliable (Thompson 1995, 47-51).

Diagnosing Learner Needs

A premise in competency-based training is that a learner's current competencies must be identified and compared to the competency profile in order to assess need and accordingly design the learning plan. The learning need is defined as the "gap between the present level of competencies and a higher level required for effective performance" (Knowles 1980, 88). In adult learning, *self-diagnosed need for learning* produces much greater motivation to learn than an externally diagnosed need such as pre-existing curriculum. Therefore, collaboration between the learner and facilitator of learning is essential. Needs are assessed through open-ended interviews, written questionnaires, paper and pencil tests, group problem analysis, and job analysis combined with performance appraisal.

Designing Learning Strategies

In conventional education, the teacher or text dispenses knowledge geared toward the average student with few provisions made for the slower or faster students. In competency-based education the responsibility is placed on the student to initiate the learning by using the teacher as a resource person. The use of learning contracts is becoming one of the more practical ways of helping learners structure their own learning. Contract learning allows individuals to set their own objectives, to identify learning resources and strategies that take into account different learning styles, and to establish ways they can collect and judge evidence to show they have accomplished their objectives (Knowles 1986). The learning contract is especially useful when accompanied by a mentor or subject matter expert who serves to facilitate and debrief the learning.

Another learning strategy involves community learning. When group training occurs, courses or seminars are prepared to focus on a single church-planter competency or a range of sub-competencies. Instructional objectives are written to help learners become certain kinds of persons and do specific tasks in church planting. Classroom-centered approaches include case studies, role play, lectures, and exercises. Field-based learning includes projects, readings, apprenticeships, and relationships to mentors.

Evaluating Change in Learners

In competency-based education, evaluation of the total program as well as the learner is an integral element of the four-part educational process. As stated above, the educational process includes a church-planter competency profile, objectives that flow out of learner needs, learning experiences, and appraisal procedures. Appraisal procedures are critical for furnishing information about the extent to which objectives are being attained and about the appropriateness of the learning experiences.

Two types of evaluation have been defined in professional literature: *summative* and *formative*. In summative evaluation, information is gathered and a final judgment is rendered. In formative evaluation, information is gathered to guide performance apart from a final judgment. Summative evaluation is useful for programs and innovations but is a less acceptable means of evaluating people. Formative evaluation, on the other hand, helps individuals uncover issues, identify directions, and provide counsel rather than judgment.

ICPC AND THE PRESBYTERIAN CHURCH IN AMERICA CASE STUDY

In 1990 the International Church Planting Center (ICPC) was started by Terry Gyger, the coordinator of Mission to North America (MNA). The goal of MNA was to start eight hundred new churches in North America by the year 2000. Due to a 40 percent failure rate in church planting experienced in the PCA, assessment centers had been implemented in the mid-1980s to screen prospective church planters. But something more was needed to jump-start mini-movements of church planting. The ICPC was given the challenge to develop a full-blown program of church-planter training that would advance church multiplication.

To fulfill its mission the ICPC developed four roles. In the *facilitating* role church-planter selection and training was developed. The *catalytic* role was designed to help "base"churches in larger cities start church-multiplying movements, which would in time start their own training base. The *problem-solving* role developed as young churches and leaders faced unique obstacles needing creative solutions. Finally a *resource-linking* role to provide support services and materials began to emerge.

The training approach employed by the ICPC reflects a commitment to learner-directed, nonformal learning. Church planters who enter the program are male seminary graduates, normally with M.Div. degrees, ordained by the PCA, and will give full time to church planting. Church planters come from various minority groups (Hispanics, African-Americans, Asians), though the largest number are Caucasian. Most of the church planting is done in suburban areas using a variety of strategies, philosophies of ministry, and church models.

Principles that undergird the training philosophy include the following: (1) *Life-related*. Learning that is meaningful and life changing ties into the life situation and perceived needs of the church planter. (2) *Individualized*. Learning is personal and incremental. Therefore the church planter participates in self-assessment and identifying the "just in time" training need. This results in a *personalized* curriculum and a *motivated* learner. (3) *Competency-based*. The training program is based on a comprehensive model of what a church planter believes, does, thinks, and feels to help produce high performance. This benchmark provides the church planter with a model for enhancing strengths and compensating for weaknesses. (4) *Content-experience-reflection oriented*. The training includes a dynamic interplay among instruction (information, understanding, and practice), actual church ministry (experience), and dynamic reflection (analysis, synthesis, and evaluation) (*International Church Planting Center Profile* 1991).

The ICPC understands its training activities as part of a greater *church planting system* that works synergistically to maximize results. The activities listed in Figure 3 are crucial components of a system aimed at developing church planters who start reproducing churches. Some activities are directly the responsibility of the ICPC; others are carried forward by the church-planting staff of MNA. Components in the system are evaluated and updated periodically to ensure that they produce momentum and multiplication in reaching the goal of two thousand churches by AD 2000.

Church Multiplication

1 Vision Casting	2 Recruit-ment	3 Church Planter Readiness	4 Place-ment	5 Training	6 Celebration
•*Multiply* •Church Planter Conferences •Networking	•Church Leaders •Campus Ministers •Seminary students	•Screening •Assessment Centers •CP readiness ratings	•Match •Funding •Prayer base	•Events Orientation Seminars Boot camps •Modes Contracts Internships •Ch Pl curriculum	•Core group formation •Converts •First worship •Leadership Installed •Daughter church

Figure 3. Components of a Church Planting and Multiplication System (ICPCP 1991).

Visioning is the ability to provide a compelling picture of God's desire for a broken world. In MNA this vision is communicated through *Multiply*, the magazine dedicated to telling the stories of church planters, and through quarterly prayer communiques. The church-planter conferences held across North America and led by church planters give individuals interested in church planting the opportunity to meet and talk with church planters. Networking among these key leaders attracts an increasing number of candidates to consider church planting.

Recruitment is the act of affirming persons that God has gifted them to start churches. To find these kinds of leaders one looks at ministries where evangelism and discipling is taking place. The major *fishing ponds* for church planters in the PCA are leaders in churches—pastors, associate pastors, youth leaders who have a heart for the lost. While some leaders consider their gifting to be that of maintaining and discipling a church, others look for the opportunity to start a church from scratch and influence a city with the gospel. Campus ministers in the Reformed University Fellowship gain a great deal of experience ministering to a secular audience and become excellent church planters. Seminary students focused on church planting may lack experience, but, demonstrating potential, are placed in internships and quickly enter church planting.

Church Planter Readiness is determined by a process of screening candidates using a competency-based interview and bringing those who show a high degree of readiness to an assessment center (AC). In assessment centers multiple techniques are used that provide personal and behavioral data from which a candidate's ability to plant a church can be evaluated. The process uses thoroughly trained assessors who are experienced and knowledgeable of the church-planter profile and needed abilities. Simulation exercises that tap into a variety of church-planter behaviors and interviews are utilized. In the end, judgments about a candidate's readiness are made by a consensus of the assessors, and strengths and weaknesses are discussed with the candidate.

Placement occurs when the church planter reaches the field. Prior to the move, individualized consultations and visits to the target city help the church planter determine the best placement match. The church planter's gift mix, cultural background, and the context in which the church is to be planted are carefully considered. Once funding is procured and presbytery membership is assured, the church planting begins. In MNA financial assistance is given to a church planter with the expectation of developing a self-supporting church within a two-year period.

Training is the process of bringing content, skill, and attitude development to a point that the learner is able to apply the ability with excellence in a specific church-planting context. *Readiness* indicates that the church planter has sufficient skill to launch a church plant. However, though ready and able to start a church, the church planter enrolls in his personalized training regimen. Four content areas requiring increasing mastery are highlighted: church-planting methodology, evangelism, philosophy of ministry, and ministry/leadership development in the new church. During assessment a discrepancy analysis of the self-ratings of the candidate is matched against the ratings done by his references. This profile provides a starting point for developing an individualized curriculum for the learner. "Just in time" training prioritizes the types of skills needed as the church is being planted and helps the church planter select the learning focus that will provide the most help for his specific phase of church planting. Some church planters in addition to the training conferences and learning contracts enter into internships and mentorships.

Celebration Milestones are markers indicating God's blessing and call for thanksgiving and rejoicing. Though many mini-celebrations are held, four are of particular importance: core group formation, first worship service, installation of leadership, and the beginning of a daughter church.

In the six years since its formation the ICPC has significantly contributed to the planting of numerous churches in cooperation with MNA staff and local church leaders. Figure 4 shows the number of churches added each year and the projected growth through the year 2000.

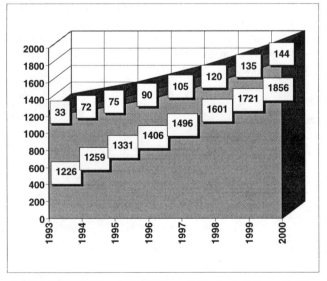

Figure 4. New Church Plants in PCA and Projected Growth Through Year 2000 (Smed 1996).

CONCLUSION

It is my firm belief that completion of the Great Commission will be accomplished by the rapid multiplication of vital churches worldwide. For this to occur we are admonished by the Lord to pray for workers (Matt. 9:37-38). Many different types of leaders are needed. We pray particularly for church multiplication movement leaders, for trainers of church planters, for church planters and pastors, and for thousands of evangelists. God is the one who calls, equips, and sends. But human instruments are used by God to mold and shape those he chooses. This is our calling as trainers of church planters.

Works Cited

Bergquist, William H., and Jack L. Armstrong. 1986. *Planning Effectively for Educational Quality*. San Francisco: Jossey-Bass Publishers.

Clinton, J. Robert. 1988. *The Making of a Leader*. Colorado Springs: Navpress.

Elliston, J. Edgar, and J. Timothy Kauffman. 1993. *Developing Leaders for Urban Ministries*. New York: Peter Lang.

Hesselgrave, David J. 1980. *Planting Churches Cross-Culturally: A Guide for Home and Foreign Missions*. Grand Rapids, Michigan: Baker Book House.

International Church Planting Center Profile. 1991. 1852 Century Pl, Suite 204, Atlanta, GA.

Knowles, Malcolm S. 1980. *The Modern Practice of Adult Education: From Pedagogy to Andragogy*. Englewood Cliffs, N.J.: Prentice Hall Regents.

_____. 1986. *Using Learning Contracts*. San Francisco: Jossey-Bass Publishers.

Smed, John. 1996. *Vision 2000*. Atlanta: Mission to North America.

Thompson, J. Allen. 1995. "Church Planter Competencies as Perceived by Church Planters and Assessment Center Leader: A Protestant North American Study. Ph.D. diss., Trinity International University.

Ward, Ted. n.d. Class notes in hands of the author.

SECTION IV

INTERNATIONAL DEVELOPMENT

*Introduction*_____

International Development

MURIEL I. ELMER

A festschrift for Ted Ward without an international development section would be most incomplete. During much of Ted's career he was, and still is, in an airplane flying to, or returning from some Two Thirds world country for a consultation, nonformal education workshop, or conference sponsored by some ministry of education, relief and development organization, or mission agency. The only difference in recent years is that he has been able to share these trips with his wife, Margaret. Ted's contribution to the field of international development was already so significant by 1975 that he was awarded the Dag Hammarskjöld Citation in Uppsala Sweden, for service in developing countries. At that time he was the only North American ever to have received the award. Also, under his leadership, Michigan State University initiated the Nonformal Education Institutes held every summer. Internationals came from all over the world to attend these highly interactive two-week workshops, taking the principles home to apply in their particular programs.

Ted's contributions to international development, especially as it relates to the mission of the church, would be difficult to measure. He has served in some sixty different countries, changing the thinking and the lives of countless host country people and Westerners working in those countries.

His deep interest in international development also found expression in the breadth of doctoral students he has mentored over the years both at Michigan State University and Trinity Evangelical Divinity School. His students, a diverse crowd from every perspective, are drawn from around the globe. Most return to apply their learning in their particular countries or corner of the United States. Ted's impact on his students has been profound. He has challenged our ideas, pushed us toward excellence (gaining him the reputation of being the most demanding professor around), affirmed our efforts, and accompanied us through some painful growing phases, always tuning in to where we were at the moment and nudging us on from there. When it came to color and gender, Ted was blind, a happy disability for someone of his international stature. Consequently, he was quick to sense injustice and fearless in rooting it out no matter where he discovered it.

Ted's capacity to ask the provocative question or draw upon a simple metaphor has stimulated many hours of dialogue and served him well in other cultures. The questions were always aimed at the heart of the issue and were rarely used twice. One particular question was quite unforgettable: "Did Jesus ever ride a bicycle?"—a question designed to explore why Jesus didn't set up a formal school for his disciples. Internationals often left his classroom with a new appreciation for the potential of nonformal education to effect change in their countries. Ted has the capacity to see all sides of an issue and argue each perspective with equal strength—a characteristic that taught his students to always expect the unexpected. With deep respect for his intellectual capacity and that ability to consider all the sides of an issue, a colleague at Michigan State University once said, "Ted is the only person I know who can dialogue with himself."

The five authors represented here, in different ways, are international or have worked internationally. All of us are grateful to have had Ted as our mentor. The essay by Frances O'Gorman challenges the old models of community development and is startling in its honesty. The chapter by Evvy Hay makes a case for better use of inquiry in medical missions, providing two fascinating illustrations of how inquiry was used to question current practice. The selection by Duane and Muriel Elmer explores the power of dialogue for development and how it can be stimulated and sustained. The chapter by Stephen Hoke explores the art of facilitating change.

We have watched and learned from Ted's example as a thoroughgoing world Christian. His truly is a "spirituality of the road." These four chapters are offered in tribute to the role that he played in showing us the way to be better servants.

Chapter Thirteen _____

The Art of Facilitating Change

STEPHEN T. HOKE

_____

The world into which I was born died dramatically in 1989. The rise of communism in the late 1940s, the cold war of the 1950s, the space race and civil rights movement of the 1960s, the energy and leadership crises of the 1970s, the global trade imbalances of the 1980s, and the cataclysmic disintegration of the communist bloc starting in 1989, left the world I entered in 1949 radically altered.

Growing up in postwar Tokyo gave me a unique vantage point on the meteoric rise of the first Asian giant—Japan. I was weaned in an environment of bullet-train speed and constant change. During the 1960s, the realization began to dawn that "the times they are a changin'." Missionaries began to forge co-worker relationships with their national counterparts. By the 1980s, most denominations and agencies had parallel national entities and were well on their way toward at least some shared planning, resourcing, and team working.

The decade of the 1980s came to be characterized by the concept of cooperative relationships and partnership. Ignited by the visible cooperation modeled by the Lausanne movement, and extended by World Evangelical Fellowship's global church network, international leaders sounded the call for long-term partnerships in which each stakeholder was to be an equal partner.

Simultaneously during the last two decades, alternate roles began emerging worldwide in the disciplines of adult education, communications, and community development. Each of these areas also witnessed gradual shifts in the roles of practitioners—from change agent to co-worker to process facilitator. At the heart of the facilitator's teaching and discipling is an "inside-out and backwards" value shift that must occur in the minds and hearts of missionaries and educators alike. This chapter defines the radical essence of the biblical model of facilitation and the value shift that one must undergo to move from a training mindset to a facilitating lifestyle, from external to internal motivation, and from technique-centered methods to relational empowerment. It presents the need for a more enlightened, biblical approach to working with people in the whole arena of Christian missions, especially in international community development.

A first step toward this value shift is *a realization of the bankruptcy of the manager model* of leading in Christian ministry and a willingness to change one's leadership model. A traditional manager is characterized as a decision-maker, a delegator, a director, and often a scheduler of the work of others. But just as American companies are in transition, so are its churches and mission agencies. Emerging from this transition is a strong movement toward using teams to improve productivity and get vital work done.

For teams to be successful, they must be led. Managers who want to make the transition to team leaders need to undergo some significant changes not only in mindset, but also in the role they play. A team leader or facilitator is more of a motivator, a guide, a helper. A facilitator gets individuals to work together closely on defined projects for certain amounts of time. For teams to be productive, leaders must draw people out, listen, and incorporate their ideas.

Fran Rees demonstrates how the functions and behaviors of the controlling manager differ greatly from those of the facilitative leader (1991, 21). Controlling leaders retain full responsibility for the work and decisions of the team. Facilitative leaders share the responsibility with team members. The controlling leader tells, sells, directs, decides, delegates, solves problems, and rewards people. The facilitating leader listens, empowers, supports, coaches, teaches, collaborates, and strives for consensus.

Accompanying the recognition of a better way of working with people must be *a desire to change one's style of relating to subordinates and peers*. This is never easy. It demands an inversion of one's learning model from information-driven to experience-driven, from top-down to working-among. Jesus' criticism of the secular leadership model of his day and the leaders who lorded it over their followers (Matt. 20:20-28) is instructive at this point. The model of serving *among* that Jesus suggested stood the disciples' learning-leading model on its head; it meant that they were to minister out of who they were rather than the position they held. The kingdom model he described was "upside-down" to the ways of the world around them. The same will be true for facilitative leaders today.

A third step in the value shift is *a willingness to develop a new set of leading-facilitating skills for working with people*. In order for teachers to function as true facilitators and not just human information delivery systems, a range of interactive strategies and methods must be developed or learned to help people learn in ways that are appropriate to their culture, age and role. Extensive lists of interactive and participatory strategies are described by other authors (Brookfield 1994; Dettoni 1994; Egan 1988; Rees 1991; Schwarz 1994), and will not be expanded here. At this point, for a genuine value shift to occur, it is mandatory that teachers/leaders recognize the importance of retooling themselves to play a significantly different role than dispensers of information, or decision-makers for the whole group. This step is difficult because it often entails walking away from a lifetime of accumulated curriculum that is neither interactive nor facilitative.

A fourth step involves *a brokenness—a breaking of one's confidence in self and personal ability*, and yielding to a total, life-long dependence on the transforming work of the Holy Spirit. For many it involves dying to self and the way we have learned to do ministry, to learning how to help others grow. The role switch is as dramatic as moving from preacher to gardener, as traumatic as moving from teller to nurturer. The goal of all teaching, preaching, and counseling in Christian ministry should be to help people transform life. Information by itself never saved anyone or transformed any organization. Scripture was given for us to know God personally, to be transformed by the Holy Spirit as we internalize Scripture and become increasingly mature in Christ. Teachers, therefore, must be aware that mere delivery of important data is not sufficient to change or transform a person into an effective disciple of Christ. There is a vital connection between personal and community transformation. Unless we are being transformed in relationship with Jesus, how can we hope to bring this to others on a broader scale?

It is precisely this values shift that is so difficult for Christians trained in the West to make. There may be several reasons for this reluctance. First, for those who hold to a high view of Scripture, that view usually comes packaged in an authoritarian style of teaching that is not easily discarded. This is the top-down, hierarchical model of leading that Jesus rejected. Second, with schooling and degrees comes a subtle temptation to rely on position and titles rather than on gifting and Spirit empowerment. "After all," we reason, "I've earned it, haven't I?" Third, with high commitment to completion of the task comes a commensurate reliance on task oriented behaviors and leadership styles designed to accomplish visible results. Rarely are leaders of large churches and movements servant-facilitators of the ministry of others. Rather, they lead by virtue of their charismatic ability to get people to follow their suggestions and methods, on their timetable. They believe that vision is something that must be imparted from outside, not something that emerges from within a community.

In addition, Western leaders who lack experience in effectively helping people to decide and act for themselves also lack confidence in approaches that seem too relational and without clear deadlines. Fifth, and most difficult, is *the reluctance to give up the power, privilege and pride that accrues to leaders in our world today,* Christian or secular. They have been in charge for so long, they like it that way. The "upside-down" approach that calls for facilitating others seems a little too nebulous, messy, and unproductive.

Finally, our reluctance to abandon the predominant leadership model for a more relational-empowerment model stems from the lack of visible models. Few of today's leaders in Christian mission were apprenticed by encourager-facilitators. Most sat at the feet of expository preachers, dynamic promoters, or scholars who presented principles and described models that ought to work in intercultural missions. Few grew up watching facilitators who modeled servant leadership very effectively. And without effective modeling of an alternate role, they fell into the mold of their mentors.

But facilitative leaders do not give up their role; on the contrary, they have important responsibilities. They have to make sure that participation is worthwhile and will make a difference to the people involved (motivation), that people's knowledge and skills are assessed and upgraded (ability), and that people have sufficient resources and authority to participate (permission).

Missionary roles engage us as teachers of the Word. We facilitate the self-discovery of people in communities of the living Christ found in the stories of Scripture. We are facilitator-missiologists who work from Scripture to culture, and from our cultural context back to Scripture, in a constantly cycling model of action-reflection learning. But the Holy Spirit remains our key resource.

Action grows out of context. What we do as facilitators is dictated by how the Spirit prompts us to respond to the needs and situations in which we find ourselves. We go as servants, to wash people's feet. Opportunities present themselves to preach, to disciple, to feed the poor, or relieve human suffering. We live out the gospel in compassionate service, responding appropriately to the needs around us, as Jesus would. It is *situational facilitation,* parallel in responsiveness to *situational leadership* (Hersey and Blanchard 1988). And, of necessity, it is ministering in chaos, often without clear roles, with mixed expectations, and a cloudy image of future success.

The art of facilitation for transformation flows out of a significant value shift. Much of our teaching in the past has come out of a great love for Scripture and a desire to share God's Word with others. But our form of teaching has been formed in the classrooms of schools, and shaped by countless hours of cognitive input, with very little involvement of the affective or behavioral domains. The result has been a teaching ministry too often characterized by one-way communication or transfer of information from our notebook to the notes of our students, with very little opportunity for life-related discussion, guided practice, or mentored experience.

The role of the encourager-facilitator is more balanced and holistic than that of a teacher who only knows the right facts. It emerges out of one's *being*—one's very character and person—and naturally results in a style of relating to and working with people in the growth process that is distinctively different from traditional teaching. It is leading with a servant's attitude, helping behind the scenes, and being clear on the biblical essentials of discipling and committed to passing them on—stripped of Western culture.

FACILITATING AS SCIENCE AND ART

Facilitating is a science, an art, and a gift. As a science, effective facilitation is based on principles that emerge from research that can be learned by study and enhanced by skillful implementation (Brookfield, Dettoni, Rees, Schwarz, et al.). Trainers tend to talk about this aspect of facilitating quite a lot, because the science of facilitating can be taught.

As an art, facilitating calls for relational sensitivity, intuition, flexibility in uncertainty, and timing. These artistic people-skills are largely natural talents but can be developed through training and practice. Donald Schon suggests that the skill of an effective teacher-artist depends on putting what one knows into day-to-day practice. The art is finely tuned by consciously thinking about (reflecting on) what one is doing, often while doing it.

Stimulated by surprise, [effective facilitators] turn thought back on action and on the learning which is implicit in action. . . . It is this entire process of reflection-in-action which is central to the "art" by which practitioners sometimes deal well with situations of uncertainty, instability, uniqueness, and value conflict (Schon 1983, 50).

In addition, the style of the encourager-facilitator is an interplay among personality and natural abilities, learned skills, and spiritual gifts. Most facilitators I know, for example, are "people persons"—warm, open, and sensitive. Many have intuitive sensitivities to people's feelings, but not all do. And not all are extroverts. Cultural styles such as deference or indirection can be accommodated as well. Many have the gift mix of teaching-encouraging, helping-encouraging or compassion-encouraging. Barnabas—the generous, accepting, and available encourager of the Jerusalem and Antioch church is the premier New Testament example of an encourager-facilitator (Acts 4:36). Sensitive to and sympathetic with weakness, accepting, available, joyful at the success of others, and contagiously positive, he had the knack of expressing the right word, the right touch, and the right response whatever the situation. It is this trait of being "apt to encourage" that distinguishes the genuine encourager-facilitator from a traditional teacher-exhorter.

The close parallel between the work of the Holy Spirit and the role of facilitator can be seen by comparing the essential similarity of their roles. The Holy Spirit comes alongside (*paraclete*) to help people live out the new life of Christ that is within them. He encourages, guides, and illumines. He is the Divine Counselor, Encourager, and Teacher. In the harvest analogy for evangelism, Paul said, "I planted the seed, Apollos watered it, but God made it grow" (1 Cor. 3:6). Similarly, the encourager-facilitator's essential role is helping others grow and develop to their fullest potential—by faith. It is a role often compared to that of a gardener—preparing the soil, watering, nurturing.

It makes sense, then, that the spiritual gifts which focus on helping others grow make up the most common giftedness mix for encourager-facilitators. Facilitating involves a special spiritual empowerment or enabling by the Holy Spirit to equip and train Christians toward maturity in Jesus Christ and effectiveness in ministry. Science can be taught, art can be developed, but a gift can only be exercised. Christian facilitators live in constant dependence upon God's Holy Spirit within to empower and sensitize them to the changing needs to which they must respond.

At the heart of the missionary or development worker's concern with optimizing human development is a crucial *attitude*: the worker's willingness to accept other people generally as fellow human beings, created in the image of God, entitled to the same respect for their wants, beliefs, needs, customs, values, and sense of personal worth, as the worker expects for his or her own. From this essential attitude, important behaviors follow.

The kind of attitude villagers attribute to the facilitator is also crucial. The people must be favorably disposed toward the facilitator and identify with him or her in some way for an effective relationship to established. In the paragraphs that follow, the focus will be on the facilitator and the vital activities in which he or she must engage that flow out of the critical internal attitudes.

THE FACILITATOR'S TASKS
IN HOLISTIC COMMUNITY DEVELOPMENT

The ministry of the facilitator flows out of who he or she is. The contribution facilitators make to the community is directly related to the kind of person they are. They bring no product. They have nothing to sell. They have adopted the concept of process—that people are on a lifelong journey of becoming who God has created them to be. They need great sensitivity to the people they have come to encourage. They seek release and transformation in the lives of those who are developing.

Facilitation is *not* primarily a matter of techniques, skills, activity, style, or personality, though it does engage each of these dimensions at different times in the facilitation process. Facilitation is coming alongside, living among, learning with—being a co-learner, a co-discoverer, facilitating learning and life-change, sensing and nurturing a learning environment and learning community. From this essential attitude and internalized value flow a set of related tasks that guide the facilitator's engagement with a community.

Ted Ward suggested in 1976 that the major determinant in selecting between teaching strategies or therapeutic interventions is the normalcy of the participants. Teaching strategies are most appropriate for people who are growing and developing naturally in their adult lives. On the other hand, people who have stopped growing or have stalemated in their development are candidates for therapy or counseling strategies. In 1987 he applied these concepts to the work of community development facilitators working with local communities in the Two-Thirds World. A list of essential facilitator tasks is given in Table 1.

THE FACILITATOR'S TASKS
IN HOLISTIC COMMUNITY DEVELOPMENT

Facilitating *appropriate for normal development*

☑ To establish a nurturing community environment: *characterized by openness, trust, and acceptance*

☑ To invite and stimulate participation: *encourage people to listen to each other*

☑ To stimulate inquiry: *avoid premature decisions*

☑ To stimulate verbalizations: *make it easy to speak up; encourage "quiet debate"*

☑ To ask why

☑ To provide experiences wherein the community situation is examined and described: *including world view and moral issues*

☑ To dialogue: *listen responsively*

☑ To explore needs (*disequilibrium states*) with those in need (*the disequilibrated*): *for example, protect those being attacked; help the poor and oppressed talk about their situation*

☑ To guide the community's gathering of appropriate information

☑ To stand alongside (*paraclete*)

☑ To guide the community in analyzing the causes of its situation

☑ To guide the community in decision-making for a new course of action

☑ To help synthesize to clarify and bring closure

Therapy *appropriate for stalemated development*
    ☒ To confront
    ☒ To challenge inconsistency
    ☒ To induce disequilibrium

Table 1. The Facilitator's Tasks in Holistic Community Development.
Stephen Hoke and Ted Ward 8.87 rev 4.93

The remaining portion of the chapter attempts to build upon Ward's developmental framework and provide practical guidelines for facilitators of change in communities.

The starting point for facilitators is *to build secure, helping relationships* with the people among whom they have the opportunity of working. The technical competence they bring into a situation from their training and background will be crucial to fostering their credibility among the people. People will respond to their openness. They must be willing to flex and change themselves, eager to accept new ideas, and willing and able to give and receive feedback. As they spend time with the people, they will gradually earn respect as persons. They will be good listeners. The realization that villagers, wherever they are, are not working in a vacuum but have accumulated vast experience in adapting to the times will place the encouragers in a learning, listening posture.

As facilitators work to establish and strengthen relationships throughout the community, they will want to establish an atmosphere characterized by reciprocity. In reciprocal relationships, both sides give and take. There is a sense of equality and mutuality between respondents that prevents one-way communication from dominating. Equal power also minimizes power plays and helps in making decisions by consensus and cooperation rather than by competition or hierarchy.

A second important guideline in working with communities is *to get involved with people.* The most obvious logical benefits derived from involving all the people (in most cases a representative group of the community members, including the key stakeholders) include building on their natural interest and commitment to their own community, gaining "buy-in" or ownership by the community members themselves, and participation in the ultimate attainment of the goal. To allow participation and input from all groups is the more democratic, ethical, moral, considerate, and just manner in which to proceed. It is founded on the biblical notion of varied gifts in the body of Christ, which have been placed there by the Father, and which when utilized draw on the energy and dynamic of the Holy Spirit.

A third requisite for facilitators is *to become involved in inquiry and study.* Too often community development workers or evangelists arrive and depart from the community without so much as having learned the language, more than a few customs, or any comprehensive picture of how their work fits into the broader scheme of things in the region or country. Encouragers must be concerned with studying and developing their own perspective of the social structure and social system in which they find themselves. They must know how to gain information about local situations. They must do more than look at the culture with interest and respect; they must develop a thorough knowledge of the main values and principal features of the community's subculture. They should have a clear idea of the nature of what is being changed.

A fourth guideline for facilitators is *to develop sensitivity to and skill in assessing local and needs and resources*. They begin with a needs assessment of the community, which they carry out with the assistance of and in cooperation with the community people themselves. They help the people identify the real difficulties and become more observant of their own setting. The people are the true experts on issues vital to their well-being, whether health, environment, food production, or spiritual condition. They are the ones best able to describe the extent of the problem and to identify which issues they wish to address first. To rely on outside observation and so-called expert opinion is foolhardy and smacks of paternalism.

A fifth task is *building and improving their own communication skills*. Once facilitators understand the basics of the communication process, they will want to practice and increase their expertise in the use of various particular skills such as active listening, questioning, and action-reflection. They will engage in dialogue with the community in an attempt to explore various problems with them. In this kind of setting, there will be opportunity to confront differences and talk them out. Encouragers will be willing to share experiences with the people in order to enlarge areas of mutual understanding. As people whose experiences differ engage in sharing, both will come to understand themselves better. Finally, facilitators will look for situations that will give them feedback on their capabilities. By helping to organize activities or by developing local organizations, they will learn to do technical tasks more effectively within the context of the local social system.

A sixth step facilitators can take is *to consider with the people the consequence and responsibilities* of the anticipated change. Facilitators should, before programs are started, engage the people in considering the potential changes in their families, their group, their community, and the society. This is why Jesus chided potential disciples to count the cost. People must together weigh the benefits and losses of change, seen and unforeseen. Change is costly. This simple procedure may serve to increase their awareness of manipulation and help them become more aware of the possibility that change agents can control the behavior of their clients.

Training responsible leaders is one of the most critical of the encourager-facilitator's tasks. Discipling new Christians is the most obvious need when the gospel invades the life of a community. It is not completed until new leaders are willing to step forward from the harvest and assume leadership responsibility in the church and community. Mentoring is the intentional process of equipping younger leaders into greater maturity and responsibility toward their full potential. This is the task Paul challenged young Timothy to pursue: "And the things you have heard me say in the presence of many witnesses entrust to reliable men who will also be qualified to teach others" (2 Tim. 2:2). Without persisting in the task of raising up the next generation of leaders, the fruit of evangelism or community development is short-lived.

Facilitators may also need to serve in the role Havelock called a *resource linkers* (1972, 9, 17-19). When facilitators make themselves available to the people, the people will feel more comfortable in seeking advice when needed and asking about the resources available outside their community.

A ninth step encourager-facilitators take is *to stand alongside the people in the growth and development process* to support and encourage them as they struggle and grow. This role is vital in the life of any newly planted church. It is the role that first Barnabas, and then Paul, played in the life of the first-century church. Enablers must be flexible, supportive, and positive. Like Barnabas encouraging the fresh church plant in Antioch (Acts 11:19-24), facilitators must be big enough to encourage initiative, give reasons for optimism, and hold high expectations of renewal and growth. As encouragers stand with people in the midst of the growth process, the people will learn to work together as equals and be able to share the benefits of improved lives and a growing community.

Effective Christian facilitators must also *model a biblical lifestyle and communication pattern*. People's perception of facilitators' competency is highest when there is congruence between what they say and what they do. A facilitator's speech will have its greatest impact when it is truth spoken in love, honesty wrapped in grace.

The epitome of the helping relationship thus described is the biblical concept designated by the Greek word *agape*. The word captures the force of vital, self-giving love. This relationship is not one in which helpers remain aloof from the people they are helping, presenting a mask and providing a sterile, neutral atmosphere. Rather, encourager-facilitators become highly involved, and, because they care so deeply, they cannot be neutral or unconditional in their responses.

The development of the concept of the two main phases of the
helping relationship—the facilitative and action phases—is a major
contribution to the field of mission and Christian community development. It is the role most consistent with the objective of holistic
human development within a Christian context. Facilitative relationships inevitably lead to action and change. The encourager facilita
tor role is the means to community development and working with
people most consistent with the end of optimal human development.
It will become a required art for missionaries in the twenty-first century.

Works Cited and Selected Resources

Belasco, James A. 1990. *Teaching the Elephant to Dance: The Manager's Guide
Empowering Change*. New York: Penguin/Plume Books.

Biddle, William W., and Loureide J. Biddle. 1965. *The Community Development Process: The Rediscovery of Local Initiative*. New York: Holt.

Brookfield, Stephen D. 1991. *Understanding and Facilitating Adult Learning*.
San Francisco: Jossey-Bass.

Dettoni, John M. 1994. "Interactive Strategies and Methods." A paper presented at NACIE, July 1994. San Clemente: Chrysalis Ministries.

Egan, Gerard. 1988. *Change Agent Skills B: Managing Innovation and Change*.
San Diego: University Associates.

Freire, Paulo. 1980. *Education for Critical Consciousness*. New York: Continuum.

Havelock, Ronald G. 1973. *The Change Agent's Guide to Innovation in Education*. Englewood Cliffs: Educational Technology Publications.

Hersey, Paul, and Kenneth H. Blanchard. 1988. *Management of Organiza-
tional Behavior*. Englewood Cliffs: Prentice Hall.

Pritchett, Price, and Ron Pound. 1993. *High Velocity Culture Change*. Dallas:
Pritchett & Associates.

Rees, Fran. 1991. *How to Lead Work Teams: Facilitation Skills*. San Diego: Pfeiffer
& Co.

Rogers, Everett M. 1983. *Diffusion of Innovations*. 3d ed. New York: Free Press.

Schaller, Lyle E. 1972. *The Change Agent: The Strategy of Innovative Leadership*. Nashville: Abingdon Press.

Schon, Donald. A. 1983 *The Reflective Practitioner*. New York: Basic Books.

Schwarz, Roger M. 1994. *The Skilled Facilitator*. San Francisco. Jossey-Bass.

Ward, Ted. 1976. "Conducting Non-Formal Education in the Two-Thirds
World." Notes from a seminar. East Lansing, Mich.: Michigan State University.

_____. 1987. Presentation at a World Vision training conference in
Honolulu.

Chapter Fourteen

Tomorrow Emerged Yesterday

Are We Facilitators "Crabbing" the Community Development Process?

FRANCES O'GORMAN

Glistening minnows leaped mercurially out of the lucent canal. Each prosaic "plop" stirred up entrancing ripples. The clump of palms, Indian almonds and poincianas, hugging the breakwater corner where the curbed lawn broke loose into an unruly rock garden, shimmered in the morning sunlight of Angra dos Reis, on Rio de Janeiro's beach-studded coast.

A gorgeously robust horseshoe crab scuttled out from the clump, shot sideways across the lawn and came to a startled halt near the holidaying grandchildren. Everyone froze.

Feigning undauntedness, one of the tots identified the intruder: "Oh, Sebastian." All nodded knowingly, but no one dared to move.

A smaller crab edged surreptitiously toward motionless Sebastian and the mesmerized children. Breathless expectation. The tot pontificated: "Oh, Sebastianna." More wise nodding and pounding hearts.

Suddenly, looking straight ahead, Sebastian and Sebastianna beat a lightning retreat sideways back to the corner. Grandchildren dashed in the opposite direction, falling over one another and their own feet in the anxiety of flight.

Till the end of their holidays, no amount of zoography could reassure them that it was all right for crabs to look ahead while getting places by going sideways.

The crab incident touched off a disquieting question: How much of my quarter of a century of experience as facilitator has really been crabbing the community development process with the poor?

CRABBING COMMUNITY DEVELOPMENT

A recent nostalgic visit to Santa Marta, a hillside slum in Rio de Janeiro, brought to mind my intensive years of community development facilitation at the base level. Pondering Sebastian and Sebastianna's efficient sideways scurry made me wonder: Have we facilitators actually been *crabbing* community development by moving the social, economic, political, and cultural change process with the poor from today to yesterday, and not ahead into the future?

In most Latin American experiences, community development vindicates a dynamic social integration process, with and for the excluded ones, which involves actions, intentions, ideals, techniques, values, beliefs, knowledge, information, decision-making, and democratic principles. Seeking the well-being of the impoverished, it moves, or is moved, in directions sanctioned by dominant structures of society. The process implies the right of all people and the means to *make* continual (process) life-giving choices (development) in harmony with other human beings (community) from the vantage point of the impoverished. Community embraces all of us. We are co-responsible for allowing society to impoverish two-thirds of our brothers and sisters of God's unique humankind.

Looking back, it seems as though many of us, as facilitators and members of support groups of nongovernmental organizations (NGOs), have inadvertently been moving community development from one today to another today. We have been going from one here-and-now to the next here-and-now without asking some disconcerting *why* questions. The todays slipped into yesterday without our perceiving the tomorrow that was already emerging.

Catching up Sideways

Sebastian and Sebastianna moved double-quick with their sharp nails on the tips of the five pairs of legs. They scurried across the grass faster than the grandchildren! Ignoring the great unknown lawn, they scampered sideways, back and forth, building a crab kingdom around mound-encircled holes.

In Santa Marta I revisited the school aid program that had sparked off the community development process and was still going strong after seventeen years. Donor sponsorship of students has benefited hundreds of boys and girls. The money was used to buy school material, prompting children to stay in the classroom three or four hours a day and keeping them off shanty rooftops where they flew kites, fought, and got into drugs.

Many prospective dropouts are being helped to catch up with schooling, the doorway into society. At the same time, millions of marginalized children all over continue to shuffle between an alienating classroom beyond the slum and their shanty world—no further—catching up sideways within yesterdays that never spawn tomorrows.

Fernando made good use of the program. Backed by material and tutorial support he completed high school. Bright, ambitious, a dreamer, Fernando applied for admittance to the navy. He passed all the tests with flying colors except one—the medical exam. Like his unhealthy slum neighbors, Fernando's rotten teeth were beyond repair.

He tried in vain to get a steady job in the city. But Fernando not only lives in a slum, he is young, black, male, and self-assured. One day he came home to find his mother's shanty sacked. The police had staged one of their mock raids to hustle drug traffickers into paying hush money. Fernando turned his back on the society that turned its back on him He went to work for the local gang, trafficking cocaine among the residents of the luxurious beach-front condominiums.

Other faces, different stories, same underlying problems: Alex, Marco Antonia, Carmen Silvia, Lucilene. . . . Have we facilitators reneged on the true meaning of education and accommodated community development merely to catching up sideways?

Digging out the Hole

Digging holes is a cinch for Sebastian and Sebastianna—even if it means going up and down sideways!

The preschool day-care center in Santa Marta reverberates with frolicking children, as it has for many years. White, bright, and full of blue windows, it still defies the drab tin roofs hemmed in by drug dealers' hideouts and the garbage mounds—a tribute to the perseverance of the community group.

Entirely run by the slum women after years of preparation by the facilitators, the center provides working mothers with essential services for a nominal fee. Strategically located in the middle of the slum, forty stories high, it safeguards its credibility through linkages with indigenous and foreign agencies. However, it cannot keep up with the demand for a cheap, wholesome space to leave slum children when shanty doors are locked behind the mothers (where are the fathers?), who trot down the hill to launder and cook and scour in nearby posh apartments.

The needs go on, despite so many years of the community day-care center proposing to change conditions in Santa Marta. People continue to be impoverished, undernourished, unhealthy, under-employed. Families are torn apart. Poor people parrot the self-seeking popular adage "each for himself (herself), and God for all," revived with the arrival of every new narcissistic splinter church. Teachers, cooks, and child caretakers want to hold on to the monthly minimum-wage employment plus plentiful food ensured by funding agencies. The needs of the poor are not generated solely in the slum base but on all levels of society. Community development seems to have ceased while the project took over and became an end in itself. Charged with the infeasible task of bringing about transformation from the bottom up, the day-care center is actually a delightful crab hole. Sometimes we facilitators not only scurry sideways to catch up with yesterday, we naively burrow ourselves in one-way projects. It is much more reassuring to look up out of the hole than to ask what makes the hole necessary.

From Here to There

> Sebastian and Sebastianna never missed their mark speeding away on five pairs of legs, from hole to corner clump, to nooks in the rock garden, to patches of lawn.

Across the years, the Santa Marta community group also hit the mark on a series of self-help projects. The boys' carpentry shop taught skills and cultivated group identity among the adolescents. It closed down because wooden products could not compete with cheap plastic goods. Also, tips paid by drug pushers to boys to serve as go-betweens were much more enticing.

For two years, the concerts by the children of the music school were the pride and joy of Santa Marta. When funds dried up, volunteer student-teachers disappeared. The famous guitarist who initiated the project lost interest once he gained widespread publicity for his magnanimity. Disgruntled youngsters stole equipment, and people in the slum took no stand because they did not consider the project their own.

Projects such as sewing, cooking, crocheting, literacy, typing, pre-election political education, and a used-clothing bazaar, all had their story. A beginning sparked by the development process, a middle of heartening achievements, and an end brought on by social, economic, political, and cultural roadblocks.

We facilitators so spontaneously raise the myth of self-help, presenting immediate responses to assumed needs. Hardly ever do we ask the whys and wherefores of causes behind the needs.

Thus, the project in Santa Marta, as in countless experiences in Latin America, kept going from here to here, never yonder.

Pincers for Power

The grandchildren maintained a healthy awe for the pairs of legs with pincers that Sebastian and Sebastianna wiggled so menacingly. Those nippers had power to cause an "ouch"!

Empowerment has become the password for the process of community development among the impoverished: raise their power and they will transform marginalization into democracy!

In Santa Marta empowerment was realized primarily by building an informal group of participants into an organization. The UNIDAS association was officially registered, outfitted with bylaws, and allotted project funds. The members were painstakingly initiated into an anachronistic democratic election system within a slum spurned by city authorities and ruled by drug kingpins.

Walking around with Irene, one of the first and most steadfast of the UNIDAS leaders, I recalled our many struggles as community participants and facilitators to make the voice of the slum dwellers heard and heeded.

Countless demonstrations after each traffic casualty finally induced the mayor to have a stoplight installed on the busy thoroughfare at the bottom of the hill so that Santa Marta residents could cross safely. Petitions led to installing electricity lines to all the shanties, with light meters so that bills could be paid without graft. Campaigns to elect honest members to the board of the Santa Marta Residents' Association made headway until they were aborted by assassination. The UNIDAS has staunchly resisted bribery and threats by local gangsters, defending the right to an autonomous people's power within the slums, a right that is being upheld by a lifeline of external funding and facilitation. Empowerment only reaches as far as its legs can carry it—and among the impoverished this is very close to home.

Sometimes we facilitators allow ourselves to create an illusion of empowerment. Recently children and a teacher from UNIDAS were given a trip to Disneyland, sponsored by McDonalds. Everyone considered it an achievement of empowerment. Nonetheless, the sightseers returned to the same slum future, with no change in sight other than more frustrated expectations and a growing unwillingness to work for community improvement.

Pseudo-empowerment of the poor often adds to the continuing empowerment of the status quo. Power in small bits here and there is not enough to offset the powerful socioeconomic systems that affect all development.

On and On

As summer went on, the grandchildren found more and more crab holes and small newcomers in the corner by the sea wall. Only Sebastian and Sebastianna retained their titles, in deference to the First Great Confrontation. Five pairs of legs scurrying sideways, mounds of earth topping off deep holes—their activities went on and on.

In Santa Marta, Irene excitedly pointed out the captivating new UNIDAS project: a tiny room jammed with youngsters glued to the screens of discarded PCs. Having access to computer training was being held up as *the* answer to today's problems.

Would half a dozen of the trainees, who might possibly one day get an office job, bring about change in the slum? It seemed as if the crab hole this time was deeper, the mound higher, the sideways scurrying faster. The community development process was still being crabbed.

It is very hard for NGOs to go anywhere but on and on. Looking back at my twenty years with the same indigenous development NGO in Brazil, I can recall the exciting sequential stages of new approaches to working with the poor. We pursued the ideal of facilitating a process that would diminish marginalization and allow a new participatory society to come into being. But we seemed to end up hurrying up sideways, burrowing project holes, scurrying from here to here, and confusing empowerment with pincer-power. Now the NGO is repairing obsolete computers, distributing them to various poor areas of Rio de Janeiro, maintaining the equipment, and providing teachers. Society is delighted with these modern and efficient responses to impoverishment.

The centrifugal impetus of community facilitation has gone through such core activities as milk distribution, vaccination campaigns, leadership training, popular education, cooperatives, labor union organization, mini self-help projects, and now, community computer training centers for the slums. Evidently each response did have a meaning for its today—but what about the tomorrow that was emerging?

TOMORROW ALREADY EMERGED YESTERDAY

The pivotal responsibility of facilitators is to place community development processes within a perspective of tomorrow. All that has been, and is being done, with and for the poor, is basic for human fulfillment and socioeconomic advancement, but it belongs to yesterday. We tend to become so engrossed in today that we look the other way and fail to focus on the crucial questions: What are the signs of the future? And what are we doing about them?

Looking One Way, Going Another

The grandchildren eventually tamed their fears and began to observe Sebastian and Sebastianna at an arm's length, rather than from half a lawn away. But seeing the crabs apparently looking one way while going another discombobulated them right to the end.

So often we facilitators have inclined the community development process one way, that is, looking to today, while really going another way—into yesterday, without intuiting tomorrow.

Tomorrow emerged yesterday in the form of global socioeconomic structures that created Santa Marta like hundreds of other slums. It emerged yesterday in surveys and project evaluations declaring that institutionalized injustice, with roots far beyond the community, would go on crushing the life out of any transformational self-help projects. Tomorrow emerged yesterday in twenty years of recycled community development patterns in Santa Marta, revealing signs of the coming decade: increasing control by drug traffickers, frustrated consumerism goaded by TV commercials, tobogganing mobility of the poorest and underemployment. . . . Tired of community development, which promises change while wielding scant influence over the causes of impoverishment, slum dwellers tended to become callous to the idealistic appeal of "for us all." They have begun to zero in on "only me."

Why is it so difficult for facilitators to intuit tomorrow? Perhaps our NGOs have (and want) too much money and power and prestige. Maybe we are too self-righteous (it is gratifying to be patronizing with other people's money). Possibly we are too pressured to produce satisfactory quantifiable results to justify charity-sponsored salaries. It could be that, since facilitation is a role not a profession, we are easily dispensable. Who knows but that our religious principles (not necessarily spiritual) bolster our conformity when reality confounds us.

Perhaps what truly counts is that when tomorrow comes, we will probably not be around to appraise the fruit of our efforts. We like to think of ourselves as pilgrim people of God and educators of the future. Yet we balk at risking even a slight totter to lift one foot off the soft soil of today, much less to leap into the air with both feet off the ground!

Leaping Up and Making Ripples

The grandchildren took for granted the minnow leaping out of the canal, but not Sebastian's and Sebastianna's sideways zipping to and fro.

Something about those glistening fish bobbing unexpectedly out of the water made me muse, "Now what?"

The twenty-five years of community development sowed good seeds, but seeds limited to that today, while tomorrow was emerging. It is time to let go of crabbing the community development process and to take a qualitative leap in the facilitator role to perceive and respond to impoverishment from a different perspective.

Carl Jung pointed out how the human conscience develops in spurts. So long as one's present level of understanding is adequate for the immediate problem, few changes occur. But when new circumstances loom up, one's conscience takes a qualitative leap to cope. Jean Piaget observed that in human development, various concepts and aptitudes, activated at the adequate qualitative moment, cannot be imposed or anticipated, but can be stimulated. Qualitative leaps in conscience and conceptualization attune the facilitator to tomorrow.

What could impel one to leap? Perhaps becoming physically, socially, psychologically, or spiritually unseated! Letting go could happen in almost any way—through losses, dreams, achievements, disappointments, prayers, insights, failures, reading, crises, shared reflections, circumstances beyond our control that impinge on us.

Substituting, redirecting, updating, enhancing, or broadening community facilitation probably increases efficiency, but hardly ever brings about a qualitative leap in our role or in the process. An unbalancing is needed to open up new insights for tomorrow to emerge.

How could we facilitators risk being thrown off balance and let go of the present moment of our role? Perhaps by asking ourselves trenchantly: What difference is my facilitation making, today, to the immediate needs of the impoverished? To the situations and causes of impoverishment? To the other side of society which tacitly tolerates impoverishment as an inevitable transitory side-effect of the growth of capitalism?

Community development attempts to invert dehumanizing impoverishment. Why do facilitators care? Because we are committed to wanting to share the dignity and right to fulfillment of all human beings. Motivation springs from the One Source of all energy and finds expression in the universal ethical principle mantled upon all people: *Do to others what you would want them to do to you.* The essence of the educational role of facilitation is simply to activate that principle, courageously and consistently, everywhere, at all times, with all people, under all circumstances. When deep-rooted changes begin to take place, so that people uphold each other's right to fullness of life in all facets of society, we will see tomorrow emerging unexpectedly in yesterday.

As I thought over those two and a half decades of community facilitation while trying to let go of the Sebastian and Sebastianna inside of me, I felt jounced into mid-air, somewhat like the leaping minnows in the canal. When splashing back into the reality of impoverishment, perhaps some unexpected ripples will emerge.

Chapter Fifteen _____

Medical Missionaries
and the Spirit of Inquiry

Evvy Hay

_____

Few international development arenas are so intrinsically compelling, or so deeply satisfying for practitioners, as medical missions. The pain, suffering, and bewilderment of people affected by illness urge us to respond. Further, the mandate in the Gospel of Mark hurries us along with the promise: "They will place their hands on sick people, and they will get well" (Mark 16:18b).

I certainly found that compelling and satisfying mix to be true of my work as a missionary nurse in Sierra Leone. Our hospital, located on an old trade route that ran from the Atlantic to Timbuktu in Mali, combined the overwhelming with the fascinating. More than two thousand surgeries were done each year, with one physician, four nurses, and a modest auxiliary staff, while two to three hundred outpatients arrived daily. There was schistosomiasis, onchocerciasis, amoebiasis, and every other kind of helminthiasis, along with creeping eruption, Burkitts lymphoma, anthrax, and wucheraria bancrofti, which causes elephantiasis. On top of that, each day in the clinic, patients spoke at least five languages: Temne, Limba, Krio, Fullah, and Susu. Initially language study was informal. After six months in the country, I gave instructions to a patient in Krio, and was congratulating myself for doing so. It was obvious, however, that he had not understood my explanation. So I said to him, "Pa, yu no ebul fo yeri Krio?" ("Sir, don't you understand Krio?"), to which he responded distinctly and to my chagrin, "I understand Krio, but I don't understand you."

178

I have done a bladder tap on a trauma case by kerosene lantern light and started an IV by flashlight as termite flies bombarded the site because of the light. I have watched with families as numerous small children took their last breaths. As the glory departed from those small bodies, I often thought, "Oh, Father, is there no other help for these little ones?" In his book *Wishful Thinking*, Frederick Buechner reminds us that the word *vocation* comes from the Latin *vocare* meaning "to call." He says it is the work that a person most needs to do and the work that the world most needs to have done—the place where the individual's deep gladness and the world's deep hunger meet. Truly medical missions still offers a challenge to practitioners.

CHANGING MODELS OF MEDICAL MISSIONS

From the inception of the church in the book of Acts, healing ministries have been integral to its work. Mission hospitals and outpatient dispensaries, which commonly operate at frenetic levels of activity, are often major providers of health-care services in developing countries. Confronted by dramatic and pressing needs, health-care professionals and mission administrators focused historically on the delivery of services to meet those needs. An unstated question driving medical missions has been, What needs to be done so sick people can get well? The answer to that question in the early years of modern missions was the pursuit and promotion of curative services.

In 1978 an international conference on primary health care, sponsored jointly by WHO and UNICEF, was held in the Soviet Union. The resulting Declaration of Alma Ata underscored the priority of people's participation in planning and implementing their own health care. In Latin America, during that decade, Paulo Freire encouraged oppressed people, through the process of conscientization, to envision taking control of their lives (Freire 1970). Simultaneously, David Werner sought to make health services more democratic by simplifying medical services for village people (Werner 1978). Among mission agencies a dialogue on primary health care emerged that considered education, water and sanitation, maternal and child health, control of communicable diseases, and adequate drug supplies. In the 1980s, with missionary physicians like Dr. Roy Shaffer in Kenya and Dr. Dan Fountain in Zaire, the discussion shifted to programs that originated in the communities and were truly community-balanced or community-based. Often these programs have been either church-based in origin or linked to local churches (Ewert 1990).

As the dialogue has progressed from curative services through disease prevention and health promotion, and now on to holistic health efforts in connection with the church, medical missionaries have struggled with a kaleidoscope of issues: an inability to support institutions financially; increasing difficulties in recruitment and retention of career personnel; blocked currency affecting the purchase of affordable medicines; and the difficulties associated with sustaining services in situations of chronic low-intensity conflict. Daily issues beyond the realm of medical care press for attention as well: repair of a hospital generator, securing building supplies for a new hospital wing, curriculum for training programs, a community evangelistic outreach. As medical missionaries are pressed by external circumstances into being response-oriented, let me suggest a personal strategy for growing into a "cutting edge" and future-oriented role, as well as deepening personal satisfaction in service. The personal strategy is to cultivate a spirit of inquiry.

MEDICAL MISSIONARIES AS ETHNOGRAPHERS

Some years ago, I saw the following sign posted on the wall of a small clothing store:

> I know that you believe
> that you understand
> what you think I said.
> But I'm not sure you realize
> that what you heard
> is not what I meant.

Since our actions are based on our perceptions of reality, we are periodically provoked into saying, "Oh, but I thought . . . " when reality differs from our expectations. We have not, indeed, heard and understood what others assumed we heard and understood.

Those living and working cross-culturally inevitably experience both the humor and difficulties associated with adapting to the language, greetings, food, relationships, and routines of those different from themselves. In cultures other than our own, we may not only lack knowledge of why people do what they do, but commonly we even lack knowledge of what they do (Hammersley and Atkinson 1983). There is no substitute for systematic language study, reading in the field of medical anthropology, or cultural orientation. But once on the field, the strategy or habit of inquiry will provide an endless amount of data, which can lead to new insights. I have seen it practiced graciously in social situations and personally used it more rigorously in research.

Dr. Clydette Powell is a pediatric neurologist with extensive international consulting experience. On a recent trip into Serbia with her, I was fascinated with the delightful way in which she was graciously inquisitive in virtually every situation. In a van rocketing down the highway or three courses into an elaborate national meal, she had an inimitable skill for asking cordial questions about seemingly obvious factors, questions that inevitably resulted in an animated discussion with a responsive colleague about enlightening or substantive issues. There are, of course, time limits to the learner role in a new culture (Hiebert 1985), but I am referring here to the posture of inquiry that arises from a genuine interest in others and their lives, and which is not bound by time. In Philippians 2:4 the apostle Paul exhorts us to "look . . . to the interests of others," and later in the same chapter commends Timothy "who takes a genuine interest" in the welfare of others. Clydette's gift for inquiry not only provided the data we needed, but it strengthened our relationships with the ethnic Albanian health professionals with whom we had come to work.

Inquiry that solicits qualitative data, meaning data in the form of words rather than numbers, has always been a staple of the social sciences, including anthropology. After several years of living and working in Sierra Leone as a health professional, I was amazed at the way in which a few basic tools of ethnography opened the door of understanding to patient behaviors and practices. Ethnography is a reflexive process, meaning that it is part of the social world it studies. Typically it includes the selection of cases, observation and interviewing, recording and filing data, then analyzing and documenting findings. If defined as a research method to medical missionaries, it would probably be relegated to the "over there, I'm busy now" corner of the mind. But when developed as a personal professional habit, it opens the doors of enlightenment and understanding and sets us on the path for effecting change in the midst of busy circumstances, as well as nudging us toward new directions for the future.

After several years of challenging and satisfying work as a medical missionary in Sierra Leone, I stepped back to look at where I had been, this time through eyes of inquiry. I was amazed at the insights gained through simple, respectful questioning and a few tools of documentation and reflection. Aspects of life in Sierra Leone I had neither seen nor understood came into sharp focus. The significance of the baboon, goat, and monkey-skin waist charms worn by patients became clear. The peregrinations of individuals and family groups to herbalists, sorcerers, and clinics in search of relief from pain took on new meaning. The midwives' stories about beliefs surrounding childbirth explained patterns of labor and delivery behavior.

Let me share two examples of significant health behaviors of which we were unaware as medical missionaries until the simple tools of inquiry were applied. The first deals with the practice of geophagy, and the second with the reinterpretation of Western pharmaceuticals.

A CASE IN POINT: THE PRACTICE OF GEOPHAGY

Geophagy, the eating of earth, is a phenomenon that occurs in many cultures. The practice may include vespid and termite clays. In Sierra Leone, it is common during pregnancy. The geophagial clays are mineraliferous, containing magnesium, phosphorus, potassium, calcium, manganese, iron, nickel, copper, zinc, and selenium. In conditions of near-subsistence living with inadequate diet and frequent pregnancy, geophagia provides important minerals for fetal development. In one study, a farm wife eating vespid clay during her fourth pregnancy was shown to be consuming 160 percent of the recommended pregnancy supplement of zinc, 62 percent of calcium, 59 percent of manganese, 47-93 percent of iron, and 30 percent of phosphorus (Hunter, 1984). I learned of the practice in a medical geography class in graduate school, from Dr. John Hunter, who had done extensive research on the subject in Sierra Leone.

On return to Sierra Leone, I discussed the practice with medical missionary colleagues, none of whom were familiar with it, including one physician who had been raised in the country, was thoroughly acculturated, and had practiced there for twenty-five years. I inquired about geophagy by asking a young nurse, who took me to her mother's home. Women who were part of the village sodality then willingly demonstrated how they obtain and prepare geophagial clays from clay pits. The clay is dug from wet pits and is then rolled into palm-size balls, removing as much yellow and red clay as possible so that only the white clay remains. The balls are dried in the sun for several days. When eating the balls, the women separate the clay from whatever sand is present, discarding the sand and eating only the clay. The amount of clay consumed during pregnancy depends on personal preference. Some women eat a large ball each day, while others eat smaller amounts on a less regular basis. The choice between eating mineral-rich termite mound or mineral-rich clay is an individual matter.

Learning of this widespread practice, openly shared with me after inquiry, awakened me to the shallowness of my previous understanding of health practices. For several years, we had been providing vitamins to pregnant women on our monthly village visits, yet never had this widespread traditional practice resulting in mineral supplementation been discussed. Perhaps shyness or fear of disrespect about the practice had kept them from mentioning it; it awaited only respectful inquiry to bring it to the fore. In any case, simple inquiry opened the door to understanding a significant health practice.

A CASE IN POINT: THE REINTERPRETATION
OF WESTERN PHARMACEUTICALS

Inquiry also provided enlightenment on the significant health practice of reinterpretation of Western pharmaceuticals. During a particular year, approximately seventy thousand outpatients were seen in the hospital clinic. Most received drugs. The waiting area in the outpatient dispensary, which was open most days, was a colorful place. Patient services were provided in the interview area, at the drug-dispensing counter, in the laboratory, in the X-ray room, and in the doctor's clinic. In addition to some two hundred general patients, an additional twenty-five to thirty with tuberculosis came each morning for streptomycin injections. When the dispensary was closed at noon, patients could be seen stretched out resting on colorful lappa cloths on the concrete floor, chatting under trees, or simply sitting and waiting. The tiny local market outside provided food and small wares for patients: oranges, hot groundnuts, bananas, guavas, cola nuts, rice chop, cherry tomatoes, candy, cigarettes, razor blades, and even assorted medicines.

The importance of Western pharmaceuticals to these clinic patients cannot be overemphasized. Patients made the following comments. "I have come to the hospital because I was told medicines are here." "The medicine here is good." "The first time I came I had a heavy sick. You gave plenty medicine and I felt better. I believe the medicine." "When I carried [brought] my mother [here] I got medicine." "I am ready to return to my home now. I have come for medicines to carry." When an eight-year-old boy was asked what he did when sick, his reply was, "You go to the hospital and make them give you medicine. If you get sick, you take the medicine to swallow it. When the medicine is done you go back for other medicine." Both quantity and types of medicines were considered important. A patient who had been seen by a physician, and had received only one medication for his intestinal parasites, was ridiculed by his peers with the comment, "Ah, you paid Le 50 to see the doctor and you only got Le 6 worth of medicine!" Post-operative patients or those who had come from great distances commonly requested "traveling medicines" to take with them when they journeyed home. A number of factors contributed to the importance of Western pharmaceuticals in the patients' eyes. One was the earlier use of penicillin to treat yaws. In the initial stage of yaws the patients had painless ulcers. In the second stage they had skin eruptions that looked like "a hundred raspberries over the skin." Eruptions on the hands and feet made work difficult and walking painful. In the third stage, patients suffered bone deformities, liver tumors, and ulcers on the palate and nose that ate the entire nose away (McMillen 1939). The disease was frightening and five thousand people queued up in 1939 for injectable penicillin in the "yaws campaigns." Impressed by the dramatic cures, people have continued to believe that an injection is essential for any serious illness and is more efficacious than tablets.

A second factor that contributed to the importance of Western pharmaceuticals was their wide availability. The town market contained tables of chloroquine, aspirin, ampicillin, tetracycline, valium, ephedrine, and a large number of analgesics, antibiotics, and antihelminthics. Market tables in the larger cities of Makeni and Freetown contained an even wider selection of pharmaceuticals, including such prescription drugs as butazolidin, tandearil, tagamet, lasix, and vibramycin. Medication theft from government and private health facilities was described as "so widespread that it has rendered many medical facilities virtually impotent. Medications end up for sale on the street or in private drug stores and clinics of private practitioners" (Bledsoe and Goubaud 1985, 277). Pills and capsules were sold at market tables without containers or directions. Purchasers usually bought one or two tablets.

Troubled after reading the study by Bledsoe and Goubaud (1985), which concluded that people in the Mende tribe of Sierra Leone used Western pharmaceuticals inappropriately, I conducted a similar study in the Kamakwie area, which was predominantly populated by the Limba and Temne people. Having emphasized efficiency of distribution of drugs in the dispensary in the past, I now asked a different question: "How are people using the medicines that have been prescribed?" An elicitation device was made using a folder with thirty-two pharmaceuticals and traditional medicines affixed to it. Sixteen of the medicines were available in the town market and the remainder were from our dispensary. Fifty people, including patients, children, villagers, and even visitors, were asked which medicines they had seen before, what illness they were used for, and what quantities were appropriate. The purpose of the device was to stimulate discussion of customary drug use for various diseases. The findings were of great interest.

Virtually all informants recognized the red and yellow tetracycline capsule, an antibiotic. Most called it just "capsule" and agreed that it was to be put on sores or that one or two should be taken for "belly pain." Tetracycline had been in the markets for some time and was called "the old medicine," whereas the more recent ampicillin capsule was "the new medicine." Ilosone, the newest antibiotic, was described as the "most powerful." Antibiotic capsules such as keflex (green and white), chloramphenicol (white) and ilosone (orange and cream color) were assigned the same dosage and functions as the tetracycline capsules. Various informants commented that the yellow tablets (ambilhar for the disease schistosomiasis and the tranquilizer valium) were for "fever." This association probably originated with the use of yellow mepacrine tablets for the treatment of malaria. One informant identified a small orange chlorpromazine tablet, a tranquilizer, as "blood medicine," probably because of its color. Bledsoe and Goubaud's study had noted that red foods (palm oil, orange soft drinks, and dark Guiness Stout beer) as well as red medicines (vitamins, diuretics, and others) are believed to replace blood. In my inquiry, some "small" tablets, such as chlorpromazine and digoxin (a cardiac medication), were considered to be for "small" children, truly a dangerous misconception. Eleven respondents pointed to the small white digoxin tablet and called it "dry chook" (a "tablet injection"), mistakenly identifying it as the ephedrine tablets (a powerful stimulant) that are sold at many market tables. People take it when they are "tired from the farm," and it is considered effective "if you don't sleep all night." It may be used before going to an all-night dance. Two informants knew individuals who had died after taking several ephedrine tablets, not a surprising effect. The essential finding confirmed that of Bledsoe and Goubaud: people interpreted medicines consistently. However, the uses and dosages that they described were at variance with those intended by both the manufacturers and by the dispensers at the clinic. Further, people saved part of a prescription for a "next illness" or shared tablets with others who were ill. Western pharmaceuticals were being reinterpreted in light of local values related to size, color, efficacy, and purported success in treating an analogous illness.

I had assumed the role of learner in querying people about the medicines on the elicitation device. I knew that posture was successful when I overheard a respected Muslim leader tell another man, "Now explain the medicines to her, because she is trying to understand them." It did indeed give me pause to realize that our care and effort in procuring, transporting, storing, and dispensing these valuable medicines was hardly helpful if people used them incorrectly. The simple question of how people were using the medicines we dispensed had received a sobering answer (Hay 1987).

THE SPIRIT OF INQUIRY

These instances of inquiry into geophagy and pharmaceuticals demonstrated to me how significant data can be obtained simply by asking the right questions. Through this process I learned that efficiency questions that had occupied our thinking (How do we generate enough funds to cover drug purchases? What staffing needs will we have for the dispensary next year?), while necessary, were essentially the wrong place to start. There was much to be gained from asking questions of a different sort. Why are these people sick? What do they do when they are sick? Are the treatments they receive at our hospital and clinic effective? What can be done to promote good health? Christian health-care professionals working in medical missions need first to become listeners and learners, asking the right questions to understand how people's world views and perceptions shape their response to illness.

In the Bible, the book of James talks of the man "who looks at his face in the mirror" and then "goes away and immediately forgets what he looks like" (James 1:24). Too often in medical missions we have not even taken the time to look at our faces in the mirror. We're busy cutting down trees without asking whether we are in the right forest. Ethnography has its limitations. It does not study past events, nor is it suitable for large-scale or national issues. But observing, documenting our findings, and putting into print our analysis of issues we confront each day will lead us to a further collective understanding of the societies in which we serve. The great Jewish rabbis were not those with all the answers but rather the ones who asked the brilliant questions. Similarly, we need to ask the right sorts of questions about the work of medical missions. The answers we gain by cultivating a spirit of inquiry using basic ethnographic methods in everyday work will enhance our professional effectiveness, deepen the personal satisfaction that comes from partnerships based on respect, and suggest to us future directions for practice that are proactive and solution-oriented.

Works Cited

Bledsoe, C. H., and M. F. Goubaud. 1985. "The Reinterpretation of Western Pharmaceuticals Among the Mende of Sierra Leone." *Social Science and Medicine* 21(3), 275-82.

Ewert, D. M. 1990. *A New Agenda for Medical Missions*. Brunswick, Ga.: MAP International.

Freire, P. 1970. *Pedagogy of the Oppressed*. New York: Seabury.

Hammersley, M., and P. Atkinson. 1983. *Ethnography: Principles in Practice.* London: Tavistock Publications.

Hay, E. 1987. "Learning in a Mission Outpatient Dispensary in Sierra Leone: A Fieldwork Study." Michigan State University.

Hiebert, P. G. 1985. *Anthropological Insights for Missionaries.* Grand Rapids, Mich.: Baker

Hunter, John. 1984. "Insect Clay Geophagy in Sierra Leone." *Journal of Cultural Geography* 4(2), 2-13.

McMillen, S. I. 1939. "An Outpost in the War Upon Disease: The A.W.M. Hospital at Kamakwie, and Its Work." *Sierra Leone Studies* 21, 33-37.

Mission Training International, 05245 Centennial Boulevard Suite 202, Colorado Springs, CO 80919. Ph: (800)896-3710 or (719)594-0687 Fax: (719)594-4682

Werner, David. 1978. *Where There Is No Doctor.* Rep. Argentina, Mexico: The Hesperian Foundation.

Chapter Sixteen

Dialogue, Fix-it Pills, and Development

MURIEL AND DUANE ELMER

Participation has been a major discussion point in the field of international development during the last two decades, with dialogue widely recognized as a key ingredient. We've learned some lessons the hard way. The current focus on sustainability has laid bare the folly of "doing development" without participation.

While *participation* is the magic word for most internationalists, we must question the degree to which an unconscious, self-serving deception has muted its expression. Many of us still carry a "delivery system" mentality. We are task-driven. Our eyes still resolutely fix on results, programs, and systems, which receive slight cultural modifications because the local people "participated." Westerners need results, programs, and systems; external pressures reinforce these needs.

One pressure is the demands of donors (government and private), whose guidelines are full of terms like "indicators" and "outcomes." All must be carefully described before the first dollar is committed. It's a ticklish business, this "designing program with participants," when competition for dollars is so high. We teeter on a precarious tightrope, looking for balance between the donor's expectations and dollars on one hand, and authentic local participation on the other. Often we lean toward the dollars. Dialogue may be key to genuine participation, but donors rarely understand that dialogue takes time and may produce some outcomes that look very "foreign." But in the long term, dialogue will enhance local ownership and contribute to the sustainability of impact.

DIALOGUE IS KEY

As internationalists move into the twenty-first century, wisdom demands that we nurture dialogue in all programs. The skill of facilitating dialogue for participation is critical to the future of effective development. Although dialogue may be used to gather information, its real value lies in its capacity to empower people. In that sense it is not only a means to participation but an end in itself.

Gathering information cannot substitute for dialogue and participation. Assessment techniques, no matter how elegant, initiated by agency people who are still trapped in a delivery-system mentality contribute little to dialogue. Nowhere is this delivery-system mentality more evident than in the field of international health, in many places still dominated by the medical model. In the years ahead, donors, relief and development agencies and mission agencies will need to intentionally make dialogue a cornerstone of all they do—recruiting efforts, training, program design, program implementation, evaluations, and public and private discussion. Permanent changes in the behavior of missionaries and field workers demand that we be as skilled in dialoguing as we are in driving our vehicles.

All development requires change: a change in thinking, a change in habits, a change in lifestyle. Sustainable change starts within. For inner change to occur and endure, it must be nurtured through dialogue into a lifelong conviction. Reuel Howe defines dialogue as "a reciprocal relationship in which each party 'experiences the other side' so that their communication becomes a true address and response in which each informs and learns" (Howe 1963, 50). Dialogue permits people to speak of their world, dream of how to change that world, and do it with the feedback and understanding of the other party. This reciprocal "address and response" encourages people to think their thoughts aloud and to make the connections between realities and dreams, an activity that births behavior change.

Most field workers arrive at their first assignment after years of schooling—years that require a high level of skill in *getting* and *giving* information. We are all familiar with authors in the field who talk a great deal about the importance of dialogue, Paulo Freire being one of the classic contributors (Freire 1973a, 1973b). However, as a student of ours once said, "I've read a lot about Paulo Freire's concept of dialogue, I've heard a lot said in the classroom about it , but I've never seen anyone *do* Freire until you did it in this class." There are few models and few opportunities to experience dialogue within our university walls. Graduate seminars often consist of a series of individual monologues, mislabeled as discussion. Little attention is paid to that "address and response in which each informs and learns," as Howe defines it (Howe 1963, 50). Few know how to create or sustain good dialogue.

Yet, the evidence is in. As Daniel Fountain said, "Our propensity to pass out information is almost useless in bringing about real change" (Fountain 1990, 4). Still, international development workers look at the massive problems in Two-Thirds World communities and suffer acutely from what Reuel Howe has termed "agenda anxiety." We are so moved by the terrible conditions we find in the field that we can barely restrain ourselves from passing out "fix it" messages, like pills, the minute we step off the airplane. Telling becomes a gentle trap that enhances our self-esteem and satisfies our deep desire to help, while accomplishing little that lasts. Talk is cheap. Listening, the currency of dialogue, is much more expensive.

THE ANATOMY OF A DIALOGUE

Some skeptics among us today wonder if it is even possible to have authentic dialogue between people so different as a development field worker, who is an outsider, and the people, who are insiders. Questions like these are voiced by practitioners who understand very well the nature of dialogue and know the barriers in the field.

However, Ted Ward's oft-repeated proverb puts barriers in perspective: "Anything worth doing is worth doing poorly . . . the first time." Attempts at dialogue are so important that they are well worth the failures and lessons learned if we finally arrive at authentic dialogue. As we grow in our capacity to *do* dialogue, we find certain attitudes and skills combine to create those wonderful moments when we truly connect across our differences.

What attitudes contribute to true dialogue? People engaged in animated and creative discussion or dialogue tend to exhibit the following attitudes. Each treats the words of the other with considerable reverence and *respect*. This respect extends to their nonverbals, such as eye contact, posture, facial expressions of interest, and willingness to listen respectfully while the other speaks. Christians know that people are more than a mere conglomeration of atoms driven by chemical reactions. This basic respect grows out of the conviction that every human being, regardless of condition in life, carries within the image of God. That image lends an "alien dignity" (Luther) that demands they be treated with deep regard. That image also means there is something distinct, special, unique, and eternal about every individual or group of human beings. C. S. Lewis once wrote that in every human contact we are nudging each other either toward an eternal corruption or an everlasting splendor (Lewis 1949, 15). To say it differently, in every human contact we are either tearing down the image of God in that person or are building it.

Jesus himself treated the Samaritan woman at the well with deep respect by showing his acceptance of her regardless of the fact that she was an adulteress and had lost her way spiritually. Paul encourages us to follow Jesus' example in Romans 15:7 when he says, "Accept one another, then, just as Christ accepted you." Treating a person with respect builds a sense of safety into the relationship. Each perceives that he or she can approach the other without fear of being shamed or diminished in any way. Trust is enhanced, and the dialogue continues at deeper levels.

Respect springs from a sense of *humility*, the second attitude seen in good dialogue. A sober assessment of what the external agent or missionary brings or fails to bring to the development party often results in an acute sense of humility. In Romans 12:3 Paul reminds us to be humble and realistic. He warns his readers not to "think of yourselves more highly than you ought," but instead to "think of yourself with sober judgment."

Humility draws a field worker to sit figuratively, and perhaps often literally, at people's feet in order to learn from them. Unfortunately the humble learning posture, it would seem, has not been the earmark of the missionary or international worker. After building mutual trust with host-country people in various countries, we have asked them one question: "What could missionaries do to minister more effectively the gospel of Jesus Christ in your country?" Of the scores of responses, the most frequent is, "Missionaries could be more effective ministering the gospel of Jesus Christ if they did not think they were so superior to us." The lore in the field of international development is littered with stories of field workers who proudly implemented development schemes that died a quick death. There are stories of totally irrelevant Bible school courses crafted by missionaries without local input, peanut fields destroyed by worms because the agriculturalist chose not to listen to women's advice to plant during the early rather than later rains, and pristine latrines never used because they happened to face Mecca. In these cases, dialogue authentically done with humility would have avoided these "war stories" as well as the frequent charges of arrogance made against well-meaning outsiders.

Patience, in short supply in our assertive, time-oriented culture, is the third attitude that contributes to dialogue. Dialogue requires that each "hear the other out." Patience allows for protracted greeting protocols. Patience permits much of what seems to be "beating around the bush" in order to size up the other and feel safe in the relationship. Patience sits quietly during long periods of reflective silence. Patience waits, sometimes days, even months, before an invitation is made to share one's own perceptions. Patience celebrates the growing relationship even when it seems to compromise the task. Unfortunately, our "agenda anxiety" often crowds out patience. Our own agenda renders us deaf to perceptions that run contrary to our particular understanding of the truth. We discount the perceptions of others and rush to correct before listening to the whole story. In so doing, we slam the door on any further dialogue for a long time. In health development in particular, illness and death crank up our anxiety level, pressuring us to do something regardless of the costs in heightened dependency or threatened sustainability.

BASIC DIALOGICAL SKILLS

Besides the attitudes of respect, humility, and patience, dialogue demands certain skills. The first is the art of asking the right questions. The greatest challenge in productive dialogue is crafting good questions that promote discovery, or reflective thought that draws out the ideas and feelings of others. In *Listening for a Change*, Slim and Thompson (1995) describe the power of oral testimony. They suggest several types of questions that animate and guide the narrator: open questions, which give the narrator opportunity to expand; closed questions, to be used for clarification or eliciting essential information; leading questions, which can be used provocatively to draw out strong and/or contrary reactions; and precision questions, which elicit essential information.

We have found that varieties of questions crafted according to their content or purpose are also useful. Some questions seek information. The act of describing facts, happenings, and experiences help people name their world and, in so doing, see it more clearly. Other questions solicit opinions. Imbedded in the heart of an opinion lie beliefs, values, and concerns that carry inherent passion and feeling. Other questions seek to clarify meaning. This latter type, when employed consistently, guards against either party jumping to conclusions. Questions that pursue causes are critical "thinking bricks" used to change oppressive elements and build a life with more dignity, commonly called development. Freire claims that the less people are aware of causality, the lower their critical consciousness, or capacity to understand the realities of their world, an essential first step in devel-

opment. Finally, questions that explore contradictions create a disso-
nance that often expands people's thinking. These questions can be
counterproductive, however, if stated as a challenge. Care must be
taken to state them so as to explore the contradiction gently, often
from a personal perspective; for example, "Help me understand how
. . . " Varieties of questions create the "stuff" out of which dialogue is
built.

A second key skill in dialogue is the capacity to listen well and
respond appropriately. Listening requires a whole array of nonverbals
that convey interest. Eye contact, if appropriate in the culture, an
open posture that leans toward the speaker, paralanguage that signals you are tracking his or her words, and facial expressions that
respond to the content—all signal that the speaker is being heard.
Responses that clarify meaning and invite the narrator to be more
expansive also demonstrate good listening. On the other hand, evaluative responses, most frequently used by Westerners, tend to jeopardize free and open exchange. The capacity to withhold judgment
while tracking with people who are describing their reality, their
world view, and their actions will distinguish the master listener from
the rest of the pack.

Learning to use local proverbs and evocative images in the culture is a skill easily acquired during some happy leisure hours spent
with local people. Ask them to remember some of the sayings or
stories their mothers or other family members used with them as
children to teach them how to live. Proverbs, cultural stories, and
images that are part of the fabric of the culture elicit deep feelings
and encourage people to talk and describe their beliefs and values—
often far more productively than a question designed to do the same.
Finally, pictures, local songs, and stories that mirror the reality of
people's lives will often open up hours of productive dialogue.

We have occasionally used a story about a monkey that "rescued"
a fish from the water, resulting, of course, in the death of the fish.
This particular story with field workers in Bangladesh created an
animated dialogue with the central lesson being that when trying to
help people from our own frame of reference we may in fact end up
hurting them. For over a year those present at that gathering were
still echoing the caution, "Don't be like the monkey."

In this chapter we have tried to share some of the lessons we have
learned as we have tried to "do" dialogue. In so doing, we run the
risk of painting dialogue as just another technique available to the
field worker. Therefore, let us keep reminding ourselves that these
skills practiced without the underlying attitudes of respect, humility, and patience will quickly be perceived as manipulative. It is also
true that these attitudes and skills, while fitting comfortably into our

speech patterns, struggle for space in our behavior. Dialoguing is an art that takes a lifetime to refine.

Dialogue is also not the mere absence of "telling," although telling has been de-emphasized here. There are times when a field worker will need to tell. But in the spirit of true reciprocity, may that telling always be in answer to someone else's question. Reciprocity demands that the field worker remain transparent and honest when asked questions in return.

Consider the power of dialogue to facilitate authentic development. Entering into dialogue permits people to wrestle with their realities, to identify concerns, to search for solutions, and to grow in confidence. Slim and Thompson describe speaking up as an "act of power" where "people begin to voice their . . . experience, [and] can begin to understand it and to act on it" (Slim and Thompson 1995, 4) Entering into dialogue affords field workers opportunities to grow in understanding and admiration of the people among whom they work. Our little experience dialoguing with people in other cultures has created a deep sense of connectedness and level of disclosure by both parties. More work yet needs to be done in documenting lessons learned by people who practice dialogue for development and in identifying barriers to dialogue.

A DIALOGUE STILL IN PROCESS

Recently, working with World Relief, we experienced what we considered to be the beginning of an authentic dialogue in Mozambique. We had requested a meeting with the village leaders, older women, and traditional birth attendants to discuss the health of their women and children. We met in the shade of a big marula tree.

We began with one of their own Shangaan proverbs: It takes two thumbs to squash a louse. World Relief, however, we said, was limited in that it was only "one thumb." Alone, it could not squash the "louse" of disease and death in their community, although we were willing to work with them. It would take the work of a "second thumb," the community itself, to ultimately squash this terrible "louse" in their village.

We continued. We sought to explore if the World Relief "thumb" could cooperate with the village "thumb" to "kill a snake" that was troubling them. We understood how important it was to "see a snake and kill it before it bites you" (another of their proverbs). We could not build clinics or provide doctors. But we did have some experience preventing disease among mothers and small children in other countries. Was such a program something they would value in their village? Several spoke to the question. The deaths, especially among children, were high in their village. This was a year of severe drought. They would be grateful if World Relief would work with them in such a program.

We asked if they would talk with us about the major killing diseases for their little children and village mothers, and what they did about them. Since we were outsiders, there was much information we did not have. We needed to learn from them. Would they help us to understand this problem better?

We spent the bulk of that afternoon listening to one elderly woman after another teach us about the realities of illness and death in her village. We often responded with words of empathy as the stories were told. Sometimes we asked questions to explore more deeply what had been said. At one point we asked what pregnant women should or shouldn't eat. They said that there were "only two foods she must avoid, eggs and hot vegetables." We asked what would happen if a pregnant woman ate these foods. They told us that if she ate hot vegetables, the vegetables in the field would wither and die. We asked about cold vegetables. The women agreed that she could certainly eat the vegetables once the heat was gone. Also, "if she ate eggs, she would have difficulty in labor, holding back the birth of that baby. "Have you ever seen chicken about to lay an egg, how it clucks about the place and anxiously struts around, trying to keep from laying the egg? The same thing will happen to a mother in childbirth who ate eggs during her pregnancy."

Before the meeting, we, the outsiders, had agreed together not to "do any health teaching" that afternoon unless they asked directly for our opinion. They did not ask in that meeting. So, we kept our promise, for the most part, and swallowed hard to control our need to "educate." It was most difficult when one woman told us that a mother who becomes pregnant while still nursing her small child must stop breastfeeding immediately or the baby in her womb will be harmed. Most nodded their agreement. We knew that many young children die as a result of this sudden weaning. So we broke our promise not to "educate" only once that afternoon. Toward the end of the meeting our "agenda anxiety" overcame us. We made the observation that one of the health promoters had continued to breastfeed while she was pregnant and that the baby was born healthy and continued to thrive.

As these women talked of the killing diseases, they also spoke of how they coped with these problems. They brought us the leaves of the nkola tree, used as herbal medicine for diarrhea. They talked of malnutrition and malaria. They believed in breastfeeding and spacing births for at least two years and expressed sadness that they had lost the traditional practices that would allow a woman to avoid pregnancy for at least two years.

A rich dialogue emerged that left us full of wonder and respect for these women. Their wisdom shared that day gave us a marvelous window into their cultural beliefs and their understanding of health and disease. We were humbled by their resilience in face of very difficult circumstances and their willingness to be transparent with us.

The health program in that village is now underway. Both "thumbs" are working together. World Relief staff members are taking a more active role in the dialogue these days. There will be bumps ahead. Trust will need strengthening. But the dialogue continues. We have much yet to learn from these women.

This chapter could have been subtitled, "Dialogue for Mutual Development," because no one walks away from authentic dialogue unchanged. Anything less and we slip into the realm of becoming a benevolent oppressor.

Works Cited

Fountain, Daniel. 1990. *Christian Health and Healing into the Twenty-First Century*. Brunswick, Ga.: MAP.

Freire, Paulo. 1973a. *Pedagogy of the Oppressed*. New York: Seabury Press.

Freire, Paulo. 1973b. *Education for Critical Consciousness*. New York: Seabury Press.

Howe, Reuel. 1963. *The Miracle of Dialogue*. New York: Seabury Press.

Lewis, C. S. 1949. *The Weight of Glory and Other Addresses*. New York: Macmillan.

Slim, Hugo, and Paul Thompson. 1995. *Listening for a Change: Oral Testimony and Community Development*. Philadelphia: New Society Publishers.

SECTION V

CHURCH LEADERSHIP
AND RENEWAL

Church Leadership and Renewal

CATHERINE STONEHOUSE

Ted Ward has never been content with the status quo in the church. Energized by a vision of what the people of God could do to make a difference in the world, he has committed his life to the renewal of the church through investing in the education of emerging leaders. His investment continually earns dividends through the lives of former students who now serve God and the church through varied ministries. The authors of this section represent those of us who continue Ted's teaching ministry in institutions of higher education and in the local church.

Through his radically refreshing world view of faith-in-life to his equally challenging sound bites (who can forget his "Christian education is neither!"), Ted Ward has charged headlong into many a foray in hopes of salvaging valuable theological nuggets and educational truths. To his credit, the spoils of each raid survive today, in various forms; but, first and foremost, they remain through the people he has touched. That, in brief, is what makes Ted Ward a leader par excellence (Ron Habermas).

It was a scorching day in July when I stood outside the classroom and attempted to catch the eye of Dr. Ted Ward. Within a few moments, Ted and I were discussing my future plans for doctoral studies, and I was beginning to understand the importance of choosing a program by choosing a mentor. That day a dynamic relationship began that continues to nurture my personal and professional growth—in essence, a mentoring relationship.

While vigorously resisting all attempts of students to make him some kind of guru for Christian educators, ministers, and missionaries, Ted has given his life to transforming relationships. A pilgrim in the Way with his students, he has consistently kept many steps ahead of most of us, always encouraging us to venture into new territory for the Master and his people. It was Ted's modeling and teaching about nonformal education that sparked my interest in the mentoring model for development in pastoral ministry. His life and ministry continue to challenge me with the transformational power of mentoring relationships (Mari Gonlag).

As we honor Ted Ward, we remember his global perspective and the wisdom with which he skillfully integrates careful scientific inquiry with the eternal Word of God (Edward Seely).

We thank God for the legacy received from our mentor, Ted Ward. He challenged us to be both educators and theologians: to develop a sound educational philosophy in harmony with a well-developed theology. Together we engaged in this process at the steak house over lunch, wrestling with the findings of the social sciences and insights from Scripture. We experienced the value of a teacher who sat among us and led in interactive learning (Klaus Issler).

Ted respected the uniqueness of his students, their potential, and God's call on their lives. With wisdom he offered guidance that helped us discover the areas of study most pertinent to our gifts and vocation. Creatively he shaped even academic hurdles, such as comprehensive examinations, to serve our learning goals. Such experiences contributed powerfully to the formation of teachers and leaders.

Leadership, excellence in teaching, mentoring, working for change—the chapter topics in this section represent themes important to Ted Ward. He has lived these themes because he believes they are essential for the renewal of the church.

Chapter Seventeen

Producing Extraordinary Wine and Extraordinary Leaders

Ronald T. Habermas

Like the topic of good wine, talk of good leadership elicits controversy. In the last quarter century, the evangelical church has invested significant resources in the elusive study of leadership: What is it? How does sacred leadership favorably compare or contrast with secular leadership? What does a biblical leader look like? What is the meaning of servant leadership? How is such leadership developed and maintained? During these same twenty-five years, we have watched the demise of many Christian leaders, and our understanding of Christian leadership has expanded through experience with what it is not.

As we prepare for the next century, where should the church turn for guidance? No single resource ever captures the whole picture; however, certain critical elements of biblical leadership do emerge from Jesus' inaugural miracle in John 2:1-11. The essence of incarnational servanthood arises from this pristine account. Even though Jesus, at the wedding in Cana, had no intention of comparing good wine and good leadership, the careful reader of this Scripture will locate several intriguing qualities of leaders. Ten particular principles deserve attention.

1: Good leaders are not loners, but mix well with people.

Because Jesus was deity, because he was perfect, some believe he was a social isolate. Physically he was found among the crowd, these interpreters would say, yet psychologically he stood at arm's length from people. Some of these same thinkers claim that contemporary leaders should also stand somewhat aloof from their followers, with extremists cautioning against any close friendships with followers.

But John offers a different view. Jesus' mother, Jesus, and the disciples were all invited to a wedding at Cana (John 2:1-2). Without a doubt, these opening verses indicate that even early in his ministry, Christ was socially accepted. In this passage we see three aspects of this acceptance, viewed in concentric rings. First, in the inner circle, Christ came to the wedding along with his mother, indicating meaningful, nuclear family ties. Second, Jesus' association with his disciples revealed extended family connections. And third, the fact that he was part of this gala community affair demonstrates Jesus' broader social acceptance.

This first principle says much more than godly leaders "don't go it alone." Leaders must be friendly and likable, but not necessarily the most popular people. They need to relate well with many different types of people, being inclusive in thought and action. Such inclusive mindsets will be imperative for future leaders, given the increasing momentum of diversification and pluralistic agendas.

2: Good leaders are not celebrities, but celebrators.

The beauty of this first miracle is that the crowds did not seek Christ because of heavenly signs. Jesus was not invited because of his celebrity status as the "Miracle-worker" or as the "Son of God." He was recognized as a friend. How refreshing for him! We can assume that Jesus was not invited to the wedding just to say the invocation or to pronounce God's blessing on the new couple. And Jesus enjoyed himself. He spent a long time at the celebration—long enough for the wine to run out. He simply had fun.

When we translate this characteristic into contemporary life, two factors surface. On the negative side, good leaders must be very leery about seeking celebrity status; the temptation will always exist because some followers are more than eager to offer it. To restate, avoid prideful attitudes. Thankfully, I have witnessed few cases of prideful leaders, but I cringe each time I hear "leaders" awkwardly boast about their accomplishments, whether formal degrees achieved, books written, or souls saved.

On the positive side, celebration must never be equated with ungodliness. Jesus had fun at the Cana wedding, and he did not feel guilty about it. In fact, later in his life, Jesus would have entire banquets thrown in his honor. Why? The word was out: Jesus enjoyed people and he enjoyed a good party.

3: Good leaders are not subversive, but submissive.

One of the greatest temptations for godly leaders is "triangles": to create divisions between people by pitting one group against another and by joining the side that offers the greatest personal advantage. Some commentators assert that Jesus was staging a triangular relationship with his earthly mother at Cana by siding with his heavenly Father.

Yet Mary's first statement to Jesus, "They have no more wine" (John 2:3), indicated that she could count on Jesus. She could look to him in trouble. Recall that Jesus was the breadwinner of his family (based upon the tradition that says Joseph died in Jesus' early teen years). A precedent had been set. He had been proven trustworthy to Mary for many years. And since Jesus had not yet performed a miracle, his mother was not expecting a supernatural solution, as is sometimes suggested. To the contrary, because of previous domestic patterns, she anticipated the use of more conventional means. Thus, a healthy mother-son relationship is evident.

But some would push the "triangle" analogy, stating that Christ's response to Mary was confrontational, even condescending: "Dear woman, why do you involve me? . . . My time has not yet come" (v. 4). However, Christ was simply delineating his twofold obligation: first to his heavenly Father, then to his earthly mother. He did not contrast these lines of authority; he simply prioritized them.

In other words, the Son of God and son of Mary was submissive to both respective authorities. Recall that Jesus, at age twelve, had advanced the same response to both of his parents in the Temple. Here in John 2, notice Mary's affirming reply to Christ in her comment to the servants: "Do whatever he tells you" (v. 5). Implicit in Mary's command was her understanding that her son would, once again, faithfully comply with her initial request.

Contemporary leaders must likewise balance the dynamic tension between family and vocational responsibilities. They must not settle for an either-or mindset. This tension reminds all believers of the daily paradoxical struggle between the "now and the not yet."

4: Good leaders are not wasteful, but resourceful.

The Lord made sure that a half dozen twenty- to thirty-gallon jars were filled with water (vv. 6-7). The start of this initial miracle was a large-scale divine act, yet by other indicators, only the necessary amount was produced. Jesus was far ahead of his time, promoting ecologically sound behavior.

Consider, for instance, another miracle pertaining to food: John's later-recorded feeding of the five thousand. What a profound combination of generosity and mercy! Yet hidden away is a much-over-looked conclusion: Jesus commanded his followers to "gather the pieces that are left over." Why? Why bother with the scraps? The Lord's rationale was simple: "Let nothing be wasted" (John 6:12).

Godly leaders of the future virtually will have no option but to be sensitive to desperate world conditions. They must model this virtue, for depleted and polluted resources will continually affect our world and our ministry.

5: Good leaders do not do it all themselves, but involve others.

Note that Jesus chose to involve the servants in this initial miracle, asking them to fill the jars and draw out the water turned to wine. Within this context, Jesus demonstrated his educational philosophy: he valued risky, experiential instruction. He valued participatory learning. And these personal convictions were neither random nor inconsistent. Consider other examples that required participant response throughout Christ's life:

- miracles of healing (Luke 5:24; 17:11-19)
- miracles of feeding (Mark 8:7-8)
- routine instruction (Luke 20:23; John 13:6-11; Matt. 26:41)
- commissioning of his followers (Matt. 10:1-42; Luke 10:1-24).

This participatory leadership contrasts with the world's "lording-it-over" model and calls current Christian supervisors to find ways of actually involving those under their care. What evidences of real-life, risky, participatory leadership can be identified in the church? Where are the true servant-leader stories?

Ted Ward's philosophy of Christian education was simply, yet vividly, displayed on the fifth floor of Erickson Hall at Michigan State University. Immediately to the right of the double doors that eventually led to Ted's office was a large shoe box, labeled "Amigos." Within this meager cardboard container lay a wealth of stimulating entries: from personal letters of former students to provocative magazine articles, from brief memos of advice from Ted to commendable samples of current student assignments. The entire box offered an assortment with a singular purpose: it invited all to join, as friends, in the cooperative venture of lifelong learning.

It was through "Amigos" that I first became acquainted with Robert Ferris. Initially, this name was just like any other unknown name, handwritten across the top of a brief treatise on the subject of theological renewal. "Such bold thoughts!" was my first impression. Later, Bob would become one of my best friends. That was Ted's way: to introduce potential colleagues through collaborative processes. No elitism, just a standing invitation to participate.

6: Good leaders do not occupy center stage, but are found behind the scenes.

This wedding miracle was quite unpretentious. In fact, it is difficult to imagine a more humble start to public ministry, utilizing supernatural powers for a seemingly mundane purpose. And the miracle was performed in the presence of lowly servants. In some cases, Jesus commanded those who were healed to remain silent concerning his identity (see Mark 1:29-34, 3:7-12) or his actions (see Luke 5:12-14; 8:51-56). Standing in the spotlight was not Jesus' idea of success.

One contemporary notion of Christian leadership takes just the opposite position. It encourages followers to spread the news about their leaders to their friends. Such leaders seek—even solicit—popularity. But godly leaders do not emerge by trumpeting their own fanfare. They do not become true leaders by announcing their candidate status. Others put them there.

7: Good leaders do not seek rewards, for they are satisfied with a job well done.

At first, only the servants knew the source of this inaugural miracle, and they did not possess the material resources to reward Christ. They were economically and politically powerless. But Jesus was not in ministry for rewards. In fact, he called his disciples to follow his lead by being advocates for the poor. In Paul's farewell address to the Ephesian elders at Miletus (see Acts 20:17-38), the Apostle cited one of the few direct quotations of Jesus outside the gospels (perhaps based upon his Damascus Road encounter). "In everything I did," Paul reflects, "I showed you that by this kind of hard work we must help the weak, remembering the words the Lord Jesus himself said: 'It is more blessed to give than to receive'" (v. 35). Note that this rare citation focuses upon the call of advocacy for the poor versus self-enhancement.

As he closed his account of the first miracle, John stated: "This, the first of his miraculous signs, Jesus performed in Cana of Galilee. He thus revealed his glory, and his disciples put their faith in him" (John 2:11). God was glorified and the twelve began to believe; those were the results of the miracle that really mattered. Jesus was not seeking acclaim or material reward. When God was glorified, and people began to take steps toward faith, he could be satisfied with a job well done.

8: Good leaders provide first-rate service, not second-best.

Who are you when nobody's looking? This eighth principle centers on the often-discussed (yet less-expressed) virtue of integrity.

At the wedding, Jesus commanded the servants to fill the six large jars to the brim (John 2:7, Living Bible). The Lord was there to do all that he could. Jesus' miracle likewise exhibited first-rate quality. The steward at the wedding said: "You have saved the best wine till now" (v. 10). What a compliment! The Lord never settled for second best.

9: Good leaders do not concentrate on the superficial, but on the significant, human needs.

Have you ever asked, "Why did Jesus begin with this particular miracle at Cana?" I have often thought that if I had the chance to rearrange Jesus' itinerary, I would have him initiate his ministry with "all the bells and whistles," in an event such as raising Lazarus from the dead.

Why would he commence with such a relatively rudimentary act? There are at least two reasons. First, this miracle kept a wedding party from social disgrace. To not have wine at a wedding in those days was like not having a wedding cake today. People were so important to Jesus that he just wanted to lend a hand. He wanted to get a young couple off with a good start. And he did. Years later, the community would still be talking about this festivity. Second, the more comprehensive answer pertains to Christ's broader view of the nature of people. In contrast to many Christian leaders today, the Lord never distinguished between so-called spiritual needs and all other types of human requirements. No need was too small or too large for Jesus; he just did not view people that way.

Good leaders do not compartmentalize people; they picture them as holistic images of their Creator. Godly leaders do not spend a lot of time rank ordering human necessities; they roll up their sleeves and serve. Both the church and the world are looking for that kind of leader in this next generation.

10: Good leaders are not limited by myopia, but see the bigger picture of their calling.

Again, John 2:11b states, "He thus revealed his glory, and his disciples put their faith in him." Most of Christ's followers, in the course of time, trusted him for more than just his miracles. We are not sure how long it took, but they eventually claimed him as their personal Savior. Christ needed to see the trees and the forest; the immediate means, but also the ultimate ends of his earthly work.

Godly leaders can do no less. They must endlessly perform the seemingly mundane tasks of ministry, tasks that usually go unnoticed. But, at the same time, they must maintain their long-term goals of leading people to Christ and helping them grow into Christlikeness. It is not an easy tension to live with, but that is the essence of the believer's life: the paradox of the here and now—and the hereafter.

CONCLUSION

The first class I took from Ted Ward was a graduate course at Wheaton College in the summer of 1981. Ted's instruction one morning came from Matthew 25:31-46, the story of the sheep and the goats. His devotional combined several themes that, to this day, I regularly reflect upon: the value of comprehensive views of truth; empathy for the human condition; the need to view people holistically (not just as "souls"); and a desire to communicate this complete message as the gospel. I left that course wanting to be just like Dr. Ward, not just in his message but in his method; not simply using the same passage, but exhibiting his all-consuming passion.

Many experiences and reflections later, I realized that it all comes down to this: Godly leaders are not born; nor are they "made" in the sense of some cloning how to procedure. Whereas they each adhere to basic principles, godly leaders are individually sculpted by God. Mature, God-energized mentors influence them powerfully; however, they are customized by the Creator for ministry to their generation. They are fashioned through the faithful servant-leader's emulation of the Son. And, like good wine, they are typically controversial.

*Chapter Eighteen*_____

Relationships that Transform

Mentoring and Pastoral Ministry

MARI GONLAG

_____

THE CHANGING FACE OF PASTORAL MINISTRY

Pastoral ministry has long been the bastion of the great traditions of the church—solid, unshakable, sacred. For many years, one could assume the pastor beginning his or her ministry was a relatively mature Christian, raised in a Christian home, and experienced in the life of the church. The pastor was both a disciple and a discipler, a model of wholeness who would guide the flock to spiritual maturity, as well as to physical, emotional, and social wholeness.

Even a relatively brief encounter with new pastors today demonstrates that in many cases those assumptions are no longer valid. More and more pastors now come to the ministry with weighty, unresolved personal issues and significantly less experience in local church life and ministry. For many pastors, the beginning years of ministry are a time of establishing and deepening spiritual foundations and of exploring the life of the church for the very first time. God is raising up a whole new host of servants and messengers of the Word, but the changes mean that old models of equipping for ministry need to be reevaluated.

Once a generalist in the care of souls, the pastor is now expected to be the specialist, not only in biblical studies and theology, but in the areas of Christian education, evangelism, preaching, counseling, administration, and a host of other related fields. Overwhelmed by the demands of these expectations for ministry, new pastors desperately need supportive relationships to help them become established in the pastoral role.

MINISTERIAL EDUCATION:
LIMITATIONS AND POSSIBILITIES

By its very nature, ministry is both *taught* and *caught*. The church has done a credible job of the formal task of educating for ministry. Formal education, however, has its limits. Can the classroom setting truly nurture a burden for the lost, a heart for ministry to people, or a passion for the preaching of the Word? Admittedly, the Lord sometimes breaks into a formal class in an awesome way, but, more often than not, transforming moments come in the context of *doing* ministry. They take place at the bedside of a dying saint, in worship experiences of celebrating the sacraments, and in the moments when the divine Presence speaks through the preacher of the Word.

The development of a pastor requires more than the mastery of certain knowledge, abilities, and skills. Ministry is a matter of the heart, as well as of the hands and the head. It is inextricably connected to the pastor as person. The functions of ministry flow out of who we are as followers of Christ. Thus, ministerial development is an intimate, personal process of discipleship that demands the context of personal ministry for its full fruition.

Based upon a relationship, the mentoring model has much to offer in pastoral equipping since it provides for both personal and professional development. It brings together the nurturing of the pastor's own spirituality and discipleship (which are the foundation of ministry) and the development of professional skills and abilities for effective ministry. Mentoring creates an atmosphere of nurture in which beginning pastors see ministry modeled before them and find the creative space and guidance to develop their own lives and ministries.

MENTORING DEFINED

Mentoring has been defined in a variety of ways. Perhaps the most comprehensive yet focused definition comes from educator Eugene Anderson. He defines mentoring as "a nurturing process in which a more skilled or more experienced person, serving as a role model, teaches, sponsors, encourages, counsels, and befriends a less skilled or less experienced person for the purpose of promoting the latter's professional and/or personal development" (Anderson 1987).

Though this definition arises from a secular literature base, careful consideration reveals distinctively Christian concepts. First, the process described is one of nurture, a concept that is integral to a biblical understanding of the development of persons. Second, the roles of the mentor described in this definition—role model, nurturer, and care-giver—are all roles exhibited and endorsed by our Lord, as well as other leaders of the New Testament church. Finally, the context of mentoring is the arena of personal relationships. Both in word and deed, the ministry of Jesus was an intimately personal one. Thus, the development of individuals in the context of personal, caring relationships provides a model with theological integrity.

What, then, is *pastoral* mentoring? It is a relationship in which a more experienced pastor serves as a role model, nurturer, and care-giver for a less experienced pastor, generally one at the beginning of his or her ministry. The more experienced pastor (mentor) seeks to assist the less experienced pastor (protégé or protégée) in matters of personal and professional development, especially as they relate to the pastoral role.

BIBLICAL ILLUSTRATIONS OF MENTORING

Biblical illustrations of this kind of formative and transformative relationship are numerous. The central illustration is that of our Lord himself. Gathering around himself the twelve disciples, for three years he poured his life into those who would be entrusted with the ministry of the gospel. By example, nurture, and care, he sought to develop within the disciples the kind of relationship with the Father and the skills and abilities that would equip them for their monumental task.

Old Testament models such as Moses and Joshua (Exod. 17; Deut. 31), Elijah and Elisha (1 Kings 19), and Eli and Samuel (1 Sam. 3) illustrate vividly the power of the role model in preparing others for tasks of leadership and ministry. Noteworthy in each of these cases is the fact that, while the ministries of the mentors were significant, the ministries of the protégés were broader and in some senses more distinguished than their mentors. One mark of a great mentor is to allow the protégé to develop beyond the mentor's own limitations.

After our Lord, the most prominent New Testament mentor is the apostle Paul. Perhaps the most obvious mentoring relationship is that between Paul and Timothy. Paul's letters to Timothy provide a variety of fatherly advice and encouragement, from spiritual counsel to instructions concerning church leadership, relationships, money, doctrine, health, and family. Clearly a deep and trusting relationship provided the basis for the kind of counsel and encouragement revealed in these letters.

OBJECTIVES OF A PASTORAL MENTORING RELATIONSHIP

The purpose of the mentoring relationship is to enhance the development of the qualities and abilities necessary for effective pastoral ministry. This relationship is especially beneficial during the early ministry years when patterns for a lifetime of ministry are established. But if the relationship is to be beneficial, clear objectives must guide both the mentor and the protégée. In *The Pastoral Mentor*, C. David Jones outlines objectives for mentoring among seminary students (Jones 1980, 74-75). From his work we can identify the following domains as objectives for ministry development in a productive pastoral mentoring relationship.

Philosophy of Ministry

Intentional and focused ministry requires an understanding of one's philosophy of ministry. A philosophy of ministry revolves around two key issues: one's view of humanity, and one's understanding of the nature of the church. Nurturing a new pastor's philosophy of ministry is an essential component of the mentoring relationship.

Interpersonal Skills

The cultivation of interpersonal relationship skills is one of the greatest needs among new pastors, especially among young men and women who have just finished the formal education process. As has already been noted, unprecedented levels of destructive and broken relationships plague today's social structures. Few individuals seem to escape uninjured from these relational battles, and many of the scars are seen in those entering the ministry.

One of the most helpful antidotes for this dilemma is found in the modeling aspect of the mentoring relationship. Mentors should be persons of significant wholeness and maturity, and protégées need to spend time in observing how mentors interact with people. The mentoring relationship itself needs to be a model of a healthy interpersonal relationship.

The mentor should seek to cultivate the skills of the protégé in one-on-one, small-group and large-group relationships. All of these skills are crucial for effective pastoral ministry, and all must be the object of intentional development within the mentoring relationship.

Ministry Skills

While interpersonal skills are certainly a part of *ministry skills*, the term ministry skill refers here to the functional skills for the specific duties of pastoral ministry. Ministry skill categories might include preaching, teaching, worship, leadership, administration, counseling, visitation, and other specific categories, some of which may vary with the pastor's church appointment.

Personal and Professional Accountability

The mentoring model, with its emphasis on the relational aspect, is uniquely suited to foster accountability in a positive manner. As with Wesley's class meetings, the nurturing, caring nature of the relationship provides an environment in which such accountability can be expected and can be used to challenge and foster growth.

Accountability in the mentoring relationship should focus on both personal and professional dimensions. Personal accountability might involve such areas as the practice of spiritual disciplines, the management of personal time and finances, and the development of family relationships. Professional accountability issues could include time management, goal-setting, planning, and decision-making. This dimension of the mentoring relationship is perhaps the most essential one because it has the potential for eliminating the risk of unbiblical "Lone Ranger" models of ministry, which too often have led to ineffectiveness, stagnation, and moral collapse.

THE ROLE AND FUNCTION OF MENTORS

The role and function of mentors vary considerably with the arena of the mentoring relationship. A useful model for mentoring in pastoral ministry is that proposed by Anderson and Shannon for the educational community (Anderson and Shannon 1988, 40-41). They define the mentor's role in three dimensions. The mentor is, first, a role model to the protégé, something that a new pastor desperately needs to aid in the development of his identity as a pastor. Second, the mentor serves as a nurturer, seeking to help the protégé develop as a person and a professional. Finally, the mentor is a care-giver. The value of this role is that of being a pastor to pastors. The many difficulties and defeats that new pastors encounter in their early years of ministry often threaten their persistence in ministry unless they have a pastor to care for them and offer support and encouragement. The care-giving role provides just such support.

The functions of mentoring defined by the model of Anderson and Shannon also fit well into a program for mentoring in pastoral ministry. As a teacher, the mentor models both the personal and the professional aspects of ministry. He or she seeks to inform the protégée with increased knowledge, to confirm or correct understandings and ideas, to prescribe possible courses of action, and to question her thoughts, attitudes, and actions in such a way as to lead her to new discoveries.

In the sponsoring function, the mentor protects and supports the protégé. The mentor seeks to promote the new pastor within the ministry in which God has placed him.

Functioning as an encourager, the mentor becomes a cheerleader, affirming and inspiring the protégée to further development. This function also demands that the mentor sees latent potential and challenges the protégée to become all that she can be, often in ways which are beyond the protégée's own expectations.

The counseling function requires that the mentor listen to the protégé, probe his thoughts and feelings, help the protégé to clarify issues, and advise the protégé both in terms of personal and professional matters.

Befriending, the final mentoring function in this model, involves accepting the protégée and relating to her in a positive manner. While Anderson and Shannon see this aspect as a function, it might be classified more appropriately as the nature of the relationship in which all other functions occur. In order to teach, encourage, sponsor, and counsel, one must operate in the context of real friendship.

CONCLUSION

The mentoring model offers a creative approach to continuing pastoral education designed to aid in the development of the whole person, while at the same time advancing the competency of pastors in their ministerial roles. While not a panacea for all of the inadequacies of ministerial education or the lack of competency among new pastors, the mentoring model proposes a strategy with both educational and theological integrity. Indeed, the apostle Paul recognized the power of the mentoring relationship and the multiplication of that power through the developing protégé. His instructions to young Timothy reveal the heart of a mentor encouraging and directing his protégé. They commend the mentoring relationship as one with the power to transform the young and the inexperienced into godly leaders for the future of the church.

> Command and teach these things. Don't let anyone look down on you because you are young, but set an example for the believers in speech, in life, in love, in faith, and in purity. Until I come, devote yourself to the public reading of Scripture, to preaching and to teaching. Do not neglect your gift, which was given you through a prophetic message when the body of elders laid their hands on you.
>
> Be diligent in these matters; give yourself wholly to them, so that everyone may see your progress. Watch your life and doctrine closely. Persevere in them, because if you do, you will save both yourself and your hearers (1 Tim. 4:11-16).

Works Cited

Anderson, Eugene. 1987. "Definitions of Mentoring." Cited in Anderson and Shannon 1988: 38-42.

Anderson, Eugene M., and Anne L. Shannon. 1988. "Toward a Conception of Mentoring." *Journal of Teacher Education* 39 (January/February): 38-42.

Jones, C. David. 1980. *The Pastoral Mentor*. Richmond, Va.: Skipworth Press.

For Further Reading

Bova, Breda Murphy, and Rebecca R. Phillips. 1984. "Mentoring as a Learning Experience for Adults." *Journal of Teacher Education* 35 (May/June): 16-20.

Coughlin, Robert. 1986. "Master Teacher/Mentor Teacher: Approaches to Educational Excellence." *Thrust for Educational Leadership* 15 (February/March): 41-43.

Daloz, Laurent A. 1983. "Mentors: Teachers Who Make a Difference." *Change* 15 (September): 24-27.

Galvez-Hjornevik, Cleta. 1986. "Mentoring Among Teachers: A Review of the Literature." *Journal of Teacher Education* 37 (January/February): 6-11.

Merriman. S. 1983. "Mentors and Protégés: A Critical Review of the Literature." *Adult Education Quarterly* 33 (3): 161-73.

Phillips-Jones, L. 1983. "Establishing a Formalized Mentoring Program." *Training and Development Journal* 37 (2): 38-42.

Zey, M. G. 1984. *The Mentor Connection*. Homewood, Ill.: Dow Jones-Irwin.

Chapter Nineteen

Habits of
the Excellent Teacher

KLAUS ISSLER

How do we best improve our teaching as we approach the twenty-first century? To be sure, exciting educational resources will continue to emerge from the overflow of our technological advances—there will be no lack here. But will an exclusive focus on method or curriculum innovation yield the most important learning dividends? Scripture seems to direct our attention elsewhere, to foundational issues relevant for teachers whether living in the first century or the twenty-first century. "A student is not above his teacher; but everyone who is fully trained will be *like his teacher*" (Luke 6:40). It is the *character* of the teacher that will largely influence what kind of student outcomes we can expect.

In Luke 6:39-49, Jesus warned his disciples not to follow the Pharisees, the blind who led their followers into a pit (v. 39). Instead, Jesus inferred that if they learned of him, they would be like him when they were fully trained. Then, in verse 45, our Lord pointed to the inward source of outward conduct, "The good man brings good things out of the good stored up in his heart, and the evil man brings evil things out of the evil stored up in his heart. For out of the overflow of his heart his mouth speaks."

This chapter places the spotlight on a crucial element in our pursuit of educational excellence: to help teachers become better persons so that out of their being, relating, and doing in the practice of teaching, the lives of students will be affected.

CHARACTER AND EXCELLENCE

Excellence, what is it? We usually expect excellent teachers to meet high standards worthy of our praise.[1] Such standards involve ongoing innovation, new insight, and creativity. Second, the excellent teacher is one who typically goes beyond the call of the routine, expending extra effort to do what is best for students. These two factors of reaching for higher standards and regularly going beyond the routine are matters of the heart, not just the head, of character, not just technique. Teaching involves more than performing educational skills; it involves a life influencing a life.

Some may wish to equate "effective teacher" with "excellent teacher." The concept of effective teacher draws our focus to means-end concerns, the consequences of teaching as evidenced in student outcomes. These indicators are largely identified with short-term outcomes within the scope of a unit, a semester, or a year of study. But by such a limited criterion, Jesus must be regarded as an ineffective teacher during his earthly ministry.[2] The Gospel writers seem to go out of their way to underscore how slow the disciples were to learn (for example, Mark 8:14-21, 31-33; Luke 22:24-27; John 14:8-9). So, when we think about the excellent teacher, we must use a broader set of criteria and include both short-term and long-term effects.

In addition, the term *effective* seems to be associated primarily with what can be validated exclusively through empirical research. But there are other sources of knowledge from which we can glean truths about excellent teachers and teaching (for example, the Bible or our conceptual analysis of the topic). Effectiveness contributes to excellence, but there is more to excellence that effectiveness research cannot tell us.[3]

A MODEL OF HUMAN FLOURISHING

To elaborate the concept of excellent teaching which involves the life of the teacher, we must first know what kind of human functioning or flourishing is possible; that is, we must articulate a view of human nature. Ronald Habermas and I have proposed a "4-C" model of Christian maturity (Issler and Habermas 1994, 173), which I will use here to mark out general arenas of human flourishing (see Figure 1 below). At the core of the model is God, the source of all life and the focus of our lives. When we are rightly related to God (communion), we open the door to all the potentialities of human flourishing. Our nature equips us to grow in our being (character), in our relating

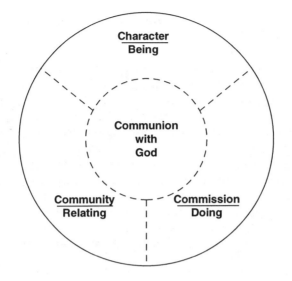

Figure 1: 4-C Model of Chirstian Maturity

with others (community), and in our doing (commission). As we grow in all four components, we live a balanced life as God intended. Applying the outer components of the model specifically to teachers, we arrive at these important focal points:

Being: The Teacher as Student

Relating: The Teacher as Friend

Doing: The Teacher as Skilled Artisan

The purpose of this chapter is to suggest certain habits or dispositions within each of these arenas that undergird the teaching ministry. Space permits only a brief survey and two illustrative metaphors for each general category, with the hope that readers will expand the list as a follow-up exercise.[4] An excellent teacher is one who increasingly embodies the dispositions discussed here, exemplifying high standards and regularly going beyond the routine.

BEING: THE TEACHER AS STUDENT[5]

Truth or subject matter is an essential ingredient in teaching. We forfeit our right to teach if we ever stop being lifelong learners ourselves.

The Teacher as Expert in Process

A traditional role for the teacher is to be a subject-matter specialist, and I want to affirm this element as foundational. Without some degree of expertise, we cannot claim to be teachers. Even the small-group leader moderating a discussion must (or should) know how to facilitate the interaction. Having such expertise does not always lead to authoritarian arrogance. In fact, a genuine humility should settle on our spirit, since the more we come to know, the more we recognize how much we do not know.

One of the best ways to increase our knowledge is by reading—one of those "glory of the grind" habits. Our study and meditation in Scripture must take first place. Jesus freely quoted the Old Testament in his teaching ministry (for example, Matt. 5, 11, 15). He even chided the religious teachers for their biblical illiteracy (Matt. 22:29). Would our Lord charge us with the same crime? The best kind of reading program consists of both fiction and non-fiction writings and includes the classics, which have stood the test of time, as well as the best contemporary offerings. Teachers must be readers.[6]

The Teacher as Critical Thinker

Bloom et al. (1956) developed a taxonomy of the cognitive domain proposing that our knowledge of something can range anywhere from a simple awareness to much higher levels of synthesis, and evaluation. To lead our students into the higher levels of critical thinking, we must engage in analysis, synthesis and evaluation ourselves. Much of the shock-therapy teaching our Lord used stemmed from a desire to critique the prevailing assumptions of his day (for example, Luke 14:26, the family is ultimate; Matt. 19:23-24, wealth is a sign of God's favor).

But let us be honest; worthy reading and good thinking are hard work. What compels us to these tasks? After I settled into my teaching routine (first as a church staff member, and now as a professor), my teaching has been kept alive by the questions about the Christian life that will not let me go. One way to enter into the discipline of wrestling with issues is to frame the basic question(s) that our class or lesson answers. This simple practice can make our teaching more focused, and it can open up new ways to respond to such probing. Questions that perplex us can launch us into further reading and study. Asking good questions is at the core of being a good student (cf. Luke 2:46).[7]

RELATING: THE TEACHER AS A FRIEND

The teachers who influenced us the most were typically the ones who showed extra concern for us. The student-teacher relationship is a significant catalyst for educators, greatly increasing the potential for learning. Yet the particular dispositions listed below may be the most difficult to pursue.

The Teacher as Mentor

One of the best gifts a teacher can offer a student is to provide discerning, evaluative comments regarding how well he or she is learning. Students do not need a teacher who just dispenses information; they can turn to books or audio tapes for that. What is really needed is someone to supervise the learning process, to guide students into taking the next step. Timely correction offers assistance and direction for improvement. Genuine affirmation encourages continuing student effort to learn.

Jesus' most explicit words on servanthood came as a censure to the disciples' inner rivalry about who was the greatest (Matt. 20:25-28; Luke 22:25-27). But he also affirmed them. As he concluded the first phase of disciple training, our Lord popped the critical exam question, "Who do you say I am?" (Matt. 16:15). Peter, speaking for the twelve, boldly acknowledged his deity, and Jesus affirms Peter with praise (16:17-19).

I think most teachers agree that the evaluation and grading task is the most difficult one. Yet we cannot shirk this important duty. As students indicate their level of understanding in the questions asked and comments made or in the assignments submitted, we can provide the evaluative feedback they desire. I have learned that I need a clear standard of excellence to guide me in the act of evaluation. As we commit ourselves to this important practice, we give our students what few are able or willing to offer: pertinent and personal reflections on their pilgrimage.

The Teacher as Colleague

Even though we may be experts and mentors, our theology reminds us that we are fellow-learners in the grace of life. The humble posture of fellow-learner invites our students to come to us freely and without fear. Are students willing to risk sharing their ignorance by asking questions or by expressing new thoughts? How much effort do we expend to identify with our students, to look at the issue from their point of view? Since Jesus, our very God, took on human form to identify with us, we have an example to follow.

But how can we grow in humility? How do we come to empathize with our students' life situations? If we take the lead from our Lord's incarnational ministry, we glean at least two guidelines. First, we realize that no task is too menial; nothing is beneath our dignity. Remember how Jesus washed the disciples dirty feet? So let us help clean up after class, or receive a student's criticism without defensiveness. Until it comes naturally, we may need to look for menial tasks to do—not for show, of course, but as a school for learning humility. Second, we can be with our students in a non-teacher capacity, where we relate as two members of the family of God. Since we may have to break through cultural perceptions of the teacher-student roles, we probably should take the initiative here.

DOING: THE TEACHER AS SKILLED ARTISAN

The excellent teacher, in wisdom and mastery, creatively crafts the teaching experience as an extension of his or her personality, passion, and teaching abilities.

The Teacher as Doctor

Out of the "black bag" repertoire of instructional strategies, knowledge, and life experience, the teacher is able to diagnose and prescribe the best remedy at the time to meet student needs. Jesus was a master at this, constantly prepared for the "teachable moment." It seemed he always had a story or a pithy saying on hand. The classic parable of the Good Samaritan was in response to the question, "And who is my neighbor?" (Luke 10: 29). When James and John requested the best seats near Jesus in the kingdom (Mark 10:37), he offered a different model of leadership—to serve others.

To be ready for such moments, we need to have a clear idea of our overall plan for student learning—not just the bite-size piece that is up for the next session. With that larger framework in mind, we can easily use any relevant opportunity, whether or not it fits exactly into today's lesson plan (cf. Mark 8: 14-21). Out of the reading and study program we have carved out for ourselves will flow needed wisdom.

Events that stimulate a teachable moment may not always happen in class, but we can bring them to class by referring to cultural practices and recent events that affect class topics. To be alert for such items, we need to be aware of our culture, to become sensitive to what is happening, both locally and around the world. We could set a goal of finding at least one such item each week until it becomes a regular habit. Thus, we make all of life our classroom, and all of our own life experiences become grist for the teaching mill.

The Teacher as Partner

This final disposition may seem a bit strange, but we must ask two fundamental questions: What right do we have to teach, to attempt to bring about changes in another? In bringing about any changes, who determines toward what ultimate ends we strive in our teaching? If there is no God, then everyone is king and anyone has that authority. But if there is a God, then only God has ultimate authority.

As Jesus was appointed for his ministry on this earth, so we have been appointed for ours (John 17:8; Matt. 28:18-20). That is our ultimate authority; it does not come from a local church, an educational institution, or the state.

Yet we do stand under various degrees of delegated authority, and we are called to a spirit of cooperation and coordination with these partners. There is no room for "Lone Rangers" or prima donnas. We must hold hands and work together to accomplish the task. We stand on the shoulders of our forebears, who have taught us and given us the insights we use. And we stand side-by-side with fellow teachers who share this grand project.

An honest recognition of our ultimate commission and our necessary partnership can nurture a posture of humility before our students. Since we are not God's sole gift to humanity, we can urge our students to take classes from other teachers to round out their education. We may wish to invite fellow teachers to share their expertise in our classroom, so students are not hindered by our own foibles and whims. We pursue the best for our students by not claiming exclusive rights to them. They will rise up to new heights through the labors of many human teachers, not just one.[8]

A century ago, American public educators were required to have "exhibited testimonials of Good Moral Character"[9] as an essential qualification. Currently, certification is based primarily on one's level of subject mastery and skillful technique. We who, with kingdom priorities, lead teachers into the twenty-first century must be concerned about more than mastery and techniques. We should keep our standards high, for "everyone who is fully trained will be like his teacher" (Luke 6:40).

Notes

1. For a more nuanced and detailed discussion of praiseworthy actions, see Swinburne 1989, chap. 2 ("Moral Responsibility and Weakness of Will").

2. "Jesus was an accomplished yet ineffective teacher. He taught well, even masterfully in respects, yet the learning that came about did not correspond to the quality of the teacher" (Dillon 1995, 161).

3. Research related to short-term learning outcomes can help us improve our teaching for certain kinds of effects, such as cognitive outcomes. Yet consideration of a longer scope is necessary for assessing teaching for dispositional and attitude formation.

4. I validated each factor by looking at the teaching ministry of Jesus, a recognized excellent teacher. And I believe Ted Ward exemplifies each of these factors in his teaching practice. See Habermas and Issler (1992), chapters 9-10, for an analysis of the concept of teaching, and Issler (1983) for another approach to a discussion of excellence in teaching.

5. "As a teacher, [I] am primarily a learner, a student among students" (Hendricks 1987, 13).

6. See Adler and Van Doren (1972) for a helpful guide on skillful reading.

7. See Dillon (1988) for the best book on questions in education.

8. For the third and final phase of the disciples' training, Jesus passed on the responsibility to the Holy Spirit (cf. Acts 1:8, John 14:26). See Pazmino (1994) for a fuller treatment of the concept of authority in teaching. Pazmino also discusses the spiritual gift of teaching, an important issue for our topic that was not developed due to space limitations (1994, 71-76).

9. This is excerpted from "Teacher's Certificate" of 1882, in Wilder 1941, 306.

Works Cited

Adler, Mortimer J.. And Charles Van Doren. 1972. *How to Read a Book: The Classic Guide to Intelligent Reading.* New York: Simon and Schuster.

Bloom, Benjamin, et al. 1956. *Taxonomy of Educational Objectives.* Handbook 1: Cognitive Domain. New York: David McKay.

Dillon, J. T. 1988. *Questioning and Teaching: A Manual of Practice.* New York: Teacher's College.

Dillon, J. T. 1995. *Jesus as a Teacher: A Multidisciplinary Case Study.* Bethesda, Md.: International Scholars.

Habermas, Ronald, and Klaus Issler. 1992. *Teaching for Reconciliation: Foundations and Practice of Educational Ministry.* Grand Rapids, Mich.: Baker.

Hendricks, Howard. 1987. *Teaching to Change Lives.* Portland, Ore.: Multnomah.

Issler, Klaus. 1983. "A Conception of Excellence in Teaching." *Education* 103 (4): 338-43.

Issler, Klaus, and Ronald Habermas. 1994. *How We Learn: A Christian Teacher's Guide to Educational Psychology.* Grand Rapids, Mich.: Baker.

Pazmino, Robert. 1994. *By What Authority Do We Teach.* Grand Rapids, Mich.: Baker.

Swinburne, Richard. 1989. *Responsibility and Atonement.* Oxford: Clarendon.

Wilder, Laura Ingalls. 1941. *Little Town on the Prairie.* New York: Harper & Row.

Chapter Twenty _____

The Need for Initiating and Managing Change

EDWARD D. SEELY

We live in a milieu of constant change. "Only two things do not change," we are told, "death and taxes!" Actually, even those two phenomena are changing as technology often postpones the time of death and politicians propose tax reform. Change is inevitable.

As leaders in the church, change is at the heart of our calling. Our biblical mandate requires that we help people grow more Christlike, which involves changes in lifestyle, values, and actions (Titus 2:1-8). We are called to be change agents, but psychosocial research and our experience demonstrate clearly that people generally resist change (Bennett 1971). A closer look deepens the dilemma: some changes are going to happen anyway. The next question is, How can we manage those changes so that the outcomes are most favorable to all involved? Lyle Schaller, church consultant and author, holds that "the number-one issue facing Christian organizations on the North American continent today is the need to initiate and implement planned change" (Schaller 1994, 11). And the speed of change is not decreasing. Preparing for ministry in the twenty-first century demands that the church learn how to manage change.

One aspect of change that challenges church leaders is the introduction of innovations. How can we lead the church to do things in new ways? The field of communication and research on the diffusion of innovations provide helpful insights into the initiation and management of change. This chapter will draw upon the latest research in this field, and consider applications for initiating and managing change in the church. The field of communication is partially grounded in cross-cultural research, making this body of knowledge especially useful to the church when addressing its global mission.

INITIATING CHANGE

Diffusion research distinguishes between individual and corporate innovation decisions (Rogers 1995, 377ff.). We will look first at the corporate dimension, and then consider elements that are important to individuals and must be taken into account to realize the most effective outcomes. Findings from diffusion research apply to churches with some form of representative government and leaders who are assigned oversight for the congregation. Historic denominations are included and, according to Schaller, most Protestant congregations (1980, 27-30).

On the corporate as well as the individual plane, the innovation process consists of a series of stages, which progress in a necessary and predictable pattern. Later stages cannot be undertaken prior to the accomplishment of prerequisite stages.

Corporate Innovation Decisions

The first stage in corporate innovation decision-making is called *agenda setting*. In this phase a need is identified as well as an innovation that will meet the need. For example, leaders in one church I served proposed a switch in the time of worship and church school to meet several needs: increased attendance at both services, improved learning, and broader teacher selection. An interesting research discovery is that in organizations most innovations are driven by the awareness of innovations being used by other organizations. Thus, as a church becomes aware of an innovation operating in another church, a "need" for that change is created in the minds of some.

When the leader and others in charge become convinced of such a need, they engage in the second stage of initiation, a *matching* of the need with the proposed innovation. The purpose of this second stage is to test whether or not a good fit will occur if the change is implemented. This practice is vital, for it protects the church. Some practices that are really working in one place (according to the most vigorous proponents) will not work in another location with different people. Other practices should not be implemented for theological or philosophical reasons. If the decision not to adopt the proposed innovation occurs, the process is concluded. On the other hand, if the leader or leaders conclude the match is philosophically and theologically good and feasible, the decision to *implement* is made. In the example mentioned above, the pastor, the minister of education, the church school superintendent, and other leaders studied the proposal and weighed all conceivable factors to see whether the innovation would "work" in our church. After some time, they decided that this change should be implemented.

Implementation involves three stages. The first is *redefining/restructuring*, in which the innovation is modified to fit the local church, and/or the church makes accommodations to employ the change most effectively. In either case, the innovation is perceived as more familiar or compatible than it was before the redefining or restructuring. One accommodation made in the plan to switch worship and study time was to keep the original time slots. This allowed people to arrive at their usual time, even though some benefits would have occurred by starting earlier.

As the innovation is introduced and put into use, a clarification of how it is helping accomplish the organization's purpose, mission, and other values is necessary. This *clarifying* stage serves to strengthen commitment to the change and to reduce misgivings. Failure to engage in this process of helping members see the meaning and value of the innovation can result in the eventual abortion of the innovation, as happened in the changing of worship and church school times.

Finally, when an innovation has become established in the regular life and work of the organization, it loses its aura of being strange. In this *routinizing* stage it is seen as an integral part of the ongoing functioning of the system. Here, too, a decision to discontinue the innovation can be made. At this point leaders must consider carefully how individuals function as they are asked to adopt an innovation.

Individual Innovation Decisions

One of the most useful insights from research on the diffusion of innovations is the understanding that the decision whether or not to adopt an innovation is part of a process that occurs over time. While the three implementation stages described above are being processed in corporate decision-making, individuals are also involved in their processing (Rogers 1996). Individuals work through five key stages as they consider the changes they are being asked to make. Within this process certain kinds of communication have been found to be more effective than others in facilitating a decision to adopt.

A church leader who wants to initiate a change should bear in mind that an innovation is an idea, a service, a program, or an object that is perceived as new (Rogers and Shoemaker 1971, xvii). The leader may be familiar with a suggested innovation, but if the people in the church are not familiar with it, it is new to them and carries with it the dynamics of change. These dynamics involve uncertainty, fear, and threat, more for some people and less for others. If the change is to be implemented successfully, leaders must give careful consideration to these dynamics.

The first phase of the innovation-decision process for individuals is the *knowledge* stage, in which persons obtain information about the existence of an innovation and some understanding of how it functions. Mass media and group meetings are typical means for communicating this knowledge and are especially useful when a need exists among the members of a congregation. If the church as a whole does not yet sense a need for change, it is critical that leaders help the members discover that need.

The second stage, *persuasion*, occurs when persons form a favorable or an unfavorable attitude toward the proposed change. At this stage individuals are especially receptive to the influence of members of the congregation who are opinion leaders. Opinion leaders may or may not be appointed or elected to official positions in the church, but they are usually long-time members who are trusted and highly respected. The wise church leader who wants to facilitate the adoption of an innovation will, as early as possible, meet one-on-one with the opinion leaders in the congregation and enlist their support.

We sought out Mart, a lifelong and greatly valued member of the church, and one to whom others looked for validation of anything new. He was cosmopolitan in his perspective and well-educated, which helped him to be open to innovations. We received and used his support and that of other opinion leaders. This support was instrumental, humanly speaking, in obtaining the change we wanted.

The next phase of the process is the *decision* stage. At this point individuals make a choice either to adopt or to reject the innovation. Most people will not adopt without a probationary period during which they can experience the change yet keep the option to go back to what they had before if the new turns out to be worse than the old. We who are leaders, ministers, and change agents must, therefore, cap our desire to press for permanent adoption at first. We need to work initially to achieve acceptance on a trial basis, which is what was done in the worship and church school switch. The result at the congregational meeting was approval of the change. We thought we had it made.

This approval initiated the *implementation* stage, the phase during which an innovation is put into effect. The change is now no longer just on paper and in the mind; it is put into practice and involves altering behavior. Depending upon the nature of the innovation, people often make modifications during this stage. Since people are not omniscient and are unable to foresee all the implications of changes—and how they will feel about them—problems often occur at this point. Moreover, in organizations, including many churches, a significant number of people do not tell their leaders about these problems—until they have the chance to vote again. This stage can be the final stage in the process, but it frequently is followed by one more.

People often seek to reinforce their decision to do something new. Most everyone has heard about and many have experienced the phenomenon called buyer's remorse. When a major decision, such as the purchase of a home or car has been made, it is not uncommon for the person to wake up the next morning and regret the purchase. Such misgivings are part of many other innovation decisions as well, and when those doubts occur the adopter seeks reinforcement or *confirmation* of the decision to adopt or reasons to reject the action taken.

When we succeeded in obtaining the adoption of the change in time periods for worship and church school, we happily but wrongly concluded that the issue was settled and we could focus on other areas that needed our attention. At the next congregational meeting we were surprised and disappointed to see that many adopters had continued to reflect during the confirmation stage and now reversed their decision. Our experience illustrates how important it is for leaders to keep an ear to the ground in order to reinforce decisions once they are made.

In megachurches and others that have a polity that limits the degree to which individuals vote on an innovation, the danger of such a reversal is minimized but not removed. Members have other ways of voting, for example, with their feet and their wallets. Yet, even more important, out of love for others, leaders want to, with sensitivity, monitor the impact of change on those affected by it. Many wise leaders initiate follow-up contacts with their members, inquiring how certain decisions are being received and experienced; not a few have made modifications, if not substantial revisions, in the innovations that were implemented.

MANAGING CHANGE

As we guide the innovation-decision process, we are managing change. However, other helpful procedures exist as well.

Our work as change agents should begin and continue with prayer. The apostle James said, "The prayer of a righteous man is powerful and effective" (James 5:16b). The omniscient God can see what we can not. Out of love for the people, God will guide leaders to help them adopt the innovations that will be in the people's best interests and empower us to meet needs, avoid manipulation, and facilitate the changes that should be made.

Diffusion research has identified five attributes of innovations that are correlated with their adoptability. Understanding these attributes can help us manage change. The first is *relative advantage*, which is the degree to which an innovation is perceived as better than what it replaces. The crucial issue here is not an objective evaluation of worth, nor the leader's or agent's opinion, but the opinion of the potential adopters as to whether the change has merit. For example, though the leaders of our church were convinced it would be better for all if we had church school precede worship, the members could not see the advantage *to them*, and the innovation was ultimately rejected.

If potential adopters view an innovation as having *compatibility* with their needs, values, and previous understandings, that change is likely to be accepted. As seen above, the compatibility was apparent to the leaders and to others in the first three stages, but in the implementation and confirmation stages the members found the innovation incompatible with lifestyle schedules and other values, so they rejected the time change.

As mentioned earlier, if an innovation can be tried without committing to an irreversible decision, it will usually be adopted more quickly. New ideas presented with the *option to revert* to previous practices are perceived as less risky.

Closely associated with the option to revert is *perceived advantage*. People are more likely to adopt an innovation when they see results. These were key factors in persuading the church members to accept a switch in the time of their worship and church school services. During the persuasion stage, these characteristics of innovations are most influential.

Complexity is negatively correlated with adoption. When potential adopters perceive an innovation as being difficult to understand or implement, they are more likely to reject the proposed change. In presenting an innovation, it is important to keep the explanation as simple and concise as possible.

Managing change also involves the careful employment of opinion leaders during the implementation and confirmation stages. When opinion leaders are brought into the decision process early, they develop ownership of the innovation. They have a vested interest and help oversee the successful completion of the change process. The baby-boomer generation especially values such input, whether it is given directly or through their representatives (Murren 1990, 147ff.).

Leaders who have come from outside the church are seen by the local members as different from them. The more we can demonstrate that we are similar to the members of the church we serve, the more they will trust us and be receptive to our efforts to effect change (Rogers 1995, 18-19). Such similarity is what the apostle Paul meant when he said, "I have become all things to all men so that by all possible means I might save some" (1 Cor. 9:22). As we walk the high road and model Christlikeness, we build credibility in the eyes of those we are called to lead.

Finally, it is important to monitor innovations after they have been adopted and become routine. Innovations often have consequences that were unforeseen in the planning stages, and these unexpected outcomes are not always positive. As leaders, we have the responsibility to monitor the changes we have been instrumental in producing to make sure that the Lord's people are being served well and that God's purposes are being accomplished.

We can maximize the probability that the new changes we are initiating and managing will produce positive results as planned if we use these insights from research in the diffusion of innovations with the prayerful guidance of the sovereign Lord. "Commit to the LORD whatever you do, and your plans will succeed" (Prov. 16:3).

Works Cited

Bennett, Thomas R. 1971. "Secular Adult Education." A paper presented at the National Sunday School Association 1971 National Leadership Seminar, Chicago, Illinois. Audio tape.

Murren, Doug. 1990. *The Baby Boomerang: Catching Baby Boomers as They Return to Church.* Ventura, Cal.: Regal Books.

Rogers, Everett M. 1995. *Diffusion of Innovations.* 4th ed. New York: The Free Press.

_____. 1996. A phone conversation with the author. January 22.

Rogers, Everett M., and F. Floyd Shoemaker. 1971. *Communication of Innovations: A Cross-Cultural Approach.* New York: The Free Press.

Schaller, Lyle E. 1980. *The Multiple Staff and the Larger Church.* Nashville: Abingdon Press.

_____. 1994. *Ministry Advantage* 5, no. 5.

SECTION VI

TRIBUTES TO TED WARD

Ted Ward's Contribution
to Theological Education

John M. Dettoni

Both in his own country and on a global scale Ted Ward has made a significant impact on theological education. His influence has been felt directly through his own consulting, speaking, and writing, as well as indirectly through the ministries of his former students.

Ted has consulted with mission-sponsored and indigenous theological institutions in more than thirty countries. On some occasions, these consultations were woven into government-agency-sponsored trips to Europe, South America, Asia, Africa, and throughout North America. He has made valuable contributions to schools he has visited by encouraging them, sharing his insight into problems, and helping them find a sense of focus and direction.

During the 1960s and the early 1970s, Ted contributed to the development of theological education by extension (TEE) in Latin America and Africa through workshops sponsored by the Committee to Assist Ministry Education Overseas (CAMEO). During the late 1970s, he had a critical role in shaping the Seminary of the East (Dresher, Pennsylvania), and during the 1980s, he made a substantial investment in the evolution of the Biblical Institute for Leadership Development (BILD) in Ames, Iowa. Recently, Ted has made a two-year commitment to study Bible college education in North America and to advise the Accrediting Association of Bible Colleges (AABC) on strategies toward its revitalization. These and other projects in which Ted has been involved have been on the cutting edge, representing radical renewal in theological education.

I saw Ted's futuristic thinking and influence firsthand when I was the assistant provost for extension education, research, and development at Fuller Theological Seminary. Ted was a committee member of the Western Association of Schools and Colleges and the Association of Theological Schools, which did a ten-year evaluation of our institution. He was given the task of examining our extension program. He read the self-study we had done, visited one of the extension sites, and looked at and listened to the comments of faculty, trustees, administrators, and students. He saw quickly that the next possibility would be to offer the M.Div. on an off-campus basis. More than ten years later, Fuller did so. In the meantime, Ted was in conversations with other seminaries about similar off-campus programs. Some of these have since made their own leaps into twenty-first-century educational delivery systems.

Beyond these direct activities, Ted Ward has also contributed to theological education through the lives of his students. In the mid 1960s he began to receive a growing number of evangelical doctoral students at Michigan State University (MSU). After thirty years at MSU, Ted moved to Trinity Evangelical Divinity School to revitalize its Ed.D. program and develop a Ph.D. in intercultural studies. At both schools, he has passed on what he himself has been discovering through his research, study, teaching, and observations about theological education.

Ted Ward's former students are in positions of academic teaching and administration on all levels of theological education. They serve in little-known Bible schools in developing countries and in the so-called prestigious institutions of the West. They continue to expand and extend Ted's ministry.

Whether directly, through his consulting and writing, or indirectly, through his students' ministries, Ted's emphases on nonformal education and the need for *doing* and *being* (not just *knowing*) have helped shape forms of theological education that combine academic excellence with hands-on experience in ministry. The impact of his often quoted and debated warning cannot be overlooked: The problem with Christian education is that too often it is neither soundly Christian nor soundly educational.

When they were beginning their lives together, Ted and Margaret Ward could not have imagined this kind of an impact. They had every intention of being missionaries and—following what appeared to them at the time to be the will of the Lord—they prepared for the mission field. Frustrated by health constraints, they continued to follow the leading of the Lord. Ted stayed in higher education and traveled the world, consulting with missions and theological education programs. And because Ted and Margaret were faithful to God's call, their contribution to international theological education has been to a degree and in a way that they never could have dreamed.

Realizing Tomorrow's Dreams

S. Joseph Levine

The call came into the motel at a little past 5 A.M. "Mr. Levine? International operator is calling." I looked over to my wife. She had been awakened the instant the phone had rung. The girls were still sound asleep. Robbie and I looked at each other. She was waiting for this call just as I was—for three long weeks in a very small motel room with our two young children. Then Ted's voice came on the line. Even with this call coming from so far away his voice had the usual reassuring sound to it.

"Joe, I think they signed the papers. You'll be out of that motel in no time at all! Here's what you have to do. Wait until about 10 o'clock and then call the Consulate in New York City. They'll let you know if the cable has been sent. If it has been sent, ask them to call the Embassy in Washington. It's the only way that it will work. Washington never reads its mail!

And so began a journey for me and my family, a journey of enormous proportions for the four of us, a journey that might never have begun if Ted Ward hadn't been sitting for three days, half a world away, in the waiting room of the Foreign Ministry's Visa Section. Sitting and waiting. Smiling every once in a while. Reading his book. Writing his notes and letters. Silently sitting there and watching what was going on. And, all the while, having his silence "loudly" proclaim to the staff that he wasn't going to leave until they signed the visa forms. That morning they had signed the forms.

Now, twenty years later, I find myself reflecting on those days and thinking we must have been out of our minds. But then I remember what convinced us to do such a crazy thing. It was the same thing that convinced the Foreign Ministry's Visa Section to sign our papers. It was Ted Ward. And it was the knowledge that Ted would be back "home" and there to listen for us that gave us the assurance that made such an adventure possible.

Ted has repeated this role over and over again in the international development arena—helping individuals, helping projects, helping communities—always helping by providing a sense of security born from his tremendous ability to bring perspective to new and different situations. He draws on his remarkable cross-cultural sensitivity to help others develop the clarity of vision that is essential as a foundation for growth and change. For Ted, international development is clearly an extension of people development, and there can be no national growth without human growth. And, as he so clearly demonstrates through his work in the developing world, the first step toward international development is to have compassion for people.

Ted has been unwavering in his challenge to the international development community to understand the complexity of the development task and the need for us all to respect such complexity—to avoid the temptation to reduce or to simplify. He works to magnify that which many take for granted.

Ted Ward's contributions to international development—whether through his writing, a seminar or workshop, the time he takes to counsel and encourage those similarly committed, or a late night call to a family about to travel to a very foreign part of the world—continue to reinforce the image of a man dedicated to making the world a place where education and learning are the keystone for the realization of tomorrow's dreams.

The Course of Theological Education

ALEMU BEEFTU

Ted Ward has served God's purpose wholeheartedly. His impact on the developing worldwide evangelical church is profound, and clearly evident in the areas of theological education, strategic leadership training, holistic development, and nonformal continuing education.

Ted changed the course of theological education through *Theological Education by Extension* (TEE). TEE continually forced abstract theology into a practical context, and so made it relevant to the local church. TEE continues its development as the most practical theological education available to meet felt needs, and so a most effective way to equip the saints for the work of ministry. TEE alone is a witness that Ted has shaped the future of the evangelical church in curriculum and its method of delivery.

On a more personal level, Ted's servant leadership has been the model for missionaries and nationals alike in developing countries. There has never been a question about Ted's focus: he championed the acceptance of potential spiritual leaders in developing countries solely on the basis of the call of God on their lives. He has proved that choice servant leaders can be built from a variety of educational backgrounds and without concern to color, social status, or gender. Ted's relationships are marked by love, respect, and trust—elements that truly unfold a person's God-given potential.

Ted has continually challenged local churches and parachurch organizations to holistic development. Preaching the Word, meeting physical needs, making economic improvements, and changing social structures have all been present when Ted brings the gospel in its wholeness to those in need. Ted has never forgotten the historic roots of his mission outlook. He is among the first to remind anyone that the early churches were committed both to preaching the gospel—"[We] will give our attention to prayer and the ministry of the word" (Acts 6:4)—and caring for the poor—"All they asked was that we should continue to remember the poor, the very thing I was eager to do" (Gal. 2:10).

Ted is a learner at heart, and he has encouraged others to become the same. His efforts to make learning—especially nonformal learning—a lifelong pursuit is changing the face of the evangelical church as its leaders grow in vision and experience through his influence.

Ted Ward is a kingdom builder. He is the most effective teacher I have encountered. Ted was always eager to make theological concepts fall in line with the practical applications of the Word. In so doing, he empowered students like me not only with a firm grip on theory, but also with ways to apply theory to transform both society and the church of Jesus Christ. Ted has stood firm in correcting inaccurate historical assumptions about cultures and missiology alike. His efforts continue to shape the present reality of the worldwide church and to prepare the way for future generations to build the kingdom until the King comes back.

Glory to the One who has used Ted to mature his church!

Back to the Future

A Mahalo Nui Loa *from Hawaii*

GREGORY J. TRIFONOVITCH

At the East-West Center in Hawaii, one of our Maori participants always pointed behind her as she spoke about the future. She was surprised that we Americans pointed in front of us when we made such references. She explained that from the Maori viewpoint we can see the past much more clearly because it is always in front of us, but we cannot see the future since it is at our backs. Ted Ward has epitomized this concept. He has had a clear vision of the past as he has directed his students toward the future. His knowledge, experience, and strong Christian principles have given direction to his students as they devise their plans for the future. He gently but resolutely keeps his grip on them until he can release them to achieve their goals.

I first met Ted Ward in 1977, when Michigan State University was listed as one of my stops for advice on international education for a new division to be implemented at the East-West Center in Honolulu, Hawaii. On that cold February morning I received advice, galoshes to cover my soaked shoes, and a new friendship with a scholar dedicated to service in Christ's kingdom.

Since that February meeting, Ted and I have cooperated in several training projects for international educators at the East-West Center. He has given his knowledge to our participants with the same selflessness that he gave me his galoshes. At the same time, we have found common ground on many issues of life, both from an earthly perspective and from the eternal.

Pacific Island navigators plot their courses among the islands by using the swells in the ocean and observing the angle of the outrigger's wake. In a similar way, Ted Ward has pointed out God's wake to students on their faith journeys. He watches vigilantly as they monitor God's path of their past and confidently continue their journey into their futures, knowing that their "island" will eventually meet them. This same strategy has been shared with other Christian organizations as Ted has served them as advisor, trustee, or board member.

God has gifted Ted with intellect, artistry, good old common sense, care, compassion, and dedication. His journey has not been without struggles and health problems, but, in the midst of them, he continues to "press toward the mark for the prize of the high calling of God in Christ Jesus" (Philippians 3:14, *KJV*).

As we say in Hawaii, *mahalo nui loa* ("a vast thank you"), Ted Ward, for being a faithful servant of God and for your powerful but gentle touch on our lives.

Bibliography of Ted W. Ward

COMPILED BY MARK E. SIMPSON

PUBLISHED ARTICLES

1956. The experimental testing of a concept of perception with implications for music education. *Abstracts of Doctoral Studies in Education: College of Education, University of Florida* (1956): 70-75.

Ward, Ted, and James Fowler. 1959. Teaching in a museum. *College of Education Quarterly: Michigan State University* 5 (3): 26-29.

1959. The hazardous communication: Criticism. *Education* 80 (2): 97-99.

Whitmer, Dana P., Ann Ess Morrow, Horton Southworth, and Ted Ward. 1959. The MSU-Pontiac student-teacher center: A symposium. *College of Education Quarterly: Michigan State University* 5 (4): 19-24.

1960. Research in teacher role emergence. *College of Education Quarterly: Michigan State University* 6 (4): 10-14.

1963. *The clinical concept in education.* East Lansing, Mich.: Learning Systems Institute and Human Learning Research Institute of Michigan State University. LSI, 2.

Ward, Ted, and Judith Lanier. 1964. *The clinical school study.* East Lansing, Mich.: Learning Systems Institute and Human Learning Research Institute of Michigan State University. LSI, 7.

1964. *The challenge to change.* East Lansing, Mich.: Learning Systems Institute and Human Learning Research Institute of Michigan State University. LSI, 4.

1964. *The clinical cycle: Paradigm of a concept.* East Lansing, Mich.: Learning Systems Institute and Human Learning Research Institute of Michigan State University. LSI, 9.

Dietrich, John E., Ted W. Ward, and Horace C. Hartsell. 1965. Media development: A part of instructional change. *Audiovisual Instruction* 10 (5): 393-94.

1965. *Establishing an effective systems for communication about school development.* East Lansing, Mich.: Learning Systems Institute and Human Learning Research Institute of Michigan State University. LSI, 18.

1965. *The professional decision simulator.* East Lansing, Mich.: Learning Systems Institute and Human Learning Research Institute of Michigan State University. LSI, 13.

Ward, Ted, and Judith Lanier. 1966. *Guidelines for building teacher behavioral research instruments.* East Lansing, Mich.: Learning Systems Institute and Human Learning Research Institute of Michigan State University. LSI, 25.

1966. *The outlook for teacher education.* East Lansing, Mich.: Learning Systems Institute and Human Learning Research Institute of Michigan State University. LSI, 22.

1967. *Clinical research: A two-way street between research and practice.* East Lansing, Mich.: Learning Systems Institute and Human Learning Research Institute of Michigan State University. LSI, 52.

Ward, Ted, and Joe Levine. 1967. *SIMULAR: Simulation and recording device for research in programmed instruction.* Learning Systems Institute and Human Learning Research Institute of Michigan State University. LSI, 57.

1968. Development of new instructional materials in the IMC network. *Exceptional Children* 35 (3): 299-302.

1968. Questions teachers should ask in choosing instructional materials. *Teaching Exceptional Children* 1 (1): 21-23.

1969. Automated braille system (Autobraille). *The Research Bulletin: American Foundation for the Blind* 19 (June): 231-33.

1969. *Encyclopedia of educational research.* American Educational Research Association. New York, N.Y.: MacMillan. S.v. "Improvement of educational practice."

1969. Music in worship. *The Sunday School Times and Gospel Herald* (March), 8-9.

Ward, Ted, Frank Cookingham, Judith Henderson, Robert Houston, and Joseph Coughlin. 1969. *Social-cultural preparation of Americans for overseas service: An approach drawn from behavioral science.* East Lansing, Mich.: Learning Systems Institute and Human Learning Research Institute of Michigan State University. LSI, 67.

1969. *The split-rail fence: An analogy for the education of professionals.* East Lansing, Mich.: Learning Systems Institute and Human Learning Research Institute of Michigan State University. LSI, 64.

Ward, Ted, Patricia Howieson, and Elaine Haglund. 1970. *Cultural adaptation of programmed instruction.* East Lansing, Mich.: Learning Systems Institute and Human Learning Research Institute of Michigan State University. HLRI, 23.

1970. *Encyclopedia of education.* New York, N.Y.: MacMillan. S.v. "Instructional devices and techniques for the handicapped."

Ward, Ted, and Frank Cookingham. 1970. *On the foundations of teacher education.* East Lansing, Mich.: Learning Systems Institute and Human Learning Research Institute of Michigan State University. LSI, 71.

1971. A new frontier: Communication. *International Christian Broadcasters Bulletin* (November): 6.

1971. Christian action in an age of despair. *Eternity* 22 (6): 20-22.

1971. Christianity and communication. *International Christian Broadcasters Bulletin* (December): 15.

1971. Communicating in the community. *Theology, New and Notes: Published for the Fuller Theological Seminary Alumni* (December), 4-10, 24.

Ward, Ted, Lois McKinney, and John Dettoni. 1971. Effective learning in nonformal modes. *Final report from the seminar on nonformal education convened by SEAMES with the cooperation of the southeast Asia development advisory group (SEADAG) and the government of Malaysia, Penang,* 11-14 October 1971, 249-62. SEAMEO/SEADAG.

Ward, Ted, and Joe Levine. 1971. *Instructional simulation: Nomenclature, viewpoint, and bias.* Learning Systems Institute and Human Learning Research Institute of Michigan State University. LSI, 73.

1971. Just who do you think you are? *Pioneer Girls Perspective* 5 (2): 4-6, 26-27.

1971. *Preparing vocational teachers for the disadvantaged: Methods used by teacher educators.* Final report updating the process and content of teacher education curriculum to reach disadvantaged youth in metropolitan areas. Project 9-0535, Grant OEG-0-9-480535-4435 (725), 15-16.

1971. The communication revolution: What it isn't. *International Christian Broadcasters Bulletin* (September): 6.

1972. Changes in society. The Standard (15 August), 18-19.

1972. Quality demands know how. *International Christian Broadcasters Bulletin* (February): 7.

Ward, Ted, and Samuel F. Rowen. 1972. The significance of the extension seminary. *Evangelical Missions Quarterly* 9 (1): 17-27.

1972. Understanding the outlook of youth. *Leader Guidebook: Christian Education Idea Book for Sunday School Leaders* (September-November), 8-10.

1972. Youth: The vocal majority. *Inter-View: An International Journal of Christian Leadership Development* 2 (1): 5-10.

1973. Cognitive processes and learning: Reflections on a comparative study of "Cognitive style" (Witkin) in fourteen African societies. *Comparative Education Review* 17 (1): 1-10.

1973. My earliest bombing mission. *Eternity* (March), 16-17.

1974. Christian education trends. *Leader Guidebook* (December 1974, January, February 1975), 31.

1974. Christian education trends. *Leader Guidebook* (June, July, August), 31.

1974. Christian education trends. *Leader Guidebook* (March, April, May), 31.

1974. Christian education trends. *Leader Guidebook* (September, October, November), 31.

Ward, Ted, and Lois McKinney. 1974. Master. *The Other Side* 10 (5): 8-10.

1974. Theological education by extension: Much more than a fad. *Theological Education* 10 (4): 246-58.

1975. Christian education trends. *Leader Guidebook* (June, July, August), 31.

1975. Christian education trends. *Leader Guidebook* (September, October, November), 31.

1975. Fuzzy fables or communications that count. *Spectrum* 1 (1): 10-11, 25.

Ward, Ted, and Lois McKinney. 1975. Teacher. *CAM* (January), 10-11.

1975. The Christian family at late-century. *Evangelical Newsletter* 2 (26): 4.

1976. China is open to the gospel. *Evangelical perspectives on china.* Occasional publications on China Series, no. 1. Farmington, Mich.: Evangelical China Committee.

1976. Christian education trends. *Leader Guidebook* (June, July, August), 31.

1976. Christian education trends. *Leader Guidebook* (March, April, May), 31.

1976. Christian education trends. *Leader Guidebook* (September, October, November), 31.

1976. Developmental implications for parents and teachers. *Asbury Seminarian* 31: 30-37.

Ward, Ted, and Rodney McKean. 1976. Six models of teaching for moral development. *Georgia Social Science Journal* 8 (1): 10-30.

1976. Strategy for the family. *The Christian Reader* 14 (6): 8-13.

1976. The Bible and moral values. *Bryan Life* 1 (3), 6-8.

1976. The Bible and moral values. *Biblical Issues and Moral Development*.

1976. To meet your needs. *The Christian Executive* 1 (4), 1, 6-7.

Ward, Ted, and Kathleen Graham. 1977. Acts of kindness: Motives and relationships. Farmington, Mich.: Associates of Urbanus.

1977. Beautiful people who smile. *Decision* 18 (12), 4.

1977. Christian education trends. *Leader Guidebook* (December 1977, January, February 1978), 31.

1977. Christian education trends. *Leader Guidebook* (June, July, August), 31.

1977. Christian education trends. *Leader Guidebook* (March, April, May), 31.

1977. The do-it-yourself culture shock survival kit. *Wherever* 2 (2), 2-5.

1977. Types of TEE. *Evangelical Missions Quarterly* 13 (2): 79-86.

1978. Christian education trends. *Leader Guidebook* (March, April, May), 31.

1978. Lifeboats, water holes, and earthquakes: The crisis in values: A response to the address by David L. McKenna. In *Evangelicals face the future: Scenarios, addresses, and responses from the Consultation on Future Evangelical Concerns, Atlanta, Georgia, 14-17 December 1977*, ed. Donald E. Hoke, 104-109. Pasadena, Calif.: William Carey Library.

1979. The church in the intermediate future. *Christianity Today* 29 (June), 14-18.

1980. Beyond the pith helmet. *HIS* (January), 10-11.

1980. Education that makes a difference. *The Bethel Focus* (May), 9-11.

1980. Foreword to *Patterns in moral development*, by Catherine Stonehouse. Waco, Tex.: Word, Inc.

1980. Innovations in education: What next? *FOCUS on Adults* (October), 14-15.

1980. Learning right from wrong: An FLT interview with Dr. Ted Ward. Interview by Family Life Today. *Family Life Today* 6 (10): 23-25, 32.

1980. Missions toward the 21st century: A global overview. *World in View* (October), 10-15.

1980. The year of the child—who cares? *Christian Standard* 115 (9): 4-6.

Institute of Society, Ethics, and the Life Sciences. 1981. Review of *The teaching of ethics in higher education*, by Ted Ward. In *Eternity* (June) 1981: 49.

1981. Hastings' hasty ethics pudding: A review of The Institute of Society, Ethics, and the Life Sciences: *The Teaching of Ethics in Higher Education*, by Hastings-on-Hudson. *Eternity* 32: 49.

1981. The church and the Christian family. *Tips for Family Ministry* 1 (4), 1,6.

1982. Are your assumptions healthy. *TEAM Horizons* (September-October), 4.

1982. Biblical metaphors of purpose: Part 1, Metaphors of spiritual reality. *Bibliotheca Sacra* 139 (554): 99-110.

1982. Botanical metaphors of development: Part 2, Metaphors of spiritual reality. *Bibliotheca Sacra* 139 (555): 195-204.

1982. Christian missions—survival in what forms? *International Bulletin of Missionary Research* 6 (1): 2-3.

1982. Evaluating metaphors of education: Part 3, Metaphors of spiritual reality. *Bibliotheca Sacra* 139 (556): 291-301.

Beeftu, Alemu, and Ted Ward. 1983. A review of *Evangelicals and development: Toward a theology of social change and Lifestyle in the eighties: An evangelical commitment to simple lifestyle,* ed. Ronald J. Sider. *International Bulletin of Missionary Research* 7 (4): 181.

1983. Metaphors of the church in troubled times: Part 4, Metaphors of spiritual reality. *Bibliotheca Sacra* 140 (557): 3-10.

Ward, Ted, and Rodney McKean. 1983. Six models of teaching for moral development. *Christian Education Journal* 3 (2): 10-29.

1983. Where to go to college. *Family Life Today* (April), 30-34.

1984. Faith, hope, and love: The remaining mission of Christian higher education. *Faculty Dialogue* 1: 1-6.

1984. Teaching and writing. *Faculty Dialogue: Journal of the Institute for Christian Leadership* (Winter 1984-85) (2): 11-16.

1984. The dandelion experience. *Radio Bible Class Discovery Digest* 8 (6), 24-27.

1985. A long look over the shoulder. *Faculty Dialogue: Journal of the Institute for Christian Leadership* (Spring-Summer) (3): i-iii.

1985. Exciting rediscovery in missions. *HCJB Radio Log* (Spring): 3-5.

1985. I want to do right. *Light and Life* (April), 12-14.

1985. Service: An endangered value. *Faculty Dialogue: Journal of the Institute for Christian Leadership* (Fall) (4): 1-6.

1985. The importance of educational value added. *Faculty Dialogue* 5:3-5.

1986. Commonplace or unique? *Faculty Dialogue: Journal of the Institute for Christian Leadership* (Fall-Winter 1986-87) (7): 1-4.

1986. So what? *Faculty Dialogue: Journal of the Institute for Christian Leadership* (Spring-Summer) (6): 1-8.

1986. The importance of educational value added. *Faculty Dialogue: Journal of the Institute for Christian Leadership* (Winter 1985-1986) (5): 3-5.

1987. A Christian logic for curriculum in liberal arts education. *Faculty Dialogue: Journal of the Institute for Christian Leadership* (Spring-Summer) (8): 7-20.

1987. Developing a global view of ministry. *Moody Monthly* (April), 23-25.

1987. Educational preparation of missionaries—a look ahead. *Evangelical Missions Quarterly* 23 (4): 398-404.

1987. Foreword to *Images of Leadership, Social Responsibility and Theological Education: A Report of an International Enquiry,* Series 3, by Arthur P. Williamson. Monrovia, Calif.: MARC Publications.

Ward, Ted, Bryan Truman, Christina Lee, Nora Avarientos, and Evita Perez. 1987. Putting nonformal education to work. *Together* (July-September): 7-10.

1987. The too-well hidden agenda. *Faculty Dialogue: Journal of the Institute for Christian Leadership* (Fall) (9): 1-6.

1988. A standard of excellence. *Christian Education Today* 40 (4): 9-11.

Ward, Ted, and G. Kellor. 1988. Commonplace or unique? The four distinguishing features of a Christian college education. *Faculty Dialogue* 10:113-20.

1988. The half-life of truth. *Faculty Dialogue: Journal of the Institute for Christian Leadership* (Winter-Spring) (10): 1-4.

Issler, Klaus, and Ted Ward. 1989. Moral development as a curriculum emphasis in American Protestant theological education. *Journal of Moral Education* 18 (2): 131-43.

1989. Leadership for missions. *Inter-View: Cross-Cultural Journal of Christian Leadership* 1 (1): 5-11.

1989. Review of *Apologia: Contextualization, globalization, and mission in theological education*, by Max L. Stackhouse. *Christian Education Journal* 9: 121-23.

1989. The anxious climate of concern for missionary kid education. *International Bulletin of Missionary Research* 13 (1): 11-13.

1989. The lines people draw. *Faculty Dialogue: Journal of the Institute for Christian Leadership* Spring 1989 (11): 7-22.

1992. A final exam for Christian higher education. *Faculty Dialogue: Journal of the Institute for Christian Leadership* (Fall) (18): 5-11.

1993. Review of *The secularization of the academy*, ed. by G. M. Marsden and B. J. Longfield. *Trinity Journal* 14: 85-88.

1995. The case of the disappearing missionaries. *Trinity World Forum* 21: 1-5.

BOOKS

1958. What makes the difference: The role of the supervising teacher in a resident student teaching program. *Professional series bulletin: Department of teacher education: Bureau of educational research: College of education*, no. 34. East Lansing, Mich.: Michigan State University.

1960. You're in for a surprise: The student teacher in resident student teaching. *Professional series bulletin: Department of teacher education: Bureau of educational research: College of education*, no. 42. East Lansing, Mich.: Michigan State University.

Ward, Ted, ed. 1963. *Concern for the individual in student teaching: Forty-second yearbook of the association for student teaching*. Cedar Falls, Iowa: Association for Student Teaching.

1966. *Selective observation simulator (SOS): dissemination document no. 2 (papers of the institute no. 41)* East Lansing, Mich.: USOE/MSU Regional Instructional Materials Center for Handicapped Children and Youth.

1966. *Variable-interval sequenced-action camera (VINSAC): dissemination document no. 1 (papers of the institute no. 40)* East Lansing, Mich.: USOE/MSU Regional Instructional Materials Center for Handicapped Children and Youth.

1967. Evaluation of instructional materials. *USOE/MSU Regional Instructional Materials Center for Handicapped Children and Youth*, Position Paper No. 1. East Lansing, Mich.: Michigan State University.

1967. The talking dictionary. *USOE/MSU Regional Instructional Materials Center for Handicapped Children and Youth*, Prospectus Series No. 2. East Lansing, Mich.: Michigan State University.

1968. Articulation of information systems. *USOE/MSU Regional Instructional Materials Center for Handicapped Children and Youth*, Dissemination Document No. 13. East Lansing, Mich.: Michigan State University.

1969. Speed—listening: An introduction to speech compression. *USOE/MSU Regional Instructional Materials Center for Handicapped Children and Youth*, Dissemination Document No. 15. East Lansing, Mich.: Michigan State University.

Ward, Ted, and Margaret Ward. 1970. *Programmed instruction for theological education by extension*. Holt, Mich.: Committee to Assist Missionary Education Overseas.

1971. *Memo for the underground*. With a Foreword by Joe Bayly. Carol Stream, Ill.: Creation House.

Ward, Ted, and S. Joseph Levine. 1971. *Yours—for a better workshop!* East Lansing, Mich.: USOE/MSU Regional Instructional Materials Center for Handicapped Children and Youth.

Buker, Raymond B., Sr., and Ted Ward, eds. 1972. *The world directory of mission-related educational institutions*. South Pasadena, Calif.: William Carey Library.

Ward, Ted, John Dettoni, and Margaret Ward. 1974. *Reaching all*. Minneapolis, Minn.: World Wide Publications.

Ward, Ted, and William A. Herzog, Jr., eds. 1974. *Study team reports: Effective learning in nonformal education*. Program of Studies in Nonformal Education Series. East Lansing, Mich.: Michigan State University.

1975. Foreword to *Everything you need to know for a cassette ministry*, by Viggø B. Søgaard. Minneapolis, Minn.: Bethany Fellowship, Inc.

1975. *The influence of secular institutions on today's family*. Plenary Series: Continental Congress on the Family, St. Louis 1975. Atlanta, Ga.: Family 76 Inc.

1979. *Leader's guide for values begin at home*. Wheaton, Ill.: Victor Books.

1979. *Personal involvement workbook for individual study of values begin at home*. Wheaton, Ill.: Victor Books.

1979. *Values begin at home*. Wheaton, Ill.: Victor Books.

1984. *Living overseas: A book of preparations*. New York: The Free Press.

1989. *Values begin at home*. Wheaton, Ill.: Victor Books, 2d ed. Wheaton, Ill.: Victor Books.

CHAPTERS AND FOREWORDS

Ward, Ted, and Troy Stearns. 1961. An expanding role. In *Teacher education and the public schools: Fortieth yearbook of the association for student teaching*, 97-114. Dubuque, Iowa: Wm. C. Brown Co., Inc.

1961. The public school's expanding role. In *Teacher education and the public schools: Fortieth yearbook of the association for student teaching*, Section Four ed., Ted Ward, 95-137. Dubuque, Iowa: Wm. C. Brown Co., Inc.

Ward, Ted, and Ernest O. Melby. 1963. The challenge of individual differences. In *Concern for the individual in student teaching: Forty-second yearbook of the association for student teaching*, ed. Ted Ward, 3-15. Cedar Falls, Iowa: Association for Student Teaching.

1964. Matching student teachers with supervising teachers. In *New developments, research, and experimentation in professional laboratory experiences: Proceedings of the forty-fourth annual national conference*, ed. Curtis Nash and Yvonne Lofthouse, 144-45. Cedar Falls, Iowa: The Association for Student Teaching Bulletin 22.

1966. Professional integration and clinical research. In *The supervisor: Agent for change in teaching*, ed. James Raths and Robert R. Leeper, 57-84. Washington, D.C.: Association for Supervision and Curriculum Development.

1968. Developing teacher behavior in clinical settings. In *Internships in teacher education: Forty-seventh yearbook of the association for student teaching*, 145-58. Washington, D.C.: The Association for Student Teaching.

1968. Programmed learning techniques. In *Seminary Extension Education Workshop Report—Wheaton, Illinois, 19-21 December 1968*, 70-90. Denver, Colo.: Committee to Assist Missionary Education Overseas.

1968. Teacher behavior and teacher education. In *Readings in distributive education: Papers from the National Seminar in Distributive Education, East Lansing, Mich. 1967*, 152-60. East Lansing, Mich.: Michigan State University.

1969. Programmed learning techniques. In *Theological education by extension*, ed. R. Winter, 311-25. Pasadena, Calif.: William Carey Press.

1970. Curricular accountability through testing. In *Using tests in curriculum evaluation: Addresses delivered at the Michigan school testing conference, Rackham building, the University of Michigan, 18 February 1970*, by the University of Michigan Bureau of School Services, 3-10.

1971. Options for overseas service in world evangelism. In *Christ the liberator*, ed. John R. W. Stott, et al., Urbana 70, 133-144. Downers Grove, Ill.: InterVarsity Press.

1973. Designing effective learning in nonformal modes. In *New strategies for educational development*, ed. Cole Brembeck, 111-24. New York: Lexington Books.

1974. A lesson from American education. In *Japan and America: Readings on education*, ed. Shigeo Imamura, Takashi Watanabe, and Tamotsu Fujiwara, 29-36. Tokyo, Japan: Bunri Co., Ltd.

Ward, Ted, F. Donald Sawyer, Lois McKinney, and John Dettoni. 1974. Effective learning: Lessons to be learned from schooling. In *Study team reports: Effective learning in nonformal education*, ed. Ted Ward and William Herzog, Jr., 14-64. Program of Studies in Nonformal Education Series. East Lansing, Mich.: Michigan State University.

Ward, Ted, and John Dettoni. 1974. Increasing learning effectiveness through evaluation. In *Study team reports: Effective learning in nonformal education*, ed. Ted Ward and William Herzog, Jr., 198-288. Program of Studies in Nonformal Education Series. East Lansing, Mich.: Michigan State University.

Ward, Ted, Lois McKinney, John Dettoni, James Emery, and Norman Anderson. 1974. Planning for effective learning in nonformal education: A learning systems approach. In *Study team reports: Effective learning in nonformal education*, ed. Ted Ward and William Herzog, Jr., 65-126. Program of Studies in Nonformal Education Series. East Lansing, Mich.: Michigan State University.

Ward, Ted, and Lois McKinney. 1974. Relating instructional procedures to learner characteristics: An experimental illustration in Brazil. In *Study team reports: Effective learning in nonformal education*, ed. Ted Ward and William Herzog, Jr., 127-97. Program of Studies in Nonformal Education Series. East Lansing, Mich.: Michigan State University.

Ward, Ted, and Donald Sawyer. 1974. The case of the disappearing distinction: Formal and nonformal education in China. In *Study team reports: Effective learning in nonformal education*, ed. Ted Ward and William Herzog, Jr., 324-68. Program of Studies in Nonformal Education Series. East Lansing, Mich.: Michigan State University.

1976. *Biblical issues in moral development.*

1976. The Christian's family in society. In *Living & growing together: The Christian family today*, ed. Gary R. Collins, 97-105. Waco, Tex.: Word Books.

1977. Facing educational issues. In *Church leadership development*, The National Christian Education Study Seminar, 31-46. Glen Ellyn, Ill.: Scripture Press Ministries.

1978. Views of the future as reflected in reports to the club of Rome: Scenario, Response Group 5. In *Evangelicals face the future: Scenarios, addresses, and responses from the Consultation on Future Evangelical Concerns, Atlanta, Georgia, 14-17 December 1977*, ed. Donald E. Hoke, 23-25. Pasadena, Calif.: William Carey Library.

1979. The future of missions: Hangovers, fallout, and hope. In *New horizons in world mission: Evangelicals and the Christian mission in the 1980s: Papers and responses prepared for the second consultation on theology and mission, Trinity Evangelical Divinity School, 19-22 March 1979*, ed. David J. Hesselgrave. Grand Rapids, Mich.: Baker Book House.

1979. The future of the church: In a secular society. In *An evangelical agenda: 1984 and beyond: Addresses, responses, and scenarios from the Continuing Consultation on Future Evangelical Concerns, Overland Park, Kansas, 11-14 December 1979*, 109-130. Pasadena, Calif.: William Carey Library.

1984. Nonformal education: What is it? In *Nonformal education: Reflections on the first dozen years*, ed. Ted Ward, S. Joseph Levine, Lynn Joesting, and Dick Crespo, 2-7. East Lansing, Mich.: Michigan State University.

1984. Servants, leaders. and tyrants. In *Missions & theological education*, ed. Harvie M. Conn and Samuel F. Rowen, 19-40. Farmington, Mich.: Associates of Urbanus.

1985. Foreword to *Social responsibility and theological education*, by Arthur Williamson. Grand Rapids, Mich.: Zondervan.

1985. Religion, research, and family: A corner turned; a step to take. In *Family building: Six qualities of a strong family*, ed. George Rekers, 333-42, Ventura, Calif.: Regal Books.

1986. The implications of developing mission strategies for MKs. In *Compendium of the international conference on missionary kids: New directions in missions: Implications for MKs, Manila, Philippines, November 1984*, ed. Beth A. Tetzel and Patricia Mortenson, 1-10. West Brattleboro, Vt.: International Conference on Missionary Kids.

1987. More to learn. In *Stepping out: A guide to short-term missions*, 137-39. Evanston, Ill.: Short-Term Missions Advocates, Inc.

1989. Getting the moral message across. In *The blackboard fumble: Finding a place for values in public education*, ed. Ken Sidey, 25-36. Christianity Today Series. Wheaton, Ill.: Victor Books.

1990. Coping with cultural differences: A major task for theological education. In *Summary of Proceedings of the 44th Annual Conference of ATLA, Northwestern University, Garrett-Evangelical Theological Seminary & Seabury-Western Theological Seminary, Evanston, Illinois, 24-28 June*, 123-29. Evanston, Ill.: American Theological Library Association.

1990. Foreword to *Sojourners: Families on the move*, by Sam Rowen and Ruth Rowen. Farmington, Mich.: Associates of Urbanus.

1990. Into the future: To discern without dichotomizing. In *Practical theology and the ministry of the church—1952-1984: Essays in honor of Edmund P. Clowney*, ed. Harvie M. Conn, 275-86, Phillipsburg, N.J.: Presbyterian and Reformed Publishing Co.

1995. Foreword: Rudiments for educational theory that is Christian. In *Nurture that is Christian*, ed. James C. Wilhoit and John M. Dettoni, 7-17. Wheaton, Ill.: Bridgepoint/Victor Books.

UNPUBLISHED MANUSCRIPTS: TEXTS FROM LECTURES AND LIMITED CIRCULATION PAPERS

1964. *One answer for conant*. Address presented at the Supervising Teachers Banquet, Wheaton College, Wheaton, Illinois, 20 March 1964. Personal collection of Ted Ward. 16 pages.

1964. *Research and the applied science of education*. Address presented at the Intern Consultant Workshop, Gull Lake, 27 May. Personal collection of Ted Ward. 12 pages.

1965. *Presentation to supervising teachers*. Michigan State University, 16 September. Personal collection of Ted Ward. 21 pages.

1967. *Internship as a source of knowledge about teacher behavior and pupil learning*. Address presented at the AST Summer Workshop, University of Rhode Island, 1967. Personal collection of Ted Ward. 14 pages.

1968. General session speech presented at the Instructional Materials and Media Fair, 4 May, John Marshall High School, Indianapolis, Indiana. Indiana Department of Public Instruction, Division of Special Education.

1968. *Instructional materials and teaching*. Address presented at the Indiana State Department of Education Annual IM Conference, 1968. Personal collection of Ted Ward. 14 pages.

1969. *Truth without consequences*. Address presented at the Space-Age Communication Conference, San Bernardino, California, June 1969. Personal collection of Ted Ward. 12 pages.

1970. *Requirements for instructional theory in special education*. Michigan State University, 20 June. Personal collection of Ted Ward. 12 pages.

1970. *The elegant non-conformist*. Address presented at the Honors Convocation, Wheaton College, Wheaton, Illinois, 2 December. Personal collection of Ted Ward. 5 pages.

1970. *The amazing personality*. Address presented at Wheaton College Chapel, Wheaton, Illinois, July 1970. Personal collection of Ted Ward. 3 pages.

1970. *Who is a missionary?* Address presented at Wheaton College Chapel, Wheaton, Illinois, 27 February. Personal collection of Ted Ward. 8 pages.

1970. *Words, meanings, and you*. Address presented at Wheaton College Chapel, Wheaton, Illinois, 26 February. Personal collection of Ted Ward. 10 pages.

1971. *Christian camping*. Address presented at Lake James Christian Assembly, Angola, Indiana. 1971. Personal collection of Ted Ward. 7 pages.

1971. *Creative Christian Communication*. Bueermann-Champion Lectureship at Western Conservative Baptist Seminary, Portland, Oregon. Portland, Oreg.: Western Conservative Baptist Seminary.

1971. *Nonformal education: Problems and promises*. Address presented at the Nonformal Education Conference, New York City, January. Personal collection of Ted Ward. 13 pages.

1971. *The creative God creates*. Address presented at Wheaton College Chapel, Wheaton, Illinois, 11 August. Personal collection of Ted Ward. 8 pages.

1971. *What goes into media education*. Address presented at the Communication Education Conference, Oral Roberts University, Tulsa, Oklahoma, April. Personal collection of Ted Ward. 22 pages.

1972. [*Pedagogy for adults*]. Address presented at Society for the Advancement of Continuing Education in Ministry (SACEM). Personal collection of Ted Ward. 7 pages.

Brembeck, Cole, and Ted Ward. 1974. *Toward an expanded view of educational resources: Some observations and working hypotheses*. Michigan State University. Personal collection of Ted Ward. 3 pages.

1974. *Christ, career, and concern: The political reality of today's mission*. Wheaton College chapel address manuscript. Personal collection of Ted Ward. 4 pages.

Salah, Amed Ben, Carlos Malpica Faustor, J. P. Naik, Patrick van Rensburg, and Ted Ward. 1975. *Alternatives in education: A new conception*. Report developed for The 1975 Dag Hammarskjold Project, The Dag Hammarskjold Foundation, Uppsala, Sweden, April. 18 pages.

1975. *COPE: A procedure for preliminary planning for evaluation*. Michigan State University. Personal collection of Ted Ward. 3 pages.

1975. *International issue: The right to learn*. Michigan State University. Personal collection of Ted Ward. 4 pages.

1975. *Nonformal education: A problem of rhetoric and logic of educational reform*. Michigan State University. Personal collection of Ted Ward. 5 pages.

1975. *Public education and Christians: Traveling the same trail?* First Annual Foundation Conference, Wheaton College, Wheaton, Illinois, 7 November, address manuscript. Personal collection of Ted Ward. 9 pages.

Ward, Ted, and James McCue. 1975. *The family matter.* Michigan State University. Personal collection of Ted Ward. 4 pages.

Ward, Ted, and Avery Willis, Jr. 1976. *A vision of reform for theological education.* Michigan State University. Personal collection of Ted Ward. 30 pages.

1976. *Church leadership development: Educational issues.* Address presented at the Nordic Hills Workshop, 23 November—2 December. Personal collection of Ted Ward. 31 pages.

1976. *Knowledge-building for nonformal education.* Michigan State University. Personal collection of Ted Ward. 6 pages.

1976. *Linear models: Good news and bad news.* Michigan State University. Personal collection of Ted Ward. 4 pages.

1976. *Research on moral judgment: Developmental implications for parents and teachers.* From Biblical issues in moral development. Michigan State University. Personal collection of Ted Ward. 10 pages.

1976. *What can we know about motivation? Michigan State University.* Personal collection of Ted Ward. 3 pages.

1977. *Position paper on educational development.* Michigan State University. Personal collection of Ted Ward. 21 pages.

1977. *The effective missionary.* Address presented at the EFMA/IFMA Personnel Workshop, Farmington, Michigan, 1-3 February. Personal collection of Ted Ward. 20 pages.

1978. *Community health education.* Address presented to the Eighth International Convention on Missionary Medicine, Wheaton, Illinois, June. Personal collection of Ted Ward. 11 pages.

1980. *Education for developing nations: Equality of education opportunities.* Address presented to The Pre-Congress Conference of The IVth World Congress of The World Council of Comparative Education Societies, 3-5 July, Seoul, Korea. Korean Comparative Education Society. 15 pages.

1980. *Human commonality: The structural-developmental roots of values.* Address presented to the Comparative and International Education Society International Conference, Vancouver, B.C., March. Personal collection of Ted Ward. 12 pages.

1982. *Lone Ranger to Barnabas: Over and out.* Address presented at OMSC Role of North Americans in the Future of the Missionary Enterprise Conference, 4 May, Ventuor, N.J. 15 pages.

1983. *Facing the crisis of human need: A question of spiritual integrity.* Address presented at the 41st Annual convention of the National Association of Evangelicals, Orlando, Florida, 8-10 March. Personal collection of Ted Ward. 13 pages.

1984. *Faith, love, hope: The remaining mission of Christian higher education.* Address presented to Amigos, 1984. Personal collection of Ted Ward. 9 pages.

1985. *Promise and peril: The emergent research in moral development.* Michigan State University. Personal collection of Ted Ward. 17 pages.

1988. *The anxious climate of concern for missionary children.* Trinity Evangelical Divinity School. Personal collection of Ted Ward. 7 pages.

1989. *Endorsement review for reprint of Schooling choices: An examination of private, public, and home education by Wayne H. House.* Portland, Oreg.: Multnomah Press.

1989. *A response to "The churches and third world poverty" by Mark R. Amstutz.* Trinity Evangelical Divinity School. Personal collection of Ted Ward. 5 pages.

1990. *Taking moral development more seriously: Toward moral consensus and shared responsibility for moral education.* Address presented at the National Commission on Children, Washington, D.C., 2 July. Personal collection of Ted Ward. 6 pages.

1994. *Missionary motivation and support—Understanding today, anticipating tomorrow.* Address presented at the Overseas Missionary Study Center Conference, New Haven, Connecticut, 22-24 April. Personal collection of Ted Ward. 8 pages.

Ward, Ted, and Mark Simpson. 1994. *The final report: TEDS 2000: A project in long-range planning.* Trinity Evangelical Divinity School. Personal collection of Ted Ward. 91 pages.

Conn, Harvie, and Ted Ward. n.d. *Education for ministry: Something not-so-funny happened along the way.* Michigan State University. Personal collection of Ted Ward. 17 pages.

Ward, Ted, and Avery Willis, Jr. n.d. *A vision of reform for theological education.* Michigan State University. Personal collection of Ted Ward. 30 pages.

n.d. *Akron seminar on change.* Address presented at the Akron Seminar on Change, date uncertain. Personal collection of Ted Ward. 41 pages.

n.d. *Debriefing: Converting experience into learning.* Trinity Evangelical Divinity School. Personal collection of Ted Ward. 5 pages.

n.d. *Developmental levels of the teacher.* Michigan State University. Personal collection of Ted Ward. 7 pages.

n.d. *Facing the crisis of human need: A question of spiritual integrity.* Michigan State University. Personal collection of Ted Ward. 13 pages.

n.d. *Healer, teacher, evangelizer or revolutionist? Contending perspectives on the church and the third world.* Trinity Evangelical Divinity School. Personal collection of Ted Ward. 22 pages.

n.d. *Kinds and sources of data.* Michigan State University. Personal collection of Ted Ward. 2 pages.

Ward, Ted, and John M. Dettoni. n.d. *Nonformal education: Problems and promises.* Michigan State University. Personal collection of Ted Ward. 18 pages.

n.d. *Nonformal education as a problem of educational anthropology.* Michigan State University. Personal collection of Ted Ward. 6 pages.

Ward, Ted, and Lois McKinney. n.d. *Nonformal education and the church.* Michigan State University. Personal collection of Ted Ward. 15 pages.

n.d. *Planning a field trip for culture learning.* Trinity Evangelical Divinity School. Personal collection of Ted Ward. 5 pages.

n.d. *Schooling as a defective approach to education.* Michigan State University. Personal collection of Ted Ward. 5 pages.

n.d. *Sources of weakness in the "schooling" approach to theological education.* Trinity Evangelical Divinity School. Personal collection of Ted Ward. 1 page.

n.d. *The effective missionary.* Michigan State University. Personal collection of Ted Ward. 2 pages.

n.d. *The limits of self-reliance: Getting serious about Christian development assistance.* Trinity Evangelical Divinity School. Personal collection of Ted Ward. 4 pages.

Ward, Ted, and Lois McKinney. n.d. *The teacher.* Michigan State University. Personal collection of Ted Ward. 4 pages.

n.d. *The tip of the iceberg.* Michigan State University. Personal collection of Ted Ward. 3 pages.

n.d. *To reform Christian education: Six criteria.* Michigan State University. Personal collection of Ted Ward. 4 pages.

n.d. *Two modes of nonformal education.* Michigan State University. Personal collection of Ted Ward. 3 pages.

CASSETTES

1972. *Probing adult education.* Thesis: Creative Dimensions in Continuing Education Series. 14 min. Thesis Theological Cassettes. November 1972, 3 (10).

1972. *Prophecies of the advent of the messiah.* One Way Library Series. 60 min. each. Costa Mesa, Calif.: One Way Library.

1973. *Christian education?* Update Series. 7 min. Thesis Theological Cassettes. August 1973, 4 (7).

1973. *The numbers game.* Thesis: Creative Dimensions in Continuing Education Series. 6 min. Thesis Theological Cassettes. January 1973, 3 (12).

1978. *A 3-D view of learning.* Update Series. 10 min. Thesis Theological Cassettes. February 1978, 9 (1).

1978. *Planning for adult learning.* Update Series. 13 min. Thesis Theological Cassettes. January 1978, 8 (12).

1979. *Reflections on moral development and values clarification.* Update Series. 13 min. Thesis Theological Cassettes. February 1979, 10 (1).

1981. *Teaching values.* Teach tapes: ICL Leadership Resource. Ventura, Calif: G/L Publications. Two cassettes.

Ward, Ted, David Larson, and Karen Mains. 1986. *Having a good religious orientation.* Making Your Family Strong Series. 45 min. Ventura, Calif.: Gospel Light Publications. A243064

Ward, Ted, and R. C. Sproul. 1989. *Effective teaching.* October Conference '89: Loving a Holy God, Orlando, Florida. 45 min each. Orlando, Fla.: Ligonier Ministries. Three cassettes.

n.d. *Consortium meeting postscript.* Audio Newsletter Series. East Lansing, Mich.: Consortium on Auditory Learning Materials for the Handicapped—Michigan State University. 1 (2).

n.d. *Critical dimensions in context.* Address presented at the Christian Communications Educators Conference. Wheaton College WETN Recording. 799-413.

n.d. *Speed listening: Speech compression and expansion.* USOE/MSU Regional Instructional Materials Center for Handicapped Children and Youth. 30 min. East Lansing, Mich.: Michigan State University.

n.d. *The great imperative: Coming to grips with the communications revolution.* Address presented at the Christian Communications Educators Conference. Wheaton College WETN Recording. 799-411.

Contributing Authors and Editors

All of the editors and authors of chapters in this book completed doctoral de-grees with Ted Ward at Michigan State University (MSU), East Lansing, Michigan, or Trinity Evangelical Divinity School (TEDS), Deerfield, Illinois.

Lynn Joesting Day teaches in the Human Services Program of Western Washington University. She has worked for the 3M company in Spain, facilitated international development workshops in Central America and the Caribbean, and taught and conducted educational research at Daystar University in Kenya.

Edgar J. Elliston is Associate Dean for Academic Affairs and Professor of Leadership Development in the School of World Mission at Fuller Theo-logical Seminary. He served eighteen years in Ethiopia and Kenya. Since then he has consulted with theological education programs in Africa, Asia, Latin America, Eastern Europe, and the United States.

Duane Elmer is Professor and Chair of the Christian Education/Educa-tional Ministries Departments at Wheaton College and Graduate School. He served previously as a missionary educator with TEAM in South Africa and is currently involved in domestic and international reconcili-ation activities. He is the author of *Cross-Cultural Conflict*.

Muriel Elmer has been the Health Training Specialist for World Relief Cor-poration. She has supervised child survival and micro-enterprise pro-grams for approximately 250,000 mothers and children in seven countries. Born of missionary parents in Zimbabwe, she later served as a mission-ary in South Africa. She is co-author of *Building Relationships*.

Robert W. Ferris is Associate Dean for Doctoral Studies at Columbia Bibli-cal Seminary. He served for twenty-one years as a missionary educator in the Philippines, teaching, consulting widely, and leading Asian Theo-logical Seminary as its academic dean. He is the author of *Renewal in Theological Education*.

Mari Gonlag is Professor and Program Director for the Christian Educa-tion Program at Bethany Bible College in New Brunswick. For the past six years she has served as Director of Ministerial Studies for The Wesleyan Church (North America).

Ronald Habermas serves as the McGee Professor of Biblical Studies at John Brown University. He previously taught at Liberty University and Columbia Biblical Seminary. He is co-author of five books, including *Teaching for Reconciliation*.

Evvy Hay is Associate Professor of Missions and Intercultural Studies at Wheaton College Graduate School. Prior to this she was Director of International Health and Educational Services for MAP International. She also was a missionary with Wesleyan Church in Sierra Leone.

Stephen T. Hoke serves as Vice President of Staff Development and Training with Church Resource Ministries (CRM). Raised by missionary parents in Japan, he taught missions at Seattle Pacific University, was Associate Director of Training for World Vision International, and, most recently, served as President of L.I.F.E. Ministries (Japan).

Klaus Issler is the Director of the Talbot School of Theology Ed.D. program at Biola University. He has been an associate pastor, an instructor for Walk Thru the Bible and serves on the board of BEE International. He is co-author (with Ronald Habermas) of *Teaching for Reconciliation* and *How We Learn*.

Lois McKinney is Professor of Mission at Trinity Evangelical Divinity School. She previously taught for eight years at Wheaton College Graduate School and served for twenty-three years with Conservative Baptist International as a theological educator in Portugal, Brazil, and in an international consulting ministry.

Frances O'Gorman is a Brazilian educator. She has worked many years facilitating community groups in the *favelas* (slums) of Rio de Janeiro and consulting for relief and development agencies. She has authored *Charity and Change* and *Hillside Woman*.

James E. Pleuddemann is President of SIM International. During thirteen years of missionary service in Nigeria, thirteen years of teaching at Wheaton College Graduate School, and now as a mission executive, Jim has been concerned about approaches to participatory planning which stimulate reflective thinking that is congruent with biblical values.

Samuel F. Rowen is an educational consultant and author. He directs Educational Projects International, an agency that matches Western experts with overseas teaching opportunities. He has served as a theological educator and intercultural trainer, and previously taught at Reformed Theological Seminary.

Edward D. Seely is Minister of Christian Education at Christ Church of Oak Brook, Illinois. He has served as an adjunct instructor in Christian education at Western Theological Seminary (Holland, Michigan) and has traveled and lectured in Europe, the Middle East, and Russia. He is the author of *Teaching Early Adolescents Creatively*.

Yau-Man Siew serves on the faculty of Singapore Bible College. Trained as a pharmacist, Yau-Man began his theological education in Singapore, then served four years with the Fellowship of Evangelical Students in

Malaysia before pursuing graduate studies in Canada and the United States.

Mark E. Simpson teaches administration and leadership as Assistant Professor and Associate Dean for Doctoral Studies in Christian Education at the Southern Baptist Theological Seminary. He has served as Associate Dean for Nontraditional Education and Academic Doctorate Programs Coordinator at Trinity International University.

Catherine Stonehouse is Orlean Bullard Beeson Professor of Christian Education at Asbury Theological Seminary. Prior to this, she served the Free Methodist Church of North America as General Director of Christian Education and as its publishing house's Director of Curriculum Ministries. She is the author of *Patterns of Moral Development*.

J. Allen Thompson is President of the International Church Planting Center in Atlanta, and coordinator of multicultural church planting for Mission to North America of the Presbyterian Church in America. As an executive with Worldteam, Allen helped the organization to focus on a strategy for training and deploying national workers in church planting in fourteen countries.

Mark S. Young teaches world missions and intercultural studies at Dallas Theological Seminary. Previously he served for fourteen years with Conservative Baptist International in Eastern Europe with Biblical Education by Extension, and then as founding Academic Dean of the Biblijne Seminarium Teologiczne in Wroclaw, Poland.

MARC

Bringing you key resources on the world mission of the church

MARC books and other publications support the work of MARC (Mission Advanced Research and Communications Center), which is to inspire fresh vision and empower Christian mission among those who extend the whole gospel to the whole world.

New MARC titles include:

Children in Crisis: A New Commitment, Phyllis Kilbourn, editor

Will alert you to the multiple ways in which children are suffering today and give you new reasons for responding. Will inspire you and equip you to reach out to children in crisis around the world. **304 pages $21.95**

By Word, Work and Wonder: Cases in Holistic Mission,
Thomas H. McAlpine

A fresh look at holism in mission. Several case studies from around the world focus on innovative mission practices that are sure to broaden your understanding of mission. **147 pages $15.95**

Costly Mission, Michael Duncan

A candid narrative that offers profound insight into the inner struggles of a missionary called to the slums. An excellent reminder that mission is indeed costly—many times on a personal level. **144 pages $7.95**

Directory of Schools and Professors of Mission
in the USA and Canada, John A. Siewert, editor

Your complete networking resource. Everything you need to contact mission schools and professors in North America, including all essential addresses, names and numbers. **124 pages $17.95**

Caring for the Whole Person, E. Anthony Allen

Combines the spiritual, psychological and social aspects of life to challenge Christian health workers to address to total needs of the whole person. Excellent for anyone struggling to integrate their faith with their vocation.
100 pages $9.95

Serving With the Poor in Asia: Cases in Holistic Ministry,
T. Yamamori, B. Myers & D. Conner, editors

Several of today's leading mission thinkers analyze real cases presented from different ministry contexts from Asia. Shows the powerful impact of holism on mission and other disciplines. **216 pages $15.95**

God So Loves the City: Seeking a Theology for Urban Mission,
Charles Van Engen and Jude Tiersma, editors

An international team of experienced urban practitioners explore the most urgent issues facing those who minister in today's cities. Each team member shares a story that illustrates the challenges to urban ministry in the face of injustice, marginalization and urban structures. From a retelling of these stories through the lens of Scripture, we see the first steps toward a theology of mission for the city.   **315 pages $21.95**

Transforming Health: Christian Approaches to Healing and Wholeness, Eric Ram, editor

Explores how God is bringing about health, healing and wholeness throughout the world today. Dr. Ram encouraged more than twenty of his health care colleagues around the world to share their newest insights on practices of health and healing.   **350 pages $21.95**

Survival of the Fittest: Keeping Yourself Healthy in Travel and Service Overseas, Dr. Christine Aroney-Sine

No one wants their ministry hindered by illnesses that can be prevented. This informative guide helps you prepare for trips and take preventative measures against common illnesses. Once abroad, it will help you maintain your physical, emotional and spiritual well-being.   **112 pages $9.95**

Bridging the Gap: Evangelism, Development and *Shalom*,
Bruce Bradshaw

From a holistic approach to Christian ministry, the author seeks to bridge the gap that occurs between evangelism and development when we perceive the two as separate enterprises of Christian mission. Examines the biblical concepts of creation, redemption and *shalom* and searches for a fuller understanding of God's redemptive plan for all creation.
                183 pages $11.95

Ask for the MARC newsletter and complete publications list

MARC

a division of World Vision International
800 W. Chestnut Ave.
Monrovia, CA 91016-3198
Fax: (818) 301-7786 • E-Mail: MARCpubs@wvi.org
WWW: http://www.wvi.org/marc

Order Toll Free: 1-800-777-7752